The Earthly Paradise by William Morris

A Poem

Part III

William Morris was born in Walthamstow, London on 24th March 1834 he is regarded today as a foremost poet, writer, textile designer, artist and libertarian.

Morris began to publish poetry and short stories in 1856 through the Oxford and Cambridge Magazine which he founded with his friends and financed while at university. His first volume, in 1858, The Defence of Guenevere and Other Poems, was the first published book of Pre-Raphaelite poetry. Due to its luke warm reception he was discouraged from poetry writing for a number of years.

His return to poetry was with the great success of The Life and Death of Jason in 1867, which was followed by The Earthly Paradise, themed around a group of medieval wanderers searching for a land of everlasting life; after much disillusion, they discover a surviving colony of Greeks with whom they exchange stories. In the collection are retellings of Icelandic sagas. From then until his Socialist period Morris's fascination with the ancient Germanic and Norse peoples dominated his writing being the first to translate many of the Icelandic sagas into English; the epic retelling of the story of Sigurd the Volsung being his favourite.

In 1884 he founded the Socialist League but with the rise of the Anarachists in the party he left it in 1890.

In 1891 he founded the Kelmscott Press publishing limited edition illuminated style books. His design for The Works of Geoffrey Chaucer is a masterpiece.

Morris was quietly approached with an offer of the Poet Laureateship after the death of Tennyson in 1892, but declined.

William Morris died at age 62 on 3rd October 1896 in London.

Index Of Contents

SEPTEMBER

O come at last, to whom the spring-tide's hope
Looked for through blossoms, what hast thou for me?
Green grows the grass upon the dewy slope
Beneath thy gold-hung, grey-leaved apple-tree
Moveless, e'en as the autumn fain would be
That shades its sad eyes from the rising sun
And weeps at eve because the day is done.

What vision wilt thou give me, autumn morn,
To make thy pensive sweetness more complete?
What tale, ne'er to be told, of folk unborn?
What images of grey-clad damsels sweet
Shall cross thy sward with dainty noiseless feet?
What nameless shamefast longings made alive
Soft-eyed September will thy sad heart give?

Look long, O longing eyes, and look in vain!
Strain idly, aching heart, and yet be wise,
And hope no more for things to come again
That thou beheldest once with careless eyes!
Like a new-wakened man thou art, who tries
To dream again the dream that made him glad
When in his arms his loving love he had.

Mid young September's fruit-trees next they met,
With calm hearts, willing such things to forget
As men had best forget; and certainly

E'en such a day it was when this might be
If e'er it might be; fair, without a cloud,
Yet windless, so that a grey haze did shroud
The bright blue; neither burning overmuch,
Nor chill, the blood of those old folk to touch
With fretful, restless memory of despair.
Withal no promise of the fruitful year
Seemed unfulfilled in that fair autumn-tide;
The level ground along the river-side
Was merry through the day with sounds of those
Who gathered apples; o'er the stream arose
The northward-looking slopes where the swine ranged
Over the fields that hook and scythe had changed
Since the last month; but 'twixt the tree-boles grey
Above them did they see the terraced way,
And over that the vine-stocks, row on row,
Whose dusty leaves, well thinned and yellowing now,
But little hid the bright-bloomed vine-bunches.

There day-long 'neath the shadows of the trees
Those elders sat; chary of speech they were,
For good it seemed to watch the young folk there,
Not so much busied with their harvesting,
But o'er their baskets they might stop to sing;
Nor for the end of labour all so fain
But eyes of men from eyes of maids might gain
Some look desired.

So at the midday those
Who played with labour in the deep green close
Stinted their gathering for a while to eat;
Then to the elders did it seem most meet
Amidst of these to set forth what they might
Of lore remembered, and to let the night
Bury its own dead thoughts with wine and sleep;
So while the loitering autumn sun did creep
O'er flower-crowned heads, and past sweet eyes of grey,
And eager lips, and fresh round limbs that lay
Amid the golden fruit—fruit sweet and fair
Themselves, that happy days and love did bear
And life unburdened—while the failing sun
Drew up the light clouds, was this tale begun,
Sad, but not sad enow to load the yoke,
E'en by a feather's weight, of those old folk.
Sad, and believed but for its sweetness' sake
By the young folk, desiring not to break
The spell that sorrow's image cast on them,
As dreamlike she went past with fluttering hem.

THE DEATH OF PARIS

ARGUMENT

Paris the son of Priam was wounded by one of the poisoned arrows of Hercules that Philoctetes bore to the siege of Troy; wherefore he had himself borne up into Ida that he might see the nymph Œnone, whom he once had loved, because she, who knew many secret things, alone could heal him: but when he had seen her and spoken with her, she would deal with the matter in no wise, wherefore Paris died of that hurt.

In the last month of Troy's beleaguerment,
When both sides, waiting for some God's great hand,
But seldom o'er the meads the war-shout sent,
Yet idle rage would sometimes drive a band
From town or tent about Troy-gate to stand
All armed, and there to bicker aimlessly;
And so at least the weary time wore by.

In such a fight, when wide the arrows flew,
And little glory fell to any there,
And nought there seemed for a stout man to do,
Rose Philoctetes from the ill-roofed lair
That hid his rage, and crept out into air,
And strung his bow, and slunk down to the fight,
'Twixt rusty helms, and, shields that once were bright.

And even as he reached the foremost rank,
A glimmer as of polished steel and gold
Amid the war-worn Trojan folk, that shrank
To right and left, his fierce eyes could behold;
He heard a shout, as if one man were bold
About the streams of Simoeis that day—
One heart still ready to play out the play.

Therewith he heard a mighty bowstring twang,
And a shaft screamed 'twixt hostile band and band,
And close beside him fell, with clash and clang,
A well-tried warrior from the Cretan land,
And rolled in dust, clutching with desperate hand
At the gay feathers of the shaft that lay
Deep in his heart, well silenced from that day.

Then of the Greeks did man look upon man,
While Philoctetes from his quiver drew
A dreadful shaft, and through his fingers ran
The dull-red feathers; of strange steel and blue
The barbs were, such as archer never knew,
But black as death the thin-forged bitter point,
That with the worm's blood fate did erst anoint.

He shook the shaft, and notched it, and therewith

Forth from the Trojans rang that shout again,
Whistled the arrow, and a Greek did writhe
Once more upon the earth in his last pain;
While the grey clouds, big with the threat of rain,
Parted a space, and on the Trojans shone,
And struck a glory from that shining one.

Then Philoctetes scowled, and cried, "O Fate,
I give thee this, thy strong man gave to me.
Do with it as thou wilt!—let small or great
E'en as thou wilt before its black point be!
Late grows the year, and stormy is the sea,
The oars lie rotten by the gunwales now
That nevermore a Grecian surf shall know."

He spake and drew the string with careless eyes,
And, as the shaft flew forth, he turned about
And tramped back slowly, noting in no wise
How from the Greeks uprose a joyous shout,
And from the Trojan host therewith brake out
Confused clamour, and folk cried the name
Of him wherethrough the weary struggle came,

Paris the son of Priam! then once more
O'erhead of leaguer and beleaguered town
Grey grew the sky, a cold sea-wind swept o'er
The ruined plain, and the small rain drove down,
While slowly underneath that chilling frown
Parted the hosts; sad Troy into its gates,
Greece to its tents, and waiting on the fates.

Next day the seaward-looking gates none swung
Back on their hinges, whatso Greek might fare,
With seeming-careless mien, and bow unstrung,
Anigh them; whatso rough-voiced horn might dare
With well-known notes, the war-worn warders there;
Troy slept amid its nightmares through the day,
And dull with waking dreams the leaguer lay.

Yet in the streets did man say unto man,
"Hector is dead, and Troilus is dead;
Æneas turneth toward the waters wan;
In his fair house Antenor hides his head;
Fast from the tree of Troy the boughs are shred;
And now this Paris, now this joyous one,
Is the cry cried that biddeth him begone?"

But on the morrow's dawn, ere yet the sun
Had shone athwart the mists of last night's rain,
And shown the image of the Spotless One
Unto the tents and hovels of the plain

Whose girth of war she long had made all vain,
From out a postern looking towards the north
A little band of silent men went forth.

And in their midst a litter did they bear
Whereon lay one with linen wrapped around,
Whose wan face turned unto the fresher air
As though a little pleasure he had found
Amidst of pain; some dreadful, torturing wound
The man endured belike, and as a balm
Was the fresh morn, with all its rest and calm,

After the weary tossing of the night
And close dim-litten chamber, whose dusk seemed
Labouring with whispers fearful of the light,
Confused with images of dreams long dreamed,
Come back again, now that the lone torch gleamed
Dim before eyes that saw nought real as true
To vex the heart that nought of purpose knew.

Upon the late-passed night in e'en such wise
Had Paris lain. What time, like years of life,
Had passed before his weary heart and eyes!
What hopeless, nameless longings! what wild strife
'Gainst nought for nought, with wearying changes rife,
Had he gone through, till in the twilight grey
They bore him through the cold deserted way.

Mocking and strange the streets looked now, most meet
For a dream's ending, for a vain life's end;
While sounded his strong litter-bearers' feet,
Like feet of men who through Death's country wend
Silent, for fear lest they should yet offend
The grim King satisfied to let them go,
Hope bids them hurry, fear's chain makes them slow.

In feverish doze he thought of bygone days,
When love was soft, life strong, and a sweet name,
The first sweet name that led him down love's ways,
Unbidden ever to his fresh lips came;
Half witting would he speak it, and for shame
Flush red, and think what folk would deem thereof
If they might know Œnone was his love.

And now, Œnone no more love of his,
He worn with war and passion—must he pray,
"O thou, I loved and love not, life and bliss
Lie in thine hands to give or take away;
O heal me, hate me not! think of the day
When as thou thinkest still, e'en so I thought,
That all the world without thy love was nought."

Yea, he was borne forth such a prayer to make,
For she alone of all the world, they said,
The thirst of that dread poison now might slake,
For midst the ancient wise ones nurtured
On peaceful Ida, in the lore long dead,
Lost to the hurrying world, right wise she was,
Mighty to bring most wondrous things to pass.

Was the world worth the minute of that prayer
If yet her love, despised and cast aside,
Should so shine forth that she should heal him there?
He knew not and he recked not; fear and pride
'Neath Helen's kiss and Helen's tears had died,
And life was love, and love too strong that he
Should catch at Death to save him misery.

So, with soul drifting down the stream of love,
He let them bear him through the fresh fair morn,
From out Troy-gates; and no more now he strove
To battle with the wild dreams, newly born
From that past night of toil and pain forlorn;
No farewell did he mutter 'neath his breath
To failing Troy, no eyes he turned toward death.

Troy dwindled now behind them, and the way
That round about the feet of Ida wound,
They left; and up a narrow vale, that lay,
Grassy and soft betwixt the pine-woods bound,
'They went, and ever gained the higher ground,
For as a trench the little valley was
To catch the runnels that made green its grass.

Now ere that green vale narrowed to an end,
Blocked by a shaly slip thrust bleak and bare
From the dark pine-wood's edge, as men who wend
Upon a well-known way, they turned them there;
And through the pine-wood's dusk began to fare
By blind ways, till all noise of bird and wind
Amid that odorous night was left behind.

And in meanwhile deepened the languid doze
That lay on Paris into slumber deep,
O'er his unconscious heart, and eyes shut close,
The image of that very place 'gan creep,
And twelve years younger in his dreamful sleep,
Light-footed, through the awful wood he went,
With beating heart, on lovesome thoughts intent.

Dreaming, he went, till thinner and more thin,
And bright with growing day, the pine-wood grew,

Then to an open, rugged space did win;
Whence a close beech-wood was he passing through,
Whose every tall white stem full well he knew;
Then seemed to stay awhile for loving shame,
When to the brow of the steep bank he came,

Where still the beech-trunks o'er the mast-strewn ground
Stood close, and slim and tall, but hid not quite
A level grassy space they did surround
On every side save one, that to the light
Of the clear western sky, cold now, but bright,
Was open, and the thought of the far sea,
Toward which a small brook tinkled merrily.

Him seemed he lingered there, then stepped adown
With troubled heart into the soft green place,
And up the eastmost of the beech-slopes brown
He turned about a lonesome, anxious face,
And stood to listen for a little space
If any came, but nought he seemed to hear
Save the brook's babble, and the beech-leaves' stir.

And then he dreamed great longing o'er him came;
Too great, too bitter of those days to be
Long past, when love was born amidst of shame;
He dreamed that, as he gazed full eagerly
Into the green dusk between tree and tree,
His trembling hand slid down the horn to take
Wherewith he erst was wont his herd to wake.

Trembling, he set it to his lips, and first
Breathed gently through it; then strained hard to blow,
For dumb, dumb was it grown, and no note burst
From its smooth throat; and ill thoughts poisoned now
The sweetness of his dream; he murmured low,
"Ah! dead and gone, and ne'er to come again;
Ah, past away! ah, longed for long in vain!

"Lost love, sweet Helen, come again to me!"
Therewith he dreamed he fell upon the ground
And hid his face, and wept out bitterly,
But woke with fall and torturing tears, and found
He lay upon his litter, and the sound
Of feet departing from him did he hear,
And rustling of the last year's leaves anear.

But in the self-same place he lay indeed,
Weeping and sobbing, and scarce knowing why;
His hand clutched hard the horn that erst did lead
The dew-lapped neat round Ida merrily;
He strove to raise himself, he strove to cry

That name of Helen once, but then withal
Upon him did the load of memory fall.

Quiet he lay a space, while o'er him drew
The dull, chill cloud of doubt and sordid fear,
As now he thought of what he came to do,
And what a dreadful minute drew anear;
He shut his eyes, and now no more could hear
His litter-bearers' feet; as lone he felt
As though amid the outer wastes he dwelt.

Amid that fear most feeble, nought and vain
His life and love seemed; with a dreadful sigh
He raised his arm, and soul's and body's pain
Tore at his heart with new-born agony
As a thin quavering note; a ghost-like cry
Rang from the long unused lips of the horn,
Spoiling the sweetness of the happy morn.

He let the horn fall down upon his breast
And lie there, and his hand fell to his side;
And there indeed his body seemed to rest,
But restless was his soul, and wandered wide
Through a dim maze of lusts unsatisfied;
Thoughts half thought out, and words half said, and deeds
Half done, unfruitful, like o'er-shadowed weeds.

His eyes were shut now, and his dream's hot tears
Were dry upon his cheek; the sun grown high
Had slain the wind, when smote upon his ears
A sudden rustling in the beech-leaves dry;
Then came a pause; then footsteps drew anigh
O'er the deep grass; he shuddered, and in vain
He strove to turn, despite his burning pain.

Then through his half-shut eyes he seemed to see
A woman drawing near, and held his breath,
And clutched at the white linen eagerly,
And felt a greater fear than fear of death,
A greater pain than that love threateneth,
As soft low breathing o'er his head he heard,
And thin fine linen raiment gently stirred.

Then spoke a sweet voice close, ah, close to him!
"Thou sleepest, Paris? would that I could sleep!
On the hill-side do I lay limb to limb,
And lie day-long watching the shadows creep
And change, till day is gone, and night is deep,
Yet sleep not ever, wearied with the thought
Of all a little lapse of time has brought.

"Sleep, though thou calledst me! yet 'mid thy dream
Hearken, the while I tell about my life,
The life I led, while 'mid the steely gleam
Thou wert made happy with the joyous strife;
Or in the soft arms of the Greek king's wife
Wouldst still moan out that day had come too soon,
Calling the dawn the glimmer of the moon.

"Wake not, wake not, before the tale is told!
Not long to tell, the tale of those ten years!
A gnawing pain that never groweth old,
A pain that shall not be washed out by tears;
A dreary road the weary foot-sole wears,
Knowing no rest, but going to and fro,
Treading it harder 'neath the weight of woe.

"No middle, no beginning, and no end;
No staying place, no thought of anything,
Bitter or sweet, with that one thought to blend;
No least joy left that I away might fling
And deem myself grown great; no hope to cling
About me, nought but dull, unresting pain,
That made all memory sick, all striving vain.

"Thou—hast thou thought thereof, perchance anights
In early dawn, and shuddered, and then said,
'Alas, poor soul! yet bath she had delights,
For none are wholly hapless but the dead.'
Liar! O liar! my woe upon thine head,
My agony that nought can take away!
Awake, arise, O traitor, unto day!"

Her voice rose as she spoke, till loud and shrill
It rang about the place; but when at last
She ended, and the echoes from the hill,
Woeful and wild, back o'er the place were cast
From her lost love a little way she passed
Trembling, and looking round as if afeared
At those ill sounds that through the morn she heard.

Then still she stood, her clenched hands slim and white
Relaxed, her drawn brow smoothed; with a great sigh
Her breast heaved, and she muttered: "Ere the light
Of yesterday had faded from the sky
I knew that he would seek me certainly;
And, knowing it, yet feigned I knew it not,
Or with what hope, what hope my heart was hot.

"That tumult in my breast I might not name—
Love should I call it?—nay, my life was love
And pain these ten years—should I call it shame?

What shame my weary waiting might reprove
After ten years?—or pride?—what pride could move
After ten years this heart within my breast?
Alas! I lied—I lied, and called it rest.

"I called it rest, and wandered through the night;
Upon my river's flowery bank I stood,
And thought its hurrying changing black and white
Stood still beneath the moon, that hill and wood
Were moving round me, and I deemed it good
The world should change so, deemed it good, that day
For ever into night had passed away.

"And still I wandered through the night, and still
Things changed, and changed not round me, and the day—
This day wherein I am, had little will
With dreadful truth to drive the night away—
God knows if for its coming I did pray!
God knows if at the last in twilight-tide
My hope—my hope undone I more might hide."

Then looked she toward the litter as she spake,
And slowly drew anigh it once again,
And from her worn tried heart there did outbreak
Wild sobs and weeping, shameless of its pain,
Till as the storm of passion 'gan to wane
She looked and saw the shuddering misery
Wherein her love of the old days did lie.

Still she wept on, but gentler now withal,
And passed on till above the bier she stood,
Watching the well-wrought linen rise and fall
Beneath his faltering breath, and still her blood
Ran fiery hot with thoughts of ill and good,
Pity and scorn, and love and hate, as she,
Half dead herself, gazed on his misery.

At last she spake: "This tale I told e'en now,
Know'st thou 'mid dreams what woman suffered this?
Canst thou not dream of the old days, and how
Full oft thy lips would say 'twixt kiss and kiss
That all of bliss was not enough of bliss
My loveliness and kindness to reward,
That for thy Love the sweetest life was hard?

"Yea, Paris, have I not been kind to thee?
Did I not live thy wishes to fulfil?
Wert thou not happy when thou lovedst me,
What dream then did we have of change or ill?
Why must thou needs change? I am unchanged still;
I need no more than thee—what needest thou

But that we might be happy, yea e'en now?"

He opened hollow eyes and looked on her,
And stretched a trembling hand out; ah, who knows
With what strange mingled look of hope and fear,
Of hate and love, their eyes met! Come so close
Once more, that everything they now might lose
Amid the flashing out of that old fire,
The short-lived uttermost of all desire.

He spake not, shame and other love there lay
Too heavy on him; but she spake again:
"E'en now at the beginning of the day,
Weary with hope and fear and restless pain,
I said—Alas, I said, if all be vain
And he will have no pity, yet will I
Have pity—how shall kindness e'er pass by?"

He drew his hand aback, and laid it now
Upon the swathings of his wound, but she
Set her slim hand upon her knitted brow
And gazed on him with bright eyes eagerly;
Nor cruel looked her lips that once would be
So kind, so longed for: neither spake awhile,
Till in her face there shone a sweet strange smile.

She touched him not, but yet so near she came
That on his very face he felt her breath;
She whispered, "Speak! thou wilt not speak for shame,
I will not grant for love, and grey-winged Death
Meanwhile above our folly hovereth;
Speak! was it not all false? is it not done?
Is not the dream dreamed out, the dull night gone?

"Hearkenest thou, Paris? O look kind on me!
I hope no more indeed, but couldst thou turn
Kind eyes to me, then much for me and thee
Might love do yet. Doth not the old fire burn?
Doth not thine heart for words of old days yearn?
Canst thou not say—Alas, what wilt thou say,
Since I have put by hope for many a day?

"Paris, I hope no more, yet while ago—
Take it not ill if I must needs say this—
A while ago I cried; Ah! no, no, no!
It is no love at all, this love of his,
He loves her not, I it was had the bliss
Of being the well-beloved—dead is his love,
For surely none but I his heart may move."

She wept still; but his eyes grew wild and strange

With that last word, and harder his face grew
Though her tear-blinded eyes saw not the change.
Long beat about his heart false words and true,
A veil of strange thought he might not pierce through,
Of hope he might not name, clung round about
His wavering heart, perplexed with death and doubt.

Then trembling did he speak: "I love thee still,
Surely I love thee." But a dreadful pain
Shot through his heart, and strange presage of ill,
As like the ceasing of the summer rain
Her tears stopped, and she drew aback again,
Silent a moment, till a bitter cry
Burst from her lips grown white with agony.

A look of pity came across his face
Despite his pain and horror, and her eyes
Saw it, and changed, and for a little space
Panting she stood, as one checked by surprise
Amidst of passion; then in tender wise,
Kneeling, she 'gan the bandages undo
That hid the place the bitter shaft tore through.

Then when the wound and his still face and white
Lay there before her, she 'gan tremble sore,
For images of hope and past delight,
Not to be named once, 'gan her heart flit o'er;
Blossomed the longing in her heart, and bore
A dreadful thought of uttermost despair,
That all if gained would be no longer fair.

In dull low words she spake: "Yea, so it is,
That thou art near thy death, and this thy wound
I yet may heal, and give thee back what bliss
The ending of thy life may yet surround:
Mock not thyself with hope! the Trojan ground
Holds tombs, not houses now, all Gods are gone
From out your temples but cold Death alone.

"Lo, if I heal thee, and thou goest again
Back unto Troy, and she, thy new love, sees
Thy lovesome body freed from all its pain,
And yet awhile amid the miseries
Of Troy ye twain lie loving, well at ease,
Yet 'midst of this while she is asking thee
What kind soul made thee whole and well to be,

"And thou art holding back my name with lies,
And thinking, maybe, Paris, of this face
E'en then the Greekish flame shall sear your eyes,
The clatter of the Greeks fill all the place,

While she, my woe, the ruin of thy race,
Looking toward changed days, a new crown, shall stand,
Her fingers trembling in her husband's hand.

Thou I called love once, wilt thou die e'en thus,
Ruined 'midst ruin, ruining, bereft
Of name and honour? O love, piteous
That but for this were all the hard things cleft
That lay 'twixt us and love; till nought was left
'Twixt thy lips and my lips! O hard that we
Were once so full of all felicity!

"O love, O Paris, know'st thou this of me
That in these hills e'en such a name I have
As being akin to a divinity;
And lightly may I slay and lightly save;
Nor know I surely if the peaceful grave
Shall ever hide my body dead—behold,
Have ten long years of misery made me old?"

Sadly she laughed; and rising wearily
Stood by him in the fresh and sunny morn;
The image of his youth and faith gone by
She seemed to be, for one short minute born
To make his shamed lost life seem more forlorn;
He shut his eyes and moaned, but once again
She knelt beside him, and the weary pain

Deepened upon her face. "Hearken!" she said,
"Death is anear thee; is then death so ill
With me anigh thee—since Troy is as dead,
Ere many tides the Xanthus' mouth shall fill,
And thou art reft of her that harmed me still,
Whatso may change—shall I heal thee for this,
That thou may'st die more mad for her last kiss?"

She gazed at him with straining eyes; and he—
Despite himself love touched his dying heart,
And from his eyes desire flashed suddenly,
And o'er his wan face the last blood did start
As with soft love his close-shut lips 'gan part.
She laughed out bitterly, and said, "Why then
Must I needs call thee falsest of all men,

"Seeing thou liest not to save thy life?—
Yee listen once again—fair is this place
That knew not the beginning of the strife
And recks not of its end—and this my face,
This body thou wouldst day-long once embrace
And deem thyself right happy—thine it is,
Thine only, Paris, shouldst thou deem it bliss."

He looked into her eyes, and deemed he saw
A strange and awful look a-gathering there,
And sick scorn at her quivering fine lip draw;
Yet trembling he stretched out his hand to her,
Although self-loathing and strange hate did tear
His heart that Death made cold, e'en as he said,
"Whatso thou wilt shall be remembered;

"Whatso thou wilt, O love, shall be forgot,—
It may be I shall love thee as of old."
As thunder laughs she laughed—"Nay, touch me not!
Touch me not, fool!" she cried, "Thou grow'st a-cold,
And I am Death, Death, Death!—the tale is told
Of all thy days! of all those joyous days
When thinking nought of me thou garneredst praise.

"Turn back again, and think no more of me!
I am thy Death! woe for thy happy days!
For I must slay thee; ah, my misery!
Woe for the God-like wisdom thou wouldst praise!
Else I my love to life again might raise
A minute, ah, a minute! and be glad
While on my lips thy blessing lips I had!

"Would God that it were yesterday again;
Would God the red sun had died yester-eve,
And I were no more hapless now than then!
Would God that I could say, and not believe,
As yesterday, that years past hope did leave
My cold heart—that I lived a death in life—
Ah! then within my heart was yet a strife!

"But now, but now, is all come to an end—
Nay, speak not; think not of me! think of her
Who made me this; and back unto her wend,
Lest her lot, too, should be yet heavier!
I will depart for fear thou diest here,
Lest I should see thy woeful ghost forlorn
Here wandering ever 'twixt the night and morn.

"—O heart grown wise, wilt thou not let me go?
Will ye be never satisfied, O eyes,
With gazing on my misery and my woe?
O foolish, quivering heart, now grown so wise,
What folly is it that from out thee cries
To be all close to him once more, once more
Ere yet the dark stream cleaveth shore from shore?"

Her voice was a wail now, with quivering hand
At her white raiment did she clutch and tear

Unwitting, as she rose up and did stand
Bent over his wide eyes and pale face, where
No torturing hope was left, no pain, or fear;
For Death's cold rest was gathering fast on him,
And toward his heart crept over foot and limb.

A little while she stood, and spake no word,
But hung above him, with white heaving breast,
And moaning still as moans the grey-winged bird
In autumn-tide o'er his forgotten nest;
And then her hands about her throat she pressed,
As though to keep a cry back, then stooped down
And set her face to his, while spake her moan:

"O love, O cherished more than I can tell,
Through years of woe, O love, my life and bane,
My joy and grief, farewell, farewell, farewell!
Forgetfulness of grief I yet may gain;
In some wise may come ending to my pain;
It may be yet the Gods will have me glad!
Yet, love, I would that thee and pain I had!

"Alas! it may not be, it may not be,
The falling blossom of the late spring-tide
Shall hang a golden globe upon the tree
When through the vale the mists of autumn glide:
Yet would, O Love, with thee I might abide.
Now, now that restful death is drawing nigh—
Farewell, farewell, how good it is to die!"

O strange, O strange, when on his lips once more
Her lips were laid! O strange that he must die
Now, when so clear a vision had come o'er
His failing heart, and keenest memory
Had shown him all his changing life passed by;
And what he was, and what he might have been,
Yea, and should be, perchance, so clear were seen!

Yea, then were all things laid within the scale,
Pleasure and lust, love and desire of fame,
Kindness, and hope, and folly—all the tale
Told in a moment, as across him came
That sudden flash, bright as the lightning-flame,
Showing the wanderer on the waste how he
Has gone astray 'mid dark and misery.

Ah, and her face upon his dying face
That the sun warmed no more! that agony
Of dying love, wild with the tale of days
Long past, and strange with hope that might not be—
All was gone now, and what least part had he

In Love at all, and why was life all gone?
Why must he meet the eyes of death alone?

Alone, for she and ruth had left him there;
Alone, because the ending of the strife
He knew, well taught by death, drew surely near;
Alone, for all those years with pleasure rife
Should be a tale 'mid Helen's coming life,
And she and all the world should go its ways,
'Midst other troubles, other happy days.

And yet how was it with him? As if death
Strove yet with struggling life and love in vain,
With eyes grown deadly bright and rattling breathy
He raised himself; while wide his blood did stain
The linen fair, and seized the horn again,
And blew thereon a wild and shattering blast
Ere from his hand afar the thing he cast.

Then, as a man who in a failing fight
For a last onset gathers suddenly
All soul and strength, he faced the summer light,
And from his lips broke forth a mighty cry
Of "Helen, Helen, Helen!"—yet the sky
Changed not above his cast-back golden head,
And merry was the world though he was dead.

But now when every echo was as still
As were the lips of Paris, once more came
The litter-bearers down the beech-clad hill
And stood about him crying out his name,
Lamenting for his beauty and his fame,
His love, his kindness, and his merry heart,
That still would thrust ill days and thoughts apart.

Homeward they bore him through the dark woods' gloom
With heavy hearts presaging nothing good;
And when they entered Troy again, a tomb
For them and theirs it seemed.—Long has it stood,
But now indeed the labour and the blood,
The love, the patience, and good-heart are vain—
The Greeks may have what yet is left to gain.

I cannot tell what crop may clothe the hills,
The merry hills Troy whitened long ago—
Belike the sheaves, wherewith the reaper fills
His yellow wain, no whit the weaker grow
For that past harvest-tide of wrong and woe;
Belike the tale, wept over otherwhere,
Of those old days is clean forgotten there.

Alas too short seemed to those ancient men
The little span of threescore years and ten,
Too hard, too bitter, the dull years of life
Beset at best with many a care and strife
To bear withal Love's torment, and the toils
Wherewith the days of youth and joy he spoils;
Since e'en so God makes equal Eld and Youth
Tormenting Youth with lies and Eld with truth;
Well-nigh they blamed the singer too, that he
Must needs draw pleasure from men's misery;
Nathless a little even they must feel
How time and tale a long-past woe will heal,
And make a melody of grief, and give
Joy to the world that whoso dies shall live.
Moreover, good it was for them to note
The slim hand set unto the changing throat,
The lids down drooped to hide the passionate eyes
Whereto the sweet thoughts all unbid would rise;
The bright-cheeked shame, the conscious mouth as love
Within the half-hid gentle breast 'gan move,
Like a swift-opening flower beneath the sun;
The sigh and half frown as the tale was done,
And thoughts uncertain, hard to grasp, did flit
'Twixt the beginning and the end of it—
And to their ancient eyes it well might seem.
Lay tale in tale, as dream within a dream,
Untold now the beginning, and the end
Not to be heard by those whose feet should wend
Long ere that tide through the dim ways of death.

But now the sun grew dull, the south wind's breath
Ruffled the stream, and spake within the trees
Of rain beyond the hills; the images
The tale wrought changed with the changed deadening day,
Till dim they grew and vanished quite away.

Now when September drew unto its end,
Unto the self-same place those men did wend
Where last they feasted; and the autumn day
Was so alike to that one passed away,
That, but for silence of the close stripped bare,
And absence of the merry folk and fair,
Whose feet the deep grass, making haste to grow
Before the winter, minded nothing now
But for the thinned and straightened boughs, well freed
Of golden fruit; the vine-stocks that did need
No pruning more, ere eager man and maid
Brown fingers on the dusty bunches laid—
But for these matters, they might even deem
That they had slept awhile and dreamed a dream,
And woke up weary in the self-same place.

And now as each man saw his fellow's face
They 'gan to smile, beholding this same thought
Each in the other's eyes:

"Or all is nought
Whereof I think," at last a wanderer said,
"Or of my tale shall ye be well apaid;
Meet is it for this silent company
Sitting here musing, well content to see
The shadows changing, as the sun goes by:
A dream it is, friends, and no history
Of men who ever lived; so blame me nought
If wondrous things together there are brought,
Strange to our waking world—yet as in dreams
Of known things still we dream, whatever gleams
Of unknown light may make them strange, so here
Our dreamland story holdeth such things dear
And such things loathed, as we do; else, indeed,
Were all its marvels nought to help our need.

THE LAND EAST OF THE SUN AND WEST OF THE MOON

ARGUMENT

This tale, which is set forth as a dream, tells of a churl's son who won a fair Queen to his love, and afterwards lost her, and yet in the end was not deprived of her.

In Norway, in King Magnus' days,
A man there dwelt, my story says,
Who Gregory had got to name;
Folk said from outland parts he came,
Though none knew whence; he served withal
The Marshal Biorn in field and hall,
And little, yet was deft of hand
And stout of heart, when men did stand
Spear against spear; and his black eyes
Folk deemed were somewhat overwise.
For of the stars full well he knew,
And whither lives of men they drew.
So Gregory the Star gazer
Men called him, and somewhat in fear
They held him, though his daily mood
Was ever mild enow and good.
It chanced upon a summer day,
When in the south King Magnus lay,
With all his men, the Marshal sent
A well-manned cutter, with intent
To get him fish for house-keeping,

And Gregory, skilful in this thing,
The skipper over them to be;
So merrily they put to sea,
And of a little island lay,
Amidst the firth, and fished all day,
But when night fell, ashore they went
Upon the isle, and pitched their tent,
And ate and drank, and slept at last.
But while sleep held the others fast
Did Gregory waken, turning oft
Upon his rough bed nothing soft,
Till stealthily at last he rose
And crept from the tent thronged and close
Into the fresh and cloudless night,
And 'neath the high-set moon's cold light
Went softly down unto the sea;
And sleep, that erst had seemed to be
A thing his life must hope in vain,
Now 'gan to fall on him again,
E'en as he reached the sandy bay
Where on the beach their cutter lay.
Calm was the sea 'twixt wall and wall
Of the green bight; the surf did fall
With little noise upon the sand,
Where 'neath the moon the smooth curved strand
Shone white 'twixt dark sea, rocks, and turf.

There, hearkening to the lazy surf,
Musing he scarcely knew of what,
Upon a grey rock Gregory sat,
Till sleep had all its will of him,
And now at last, with slackened limb
And nodding head, he fell to dream;
And far away now did he seem,
Waked up within the great hall, where
King Magnus held right merry cheer
In honour of the Christmas-tide,
At Ladir; and on every side
His courtmen and good bonders sat.
There as folk talked of this and that,
And drank, and all were blithe enow,
Amid the drifting of the snow
And howling of the wind without,
Within the porch folk heard a shout,
And opening of the outer door;
Then one came in, who to the floor
Cast down the weight of snow, and stood
Undoing of his fur-lined hood,
And muttering in his beard the while.
The King gazed on him with a smile,
Then said at last—"What is it then?

Art thou called one of my good men,
And art thou of the country-side,
Or hast thou mayhap wandered wide?
Come sit thee down and eat and drink—
And yet hast thou some news, I think?"

The man said, "News from over sea
Of Mary and the Trinity,
And goodman Joseph, do I bring;
Nowell, Nowell, Nowell, O King!"

Inward he stalked on, therewithal,
But stopped amidmost of the hall,
And cast to earth his cloak and hood,
And there in glittering raiment stood,
While the maids went about the board
And deftly the cup's river poured,
And 'mid great clank of ewer and horn
Men drank the day when Christ was born.

Then by the King the gold-clad man
Sat, Gregory dreamed, and soon began
Great marvels of far lands to tell,
And said at last:
"Ye serve me well,
And strange things therefore will I show,
Wonders that none save ye may know;
That ye this stormy night may call
A joyful tide in kingly hall
A night to be remembered."
Then Gregory dreamed he turned his head
Unto the stranger, and their eyes
Met therewith, and a great surprise
Shot through his heart, because indeed
That strange man in the royal weed
Seemed as his other self to be
As he began this history.

In this your land there once did dwell
A certain carle who lived full well,
And lacked few things to make him glad;
And three fair sons this goodman had,
Whereof were two stout men enow
Betwixt the handles of the plough,
Ready to drive the waggons forth,
Or pen the sheep up from the north,
Or help the corn to garner in,
Or from the rain the hay to win;
To dyke after the harvesting,
And many another needful thing.
But slothful was the youngest one,

A loiterer in the spring-tide sun,
A do-nought by the fire-side
From end to end of winter-tide,
And wont in summer heats to go
About the garden to and fro,
Plucking the flowers from bough and stalk;
And muttering oft amid his walk
Old rhymes that few men understood.

"Now is he neither harm nor good,"
His father said; "there, let him go
And do what he has lust to do."

Now so it chanced the goodman had
A meadow meet to make him glad
Full oft because of its sweet grass,
Whereto an ill thing came to pass,
When else the days were drawing nigh
To hay-harvest, and certainly
Our goodman thought all would be won
Before the morrow of St. John.
For as he walked thereto one day
He fell to thinking on the way,
"A fair east wind, and cloudless sky
In scythes before two days go by."
But yet befell a grievous slip
Betwixt that fair cup and the lip,
For when he reached the wattled fence,
And looked across his meadow thence,
His broad face drew into a frown,
For there he saw all trodden down
A full third of the ripening grass,
So that no scythe might through it pass;
Then in a rage he turned away
And was a moody man that day.

But when that eve he sat at home
And his two eldest sons had come
Back from the field, he spake and said:—

"Ill-doers, sons, by likelihood
Be here about, or envious men;
I thought the last had left us, when
Skeggi's two sons put off to sea,
Yet is there left some enemy
Not bold enough on field or way
To draw the sword his debt to pay;
Therefore, son Thorolf, shalt thou go
And bear with thee the great cross-bow,
And hide within the white-thorn brake
And lie there all this night awake

Watching the great south meadow well;
Because last night it so befell
This gangrel thief thought fit to tread
The grass to mammocks by my head!"

So Thorolf rose unwillingly,
And round about his waist did tie
The case of bolts, and took adown
The mighty cross-bow tough and brown,
And in his strong belt set a knife
Lest he should come to closer strife,
And thereon, having drunk full well,
Went on his way, and thought to tell,
A goodly tale at break of day.
Thus to the mead he gat, and lay
Close hidden in the hawthorn brake,
And kept but little time awake,
But on the sorrel slept as soft
As on his truckle in the loft,
Nor woke until the sun was high,
When looking thence full sleepily
He saw yet more of that fair field,
So dealt with, that it scarce would yield
Much fodder to his father's neat
That summer-tide, of sour or sweet.
Then home he turned with hanging head,
And right few words that tide he said,
In answer to his father's scoff,
But toward the middenstead went off.

So that same night the vexed carle sent
His next son Thord with like intent;
But ere the yellow moon was down
Asleep and snoring lay our clown,
And waking at the dawn could see
The meadow trodden grievously.

Now when unto the house he came,
Speaking no word for very shame,
The good man 'gan to gibe and jeer,
Saying, that many a groat too dear
Such sleepy-headed fools he bought,
That tide when he their mother sought
With Flemish cloth and silver rings
And chains, and far-fetched, dear-bought things
The mariners had sold to him,
For which had many a man to swim
Head downward to the porpoises—
All to get gluttons like to these!

The third son John, who on the floor

Was lying kicking at the door,
Turned round and yawned, and stretched, and said,
"Alas, then, all my rest is sped,
For now thou wilt be sending me,
O father, the third watch to be.
Well, keep thy heart up, I shall know
To-morrow, what thing grieves thee so."

"Yea, yea," his father said, "truly
A noble son thou art to me!
Thou fool, thou thinkest then to win
The game when these have failed therein!
Truly a mighty mind I have
Thy bread and beer henceforth to save,
And send thee with some skipper forth,
Who brings back stockfish from the north;
Then no more dreaming wouldst thou spend
Thy days, but learn to know rope's-end,
And stumble on the icy decks
To no sweet music of rebecks.
Yet since indeed a fool may do
What no wise man may come unto,
Go thou, if thou hast any will,
Because thou canst not do me ill;
And lo, thou! if thou dost me good
Then will I fill thy biggest hood
With silver pennies for thine own,
To squander in the market-town."

Nought answered John, but turned away,
And underneath the trees all day
He slept, but with the moon arose;
Nor did he arm himself like those,
His brethren, for he thought, 'Indeed
Of bolt and bow have I no need,
For if ill-doers there should be,
Then will they slay me certainly,
If I should draw on them a bolt;
And, though my brethren call me dolt,
Yet have I no such foolish thought
For a shaft's whistle to be brought
To death—withal I shall not see
Men-folk belike, but faërie,
And all the arms within the seas
Should help me nought to deal with these;
Rather of such lore were I fain
As fell to Sigurd Fafnir's-bane
When of the dragon's heart he ate.
Well whatso hap I gain of fate,
I know I will not sleep this night,
But wake to see a marvellous sight.'

Therewith he came unto the mead,
And looked around with utmost heed
About the remnant of the hay;
Then in the hawthorn brake he lay
And watched night-long 'midst many a thought
Of what might be, and yet saw nought
As slowly the short night went by,
'Midst bittern's boom and fern-owl's cry;
Then the moon sank, the stars grew pale,
And the first dawn 'gan show the veil
The night had drawn from tree to tree,
A light wind rose, and suddenly
A thrush drew head from under wing,
And through the cold dawn 'gan to sing,
And one by one about him woke
The minstrels of the feathered folk,
Long ere the first gleam of the sun.
Then, though his watch was but begun,
E'en at that tide, as well he knew,
O'er John a drowsiness there drew,
And nothing seemed so good as sleep,
And sweet dreams o'er his eyes 'gan creep
That made him smile, then wake again
In terror that his watch was vain;
But in the midst of one of these
He started up, for through the trees
A mighty rushing sound he heard,
As of the wings of many a bird;
And, stark awake, with beating heart,
He put the hawthorn twigs apart,
And yet saw no more wondrous thing
Than seven white swans, who on wide wing
Went circling round, till one by one
They dropped the dewy grass upon.
He smiled thereat, and thought to shout
And scare them off; but yet a doubt
Clung to him, as he gazed on those,
And in the brake he held him close,
And watched them bridle there, and preen
Their snowy feathers well beseen;
So near they were, that he a stone
Might have cast o'er the furthest one
With his left hand, as there he lay.

Apace came on the summer day,
Though the sun lingered, and more near
The swans drew, and began to peer
About in strange wise, and John deemed,
In after days, he must have dreamed
Again, if for the shortest space;

For a cloud seemed to dull the place
And silence of the birds there was;
And when he next looked o'er the grass,
Six swan-skins lay anigh his hand,
And nearby on the grass did stand
Seven white-skinned damsels, wrought so fair
That John must sit and tremble there,
And flush blood-red, and cast his eyes
Down on the ground in shamefast wise,
Then look again with longings sweet
Piercing his heart; because their feet
Moved through the long grey-seeded grass
But some two yards from where he was.

A while in gentle wise they went,
Among the ripe long grass that bent
Before their beauty; then there ran
A thrill through him as they began,
In musical sweet speech and low,
To talk a tongue he did not know;
But when at last one spake alone,
It was to him as he had known
That heavenly voice for many years,
His heart swelled, till through rising tears
He saw them now, nor would that voice
Suffer his hot heart to rejoice,
In all that erst his eyes did bless
With unimagined loveliness:
Because her face, that yet had been
Alone among those girls unseen,
He longed for with such strong desire,
That his heart sickened, and quick-fire
Within his parched throat seemed to burn.

A while she stood and did not turn,
While still the music of her voice
Made the birds' song seem tuneless noise;
And she alone of all did stand,
Holding within her down-drooped hand
The swan-skin—like a pink-tinged rose
Plucked from amidst a July close,
And laid on January snow,
Her fingers on the plumes did show:
A rosy flame of inner love
Seemed glowing through her; she did move
Lightly at whiles, or the soft wind
Played in her hair no coif did bind.
Then did he fear to draw his breath
Lest he should find the hand of Death
Was showing him vain images;
Then did he deem the morning breeze

Blew from the flowery fields of heaven,
Such fragrance to the morn was given.

And now across the long dawn's grey
The climbing sun's first level ray,
Long hoped, yet sudden when it came,
Over the trembling grass did flame
And made the world alive once more;
And therewithal a pause came o'er
The earth and heaven, because she turned,
And with such longing his heart burned
That there he thought he needs must die,
And, breathless, opened mouth to cry.
And yet how soft and kind she seemed;
What a sweet helpful smile there gleamed
Over the perfect loveliness
That now his feeble eyes did bless!

Now fell the swan-skin from her hand,
And silent all a space did stand,
And then again she turned away,
And seemed some whispered word to say
Unto her fellows; and therewith
Their delicate round limbs and lithe
Began to sway in measured time
Unto a sweet-voiced outland rhyme
As they cleft through the morning air
Hither and thither: fresh and fair
Beyond all words indeed were these,
Yet unto him but images
Well wrought, fair coloured: while she moved
Amid them all, a thing beloved
By earth and heaven: could she be
Made for his sole felicity?
Yet if she were not, earth and heaven
Belike for nought to men were given
But to torment his weary heart.
He put the thorny twigs apart
A little more to gaze his fill;
And as he gazed a thought of ill
Shot through him: close unto his hand,
Nigher than where she erst did stand,
Nigher than where her unkissed feet
Had kissed the clover-blossoms sweet,
The snowy swan-skin lay cast down.
His heart thought, 'She will get her gon
E'en as she came, unless I take
This snow-white thing for her sweet sake;
Then whether death or life shall be,
She needs must speak one word to me
Before I die.'

And therewithal
His hand upon the skin did fall
Almost without his will, while yet
His eyes upon her form were set.
He drew it to him, and there lay
Until the first dance died away,
And from amid the rest thereof
Another sprang, whose rhythm did move
Light foot, long hair, and supple limb,
As the wind moves the poplars slim;
Then as the wind dies out again,
Like to the end of summer rain
Amid their leaves, and quivering now
No more their June-clad heads they bow,
So sank the rippling song and sweet,
And gently upon level feet
They swayed, and circle-wise did stand
Each scarcely touching each with hand,
Until at last all motion ceased.

Still as the dewy shade decreased,
Panting John lay, and did not move,
Sunk in the wonder of his love,
Though fear weighed on him; for he knew
That short his time of pleasance grew
Though none had told him.

Now the one
His heart was set on spake alone,
And therewith hand and arm down-dropped,
Their scarce-heard murmuring wholly stopped,
And softly in long line they passed
Unto the thorn-brake, she the last.
Then unto agony arose
John's fear, as once again all close
She was to him. The wind ran by
The notched green leaves, the sun was high,
Dappling the grass whereon he lay:
Fresh, fair, and cheery was the day,
And nought like guile or wizardry
Could one have thought there was anigh,
Till, suddenly, did all things change,
E'en as his heart, and dim and strange
The old familiar world had grown,
That blithe and rough he erst had known,
And racked and mined time did seem.

A sudden, sharp cry pierced his dream,
And then his cleared eyes could behold
His love, half-hid with hair of gold,

Her slim hands covering up her face,
Standing amid the grassy place,
Shaken with sobs, and round her woe,
With long caressing necks of snow
And ruffling plumes, the others stood'
Bird-like again. Chilled to the blood,
Yet close he lay and did not move,
Strengthening his heart with thoughts of love,
Wild as a morning dream. Withal
Some murmured word from her did fall,
Closer awhile the swans did press
Around her woeful loveliness,
As though a loth farewell they bade;
And she one fair hand softly laid
Upon their heads in wandering wise,
Nor drew the other from her eyes,
As one by one her body fair
They left, and rose into the air
With clangorous cries, and circled wide
Above her, till the blue did hide
Their soaring wings, and all were gone.

As scarce she knew that she was lone,
She stood there for a little space,
One hand still covering up her face,
The other drooped down, half stretched out,
As if her lone heart yet did doubt
Somewhat was left her to caress.
Yet soon all sound of her distress
Was silent, though thought held her fast
And nought she moved; the field-mouse passed
Close to her feet, the dragon-fly,
A thin blue needle flickered by,
The bee whirled past her as the morn
Grew later, and strange thoughts were born
Within her.

So she raised her head
At last, and, gazing round, she said:
"Is pitying love all dead on earth?
Is no heart left that holds of worth
Love that hands touch not, and that eyes
Behold not? Is none left so wise
As not to know the smart of bliss
That dieth out 'twixt kiss and kiss?"

She stopped and trembled, for she heard
The hawthorn brake beside her stirred,
Then turned round, half unwittingly,
Across the meadow-grass to flee,
And knew not whither, as, half blind,

She heard the rustling twigs behind,
And therewithal a breathless cry
And eager footsteps drawing nigh.
With streaming hair, a little way
She fled across the trodden hay,
Then failed her feet, and turning round,
She cowered low upon the ground,
With wild eyes turned to meet her fate,
E'en as the partridge doth await,
With half-dead breast and broken wing,
The winged death the hawk doth bring.

Dim with the horror of that race,
Wild eyes her eyes met, and pale face,
And trembling outstretched hands that moved
No nigher to her body loved,
Whereto they had been brought so near.
For very fear of her wild fear.

So each of other sore afraid,
There fleer and pursuer stayed,
Each gathering breath and heart to speak—
And he too hopeless, she too weak,
For a long space to say a word.

Yet first her own faint voice she heard,
For in his hand she saw the skin,
And deemed she knew what he would win,
And how that morning's deed had gone:

"What have I done? what have I done?
Did I work ever harm to thee,
That thou this day my bane shouldst be?
Why is there such hate in thine eyes
Against me?"

From his breast did rise
A dumb sound, but no word came forth;
She shrank aback yet more:
"What worth,
What worth in all that thou hast done?
For say my body thou hast won,
Art thou God, then, to keep alive,
Unless my will therewith I give?"
E'en as she spake, a look of pain
Twitched at his face; she spoke again:

"For now I see thou hat'st me not,
But thinkest thou a prize hast got
Thou wilt not lightly cast away:
O hearken, hearken!—a poor prey

Thy toils shall take, a thing of stone
Amid your folk to dwell alone
And hide a heart that hateth thee."

He shrank back from her wretchedly,
And dropped his hand and hung his head;
"Nay, now I hate thee not," she said—
"And who knows what may come to be
If thou but give mine own to me,
And free this trembling body here?
Wouldst thou rejoice if thou wert dear,
Dear unto me though far away,
And hope still fed thee day by day?"

She deemed he wept now, as he turned
Away from her, and her heart yearned
Somewhat toward him as she spake:

"And if thou dost this for my sake,
Wilt thou, for all that, deem this morn
Has made thee utterly forlorn?
Hast thou not cast thine arms round Love
At least, thy weary heart to move,
To make thy wakening strange and new,
And dull life false and old tales true;
Yea, and a tale to make thy life
To speed the others in the strife,
To quicken thee with wondrous fire,
And make thee fairer with desire?
Wilt thou, then, think it all in vain,
'The restless longing and the pain,
Lightened by hope that shall not die?
For thou shalt hope still certainly,
And well mayst deem that thou hast part,
Somewhat, at least, in this my heart,
Whatever else therein may be."

He turned about most eagerly
And gazed upon her for a while .
Wild fear had left her, and a smile
Had lit up now her softened face,
Sweet pleading kindness gave new grace
To all her beauty; fresh again
Her cheeks grew, haggard erst with pain
She saw the deep love in his eyes,
And slowly therewithal 'gan rise,
While something in her heart there moved,
Some pleasure to be well beloved,
Some pain because of doubt and fear,
Of once-loved things grown scarce so dear;
Less clear all things she seemed to see,

Her wisdom in life's mystery
Seemed fleeting, and for very shame
A tingling flush across her came.

But close unto him did she stand,
And, reaching out her little hand,
Took his, and in strange searching wise
Gazed on him with imploring eyes;
And with the sweetness of that touch
And look, wrought fear and hope o'ermuch
Within him, and his eyes waxed dim,
And trembling sore in every limb,
He slid adown, and knelt, and said:

"O sweetly certes hast thou prayed,
Nor used vain words, but smitten me
With all the greater agony
For all thy sweetness: so, indeed,
If thou art holpen well at need
By this thy prayer, yet meet it is
Ere this one moment of great bliss
Has turned to nought all life to come,
That thou shouldst hear me ere my doom,
And yet indeed what prayer to make
Thy heart amid its calm to shake,
When thou art gone—when thou art gone,
And I and woe are left alone!
What fiercest word shall yet avail
If this my first and last one fail—
Wherewith shall the hard heart be moved
If this move not, that it is loved?"

His eager hand her hand did press,
His eyes devoured her loveliness.
But silent she a short while stood,
Her face now pale, now red as blood,
While her lip trembled, and her eyes
Grew wet to see his miseries,
At last she spake with down-cast head;

"Alas, what shall I do?" she said,
"Thy prayer shall make me sorrow more
Whenas I go to that far shore
I needs must go to; for I know,
Poor soul! that thou wilt let me go,
Since thou art grown too wise and kind
My helpless soul with force to bind—
Would thou might'st have some part in me!"

She shrank aback afraid, for he
Now sprang up with a bitter cry:

"Thou knowest not my agony!
Thou knowest not the words thou say'st,
Or what a wretched, empty waste
This remnant of my life is grown,
Or how I need thee all alone
To heal the wound this morn has made!
Why tremblest thou?—be not afraid;
I will not leave thee any more:
Come near to me! My mother bore
No dreadful thing when I was born.
Fear not, thou art not yet forlorn,
As I, as I, as I shall be
If ever thou shouldst go from me."

She shrank no more, but looked adown
And said, "Alas! why dost thou frown?
Wilt thou be ever angry thus?"
Her voice was weak and piteous
As thus she spake, and in her breast
A sob there moved, yet hard she pressed
The hand she held: too sweet was love
For any word his lips to move;
Too sweet was hope that lips might dare
To touch her sweet cheek smooth and fair.
Yet with her downcast eyes she knew
That nigher ever his face drew
To hers, and new-born love did flame
Out from her heart, as now there came
A sound half sigh, half moan from him;
She trembled sore, all things 'gan swim
Before her eyes, nor felt her feet
The firm earth—for all over-sweet
For sight or hearing life 'gan grow,
As panting, and with changed eyes now,
She raised her parted lips to his.

But ere their fair young mouths might kiss,
While hand stole unto hand, and breath
Met breath, the image of cold death,
With his estranging agonies,
Smote on her heart that once was wise;
As touched by some sharp sudden sting,
Back from her love's arms did she spring,
And stood there trembling; and her cry
Rang through the morn:
"Why shouldst thou die
Amidst thy just-won joy?" she said,
"And must I see thee stark and dead
Who have beheld thy gathering bliss?
Touch me no more yet—so it is
That thy fierce heart hath conquered me,

That I no more may look on thee
Without desire—for such an end
I hitherward, belike, did wend,
Led on by fate, and knew it not—
But if thy love is e'en as hot
As thine eyes say, what wilt thou do?
Loved or loved not, still is it so,
That in thy land I may not live.
Too strong thou art that I should strive
With thee and love—Yet what say'st thou?
Art thou content thy love to throw
Unto the waste of time, and dwell
Here in thy land, and fare right well,
Feared, hated maybe, yet through all
A conquering man, whate'er shall fall—
Or, in mine own land be mine own,
Live long, perchance, yet all unknown,
Love for thy master and thy law,
Nor hope another lot to draw
From out life's urn?—Think of it, then!
Be great among the sons of men
Because I love thee, and forget
That here amid the hay we met—
Or else be loved and love, the while
Life's vision doth thine eyes beguile."

He fell upon his knees, and cried:
"Ah, wilt thou go?—the world is wide
And waste; we were together here
A while ago, and I grew dear
To thee, I deemed—what hast thou said?
Behold, behold, the world is dead,
And I must die, or ere I deal
With its dead follies more, or feel
The dead men's dreams that move men there,
Alas, how shall I make my prayer
To thee, who lovedest me time agone,
No more to leave my heart alone?"

Musing, his passionate speech she heard,
And with a strange look, half afeard,
Half pitying, did she gaze on him,
Until through tears that sight waxed dim;
At last she spake:
"No need to pray
Lest I thy love, O love, betray;
But many a thought there is in me
If I through love might clearly see;
But the morn wanes fast, dear, arise
And let me hence, lest eviler eyes
Than thine behold my body here,

And thou shouldst buy thy bliss too dear;
So bring me to some place anigh
Amid thick trees, where thou and I
May be alone a little space,
To make us ready for the place
Where love may still be happiness
Unmixed with change and ill distress."

He gazed on her, but durst not speak,
Nor noted how a sigh did break
The sweetness of her speech, but took
Her white hand with a hand that shook
For very love, and o'er the grass,
Scarce knowing where his feet did pass,
He led her, till they came at last
Unto a beech-wood, where the mast
And dry leaves, made a carpet meet,
Sun-speckled, underneath their feet.
She stopped him, grown all grave and calm,
And laid lips like a healing balm
Upon his brow and spake:
"Ah, would
That I who know of ill and good,
And thou who may'st learn e'en as much
By misery, might deem this touch
Of calm lips, joy enough to last
Till life with all its whirl were past—
This kiss, and memory of the morn
Whereon the sweet desire was born."

He trembled, and beseechingly
Gazed on her: "Ah, no, no," said she,
"No more with thee this day I strive,
E'en as thou prayedst will I give;
Belike because I may not choose,
Nay nor may let my own soul loose.
Is it enow?"
Once more he strove,
With some sweet word to bless his love
And might not; but she smiled and said:
"The lovers of old time are dead,
And so too shall it be with thee.
Yea, hast thou heard no history
Of lovers who outlived the love
That once they deemed the world would move?
And so too may it be with thee.
Nay stretch thy right hand out to me,
Poor soul, and all shall soon be done."

A gold ring with a dark green stone
Upon his finger then she set,

And said: "Thou may'st repent thee yet
The giving of this gift to-day;
Be wise then! Cast the ring away,
Give me my own and get thee gone;
For all the past, not so alone
Shall thou and I then be, as erst;
Sad, longing, loving, not accurst."

She trembled as she spake, and turned
Unto his eyes a face that yearned
With great desire, although her eyes
Seemed wonderful and overwise.
But pain of anger changed his face,
He said; "I have compelled thy grace,
But not thy love then; do to me
E'en as thou willest, and go free."

She murmured; "Nay, what wilt thou have?
Thou prayedst and the gift I gave,
Giving what I might not withhold,
In spite of wisdom clear and cold.
Alas, poor heart unsatisfied,
Why wilt thou love? the world is wide
And holdeth many a joyous thing:
Why wilt thou for thy misery cling
To that desire that resteth not
What part soever thou hast got
Of that whose whole thou ne'er shalt gain?
Alas for thee and me, most vain,
Most vain to wrangle more of this!
Come then, where wait us woe and bliss,
Give me the swan-skin, lay thee down,
Nought doubting, on the beech-leaves brown!"

What spell weighed on his heart but love
I know not, but nought might he move
Except to do her whole command;
He lay adown, and on his hand
Rested his cheek; his eyes grew dim,
Yet saw he the white beech-trunks slim
At first; and his fair-footed love
He saw 'twixt sun and shadow move
Close unto him, and languidly
Her rosy fingers did he see
About the ruffled swan-skin white,
Even as when that strange delight
First maddened him; then dimmer grew
His sight, and yet withal he knew
That over him she hung, and blessed
His face with her sweet eyes, till rest,
As deep as death as soft as sleep,

Across his troubled heart did creep;
And then a long time seemed gone by
And 'mid soft herbage did he lie
With shut eyes, half awake, and seemed
Some dream forgotten to have dreamed,
So sweet, he fain would dream again;
Then came back memory with a pain,
Like death first heard of; with a cry
And fear swift born of memory
He oped his eyes, that dazed with light
Long kept from them, saw nought aright;
But something kind, and something fair,
Seemed yet to be anigh him there,
Whereto he stretched his arms, that met
Soft hands, and his own hands were set
On a smooth cheek, he seemed to know
From days agone;
"Sweet, sweet doth blow
The gentle wind," he said, "whereas
Surely o'er blossoms it doth pass
If any there be made so sweet."

And as he spake, his lips did meet
In one unhoped, undreamed-of kiss,
The very heart of all his bliss.

Like waking from an ecstasy,
Too sweet for truth it seemed to be,
Waking to life full satisfied
When he arose, and side by side,
Cheek touching cheek, hand laid in hand,
They stood within a marvellous land,
Fruitful, and summer-like, and fair.
The light wind sported with her hair,
Crowned with a leaf-like crown of gold,
Or round her limbs drave lap and fold
Of her light raiment strange of hue
That earthly shuttle never knew;
From overhead the blossoms sweet
Fell soft, pink-edged upon her feet,
That moved the grass now, as her voice
Made the soft scented air rejoice
And made him tremble; murmuring;
"Come,
These are the meadows of my home,
My home and thine; much have I now
To tell thee of, and much to show.
Is it with thee, love, as with me
That too much of felicity
Maketh thee sad? yet sweet it is
That little sadness born of bliss

And thought of death, and memory
That even this perchance goes by."

Too glad his eyes now made his heart
To let his tongue take any part
In all his joy: afraid he felt,
As though but for a while he dwelt
Upon the outer ledge of heaven,
And scarce he knew how much was given
Of all his heart had asked, as she
Led softly on from tree to tree.
He shut his eyes that he might gain
Some image of the world of pain,
Some roughness of the world cast by,
The more his heart to satisfy,
The more to sound the depths of bliss
That now belike was ever his.

But therewithal the dream did break,
And Gregory sat up, stark awake,
And gazing at the surf-line white,
Sore yearning for some lost delight,
Some pleasure gone, he knew not what;
For all that dream was clean forgot.
So rising with a smile and sigh,
He gat him backward pensively
Unto the tent, and past between
The sturdy sleepers, all unseen
Of sleep-bound eyes, sore troubled yet
That he must needs his dream forget.
So on his rough bed down he lay,
And thought to wake until the day,
But scarce had time to turn him round
Ere the lost wonder was well found
By sleep; again he dreamed that he
Sat at the King's festivity,
Again did that sweet tale go on,
But now the stranger guest was gone
As though he had not been, and he
Himself, Star gazing Gregory,
Sat by King Magnus, clad in gold,
And in such wise the sequel told.

Midst all that bliss, and part thereof,
Full-fed with choicest gifts of love,
The happy lover lived right long
Till e'en the names of woe and wrong
Had he forgotten.—Of his bliss
Nought may we tell, for so it is
That verse for battle-song is meet,
And sings of sorrow piercing-sweet,

And weaves the tale of heavy years
And hopeless grief that knows no tears
Into a smooth song sweet enow,
For fear the winter pass too slow;
Yet hath no voice to tell of Heaven
Or heavenly joys for long years given,
Themselves an unmatched melody,
Where fear is slain of victory
And hope, held fast in arms of love,
No more the happy heart may move.
Sweet souls, grudge not our drearihead,
But let the dying mourn their dead
With what melodious wail they will!
Even as we through good and ill
Grudge not your soundless happiness,
Through hope whereof alone, we bless
Our woe with music and with tears.

Now deems the tale that three long years
John in that marvellous land abode,
Till something like a growing load
Of unacknowledged longing came
Upon him, mingled with a shame,
Which happiness slew not, that he
Apart from his own kind must be,
Nor share their hopes and fears: withal
A gloom upon his face did fall,
His love failed not to note, and knew
Whither his heart, unwitting, drew.

And so it fell that, on a day,
As musing by her side he lay,
She spake out suddenly, and said:
"What burden on thy soul is laid,
What veil through which thou canst not see,
Thinkst thou that I hide aught from thee?"

He caught her in his arms, and cried,
"What is it that from love can hide?
Thou knowest this, thou knowest this!"

"Alas," she said, "yet so it is
That never have I told to thee
What danger crept toward thee and me!
How could I spoil the lovesome years
With telling thee of slow-foot fears,
Or shade the sweetness of our home
With what perchance might never come?
But now we may not turn aside
From the sharp thorn the rose did hide."

He turned on her a troubled face,
And said, "What is it, from what place
Comes trouble on us?"
She flushed red
As one who lies, and stammering said;
"In thine own land, where while ago
Thou dwelledst, doth the danger grow.
How thinkst thou? hast thou such a heart,
That thou and I a while may part
To make joy greater in a while?"

She smiled, but something in her smile
Was like the heralding of tears,
When lonely pain the grieved heart bears.
But he sprang up unto his feet,
Glad 'gainst his will, and cried; "O sweet,
Fear nought at all, for certainly
Thy fated fellow still am I;
Tell me the tale, and let me go
The nighest way to meet the foe."

Something there was, that for a while
Made her keep silence; with a smile
His bright flushed visage did she note,
And put her hand unto her throat
As though she found it hard to breathe;
At last she spake:
"The long years seethe
With many things, until at last
From out their caldron is there cast
Somewhat like poison mixed with food;
To leave the ill, and take the good
Were sweet indeed, but nowise. life,
Where all things ever are at strife.
Thou, knowing not belike, and I,
Wide-eyed indeed and wilfully,
Through these three years have ever striven
To take the sweet of what was given
And cast the bitter half aside;
But fate his own time well can bide,
And so it fares with us to-day.
Bear this too, that I may not say
What danger threatens; thou must go
Unto thy land and nothing know
Of what shall be—a hard, hard part
For such as thee, with patient heart
To sit alone, and hope and wait,
Nor strive in anywise with fate,
Whatever doubt on thee may fall,
Unless by certain sign I call
On thee to help me: to this end

Each day at nightfall shalt thou wend
Unto that place, where thou and I
First met; there let an hour go by,
And if thereby nought hap to thee
Of strange, then deem thou certainly
All goeth, or too well or ill
For thee to help, and bide thou still."

She had arisen, side by side
They stood now, and all red had died
From out his face, most wan he grew,
He faltered forth:
"Would that I knew,
If thou hadst ever loved me, sweet!
Then surely all things would I meet
With good heart."
Such a trouble came
Across his face, that she, for shame
Of something hidden, blushed blood-red,
Then turned all pale again, and said:

"Thou knowest that I love thee well!
What shall I do then? can I tell
In one short moment all the love
That through these years my heart did move?
Come nigher, love, and look at me,
That thou in these mine eyes mayst see
If long enow this troubled dream,
That men call life, mine heart may deem
To love thee in."
His arms he cast
About her and his tears fell fast,
Nor was she dry-eyed; slowly there
Did their lips part, her fingers fair
Sought for his hand:
"Come, love," she said,
"Time wears;" withal the way she led
Unto the place where first he woke
Betwixt a hawthorn and an oak,
And said: "Lie down, and dream a dream,
That nought real, wasted then may seem
When next we meet! yet hear a word
Ere sleep comes: thou mayst well be stirred
By idle talk, or longings vain,
To wish me in thine arms again;
Long then, but let no least word slip
Of such a longing past thy lip;
For if thou dost, so strangely now
Are we twain wedded, I and thou,
And that same golden green-stoned ring
Is token of so great a thing

That at thy word I needs must come
Whereso I be unto thine home;
And so were both of us undone:
Because the great-eyed glaring sun
That lights your world, too mighty is
To look upon our secret bliss.
What more to say or e'er thou sleep?
I would I yet had time to weep
All that I would, then many a day
Would pass, or thou shouldst go away.
But time wears, and the hand of fate,
For all our weeping, will not wait.
—Yet speak, before sleep wrap thee round,
That I once more may hear the sound
Of thy sweet voice, if never more."

For all her words she wept right sore.
"What wouldest thou?" he said in turn,
"Thou know'st for thee and peace I yearn
Past words—but now thy lips have sealed,
My lips with mysteries unrevealed;
How shall I pray, this bitter morn
That joy and me atwain hath torn?
While yet as in a dream it is
Both bliss and this strange end of bliss.
Ah what more can I say thereof?
That never any end of love
I know, though all my bliss hath end;
That where thou willest I will wend,
Abide where thou wouldst have me stay,
Pass bitter day on bitter day
Silent of thee, and make no sign
Of all the love and life divine,
That is my life and knowledge now."

And with that word he lay a-low
And by his side she knelt, and took
His last kiss with a lovely look,
Mingled of utmost love and ruth
And knowledge of the hidden truth.
And then he heard her sing again
Unknown words to a soft low strain,
Till dim his senses waxed, nor knew
What things were false, and what were true,
Mid all the things he saw and heard,
But still among strange-plumaged bird,
Strange-fruited tree, and strange-clad maid,
And horrors making not afraid
Of changing man, and dim-eyed beast,
Through all he deemed he knew at least
That over him his true-love hung

And 'twixt her sobs in sweet voice sung
That mystic song, until at last
Into the dreamless land he passed
Of deep, dark sleep without a flaw
Where nought he heard and nought he saw.

Amidst unreasoning huge surprise,
Remembering nought, he oped his eyes
And leapt up swiftly, and there stood
Blinking upon a close beech-wood
As one who knew not aught of it;
Yet in a while 'gan memory flit
Across him, and he muttered low
Unwitting words said long ago
When he was yet a child; then turned
To where the autumn noon-sun burned
Bright on a cleared space of the wood,
Where midst rank grass a spruce-tree stood,
Tall, grey-trunked, leafless a long way,
And memory of another day,
Like to a dream within a dream
Therewith across his heart 'gan gleam,
And gazing up into the tree,
He raised his right arm suddenly,
E'en as he fain would climb the same;
Then, as his vision clearer came,
He muttered, 'O Nay, gone is the nest,
Nor is it spring-tide; it were best
Unto the stead to hurry back,
Or else my dinner may I lack,
For father's grip is close enow."
And therewithal, with head hung low,
Even as one who needs not sight,
And looking nor to left nor right,
Through blind ways of the wood he went,
Seeming as he were right intent
On heavy thoughts, as well might be,
But scarcely waked yet verily,
Or knowing in what place he was.
In such wise swiftly did he pass
Without a check straight through the wood,
Until on the slope-side he stood,
Where all its tangles were clean done;
There staying, while the unclouded sun
Gleamed on the golden braveries
That clad him, did he raise his eyes,
And 'neath his shading hand looked thence,
And saw o'er well-tilled close and fence
A little knot of roofs between
Dark leaves, their ridges bright and green
With spiky house-leek; and withal

Man unto man did he hear call
Afar amid the fields below;
And then a hoarse loud horn 'gan blow
No point of war, but peasant-call
To hurry toward the steaming hall.
Then as a red spark lights a flame
Among light straw, all memory came
Back-rushing on his heart, and he
'Gan think of joy and misery,
Trouble and hope, in tangled wise,
Till longing in his heart 'gan rise
Fretting with troublous ecstasy
All else to nought.

So pensively
Down the hill-side he slipped, and saw
All folk unto the homestead draw,
And noted how a homeman there
Turned round unto the hillside bare
Whereas amid the sun he went,
Then side-long to his fellow bent
And pointed, and all turned about
And stood a while, as if in doubt
Whether for him they should not stay,
Yet went at last upon their way.
Now thereat somewhat did he smile
And walked the slower for a while,
As though with something of a care
To meet outside no loiterer,
Then went on at a swifter pace:
And all things with familiar face
Gazed on him; till again the shame
Of not being of them o'er him came.

Most fair to peaceful heart was all,
Windless the ripe fruit down did fall,
The shadows of the large grey leaves
Lay grey upon the oaten sheaves
By the garth-wall as he past by;
The startled ousel-cock did cry
As from the yew-tree by the gate
He flew; the speckled hen did wait
With outstretched neck his coming in,
The March-hatched cockerel gaunt and thin
Crowed shrilly, while his elder thrust
His stiff wing-weathers in the dust
That grew aweary of the sun:
The old and one-eyed cart-horse dun
The middenstead went hobbling round
Blowing the light straw from the ground.
With curious eyes the drake peered in

O'er the barn's dusk, where dust and din
Were silent now a little space.

There for a while with anxious face,
Yet smiling therewithal, John stood,
Then toward the porch of carven wood
He turned, and hearkened to the hum
Of mingled speech that thence did come
Through the dumb clatter of the hall,
Lest any word perchance might fall
Upon his ears to tell of aught
That change or death thereto had brought,
And, listening so, deemed he could hear
His father's voice, but nothing clear,
And then a pause, and then again
The mingled speech of maids and men.
Again some word remembered
From old days half aloud he said,
And pulled his hood about his brow,
And went with doubtful steps and slow
Unto the door, and took the horn,
His own hand time past did adorn,
And blew a loud, clear blast thereon,
And pushed the door, then like a sun
New come to a dull world he stood,
Gleaming with gold from shoes to hood,
In the dusk doorway of the place
Whence toward him now turned every face.
From 'neath his hood he gazed around,
And soothly there few gaps he found;
Amidmost of the upper board
His brethren sat, Thorolf and Thord;
He saw his sire, half risen up
From the high-seat, a silver cup
In his brown hand; and by his side
His mother o'er her barm-cloth wide
Gazed forward somewhat timidly
The new-corner's bright weed to see.
Small change in these indeed, John thought,
By lapse of days had yet been wrought
And for the rest, but one or two
There were, he deemed, of faces new.
There open-eyed, beer-can in hand,
And staring did the damsels stand
As he had known them; there he saw
Haldor the Icelander half draw
His heavy short-sword forth, as he
The gleam of gold and steel did see
Flash suddenly across the door—
An old man skilled in ancient lore,
And John's own foster-sire withal.

But on one face did John's eyes fall
He needs must note—a woman leaned
O'er Thord, and though her face was screened
By his wide bush of light red hair
Yet might he see that she was fair,
And deemed his brother newly wed.

And now, as thoughts ran through his head
About the tale that he should tell,
His sire, as one who knew right well
What manners unto men were meet,
Rose up and cried from out his seat:

"Knight, or fair lord, whatso thou be'st,
If thou mayst share a bonder's feast,
Sit by me, eat and drink thy fill;
For this my hall is open still
To peaceful men of all degree."

Strange seemed his own voice there to be
To John, as he in feigned speech said:
"Thanks have thou for thy goodlihead
And welcome, goodman; certainly
Hungry and weary-foot am I,
And fain of rest, and strange withal
To this your land, for it did fall,
That e'en now as I chanced to ride
I lighted by a waterside
To slake my thirst; and just as I
Was drinking therefrom eagerly,
A blue-winged jay, new-hatched in spring,
Must needs start forth and fall to sing
His villain plain-song o'er my head;
And like a ghost come from the dead
Was that unto my horse, I trow,
Who swerved and went off quick enow,
To leave me as a gangrel churl."

"Thou seemest liker to an Earl,"
His father said; "but come to meat,
To hungry men are bannocks sweet."

So by his father's side he sat
And of that homely cheer he ate,
Remembered well; and oft he sighed
To think how far away and wide
The years had set him from all this,
And how that all-devouring bliss
Had made the simple life of old
As a dull tale too often told.

But as he sat thereby, full oft
The goodwife's eyes waxed sad and soft,
Beholding him; she muttered low:

"Alas! fair lips, I ought to know,
Like unto lips that once hung here;
Eyes like to eyes that once were dear
When all that body I could hold,
And flaxen-white was hair of gold."

So muttered she, but said not aught
Aloud. Now the fair damsel brought
Mead to the gay-clad man, and he
Beheld her beauty thoughtfully,
As she shook back her cloud of hair,
And swung aside her figure fair,
And clasped the cup with fingers slim,
And poured and reached it forth to him;
Then his heart changed again with shame
As cold cup and warm fingers came
Into his hand, the while his eyes
A look in hers must needs surprise
That made him flush, and she—the red
O'er face and neck and bosom spread
And her hand trembled; Thord the while
Gazed on her with a foolish smile
Across his wide face. So went by
The hour of that festivity,
And then the boards were set aside;
But the host prayed his guest to bide
As long as he had will thereto,
And therewith to the field did go
With sons and homemen, leaving John
Among the women-folk alone.

So these being set to rock and wool,
John sat him down upon a stool
And 'gan to ponder dreamily,
'Mid longings, on the days gone by,
And many a glance did Thord's wife steal
Upon him as she plied the reel
Not noted much, though once or twice
His pensive eyes did meet her eyes,
And troubled and abashed thereat
He reddened. But the good wife sat
Meanwhile, and ever span and span
With steady fingers, and yet wan
Her face was grown; her mouth and eyes
Seemed troubled with deep memories.
At last to Thord's wife did she turn
And said:

"If honey we would earn
Against Yule-tide, the weaving-room
Must hear the clatter of the loom;
Ere the long web is fully done;
So, Thorgerd, thither get thee gone;
Thou, Asa, to the cloth-room go
And wait me there; and for you two,
Mary and Kirstin, best were ye
Sitting in Thorgerd's company,
To give her help with reel and thread
And shuttle."
Therewith, as she said,
So did they, and went, one and all;
But in the doorway of the hall
Did Thorgerd for a moment stand,
Holding her gownskirt in her hand,
Her body swaying daintily,
Nor cared to hold aback a sigh.
Nor son, nor mother noted her,
A little time the twain sat there
Nor spake, though twice the goodwife strove,
But fear forbade her tongue to move;
Nor had he noted much forsooth
Midst his own longing and self-ruth,
Her looks of loving and of doubt.
So from the hall did she pass out,
And left him there alone, and soon
So longing dealt that afternoon
That, fallen to musing pensively,
In the lone hall, now scarce might he
Know if his heart were glad or sad;
And tunes within his head he had
Of ancient songs learnt long ago,
Remembered well through bliss and woe,
And now withal a lovesome stave
He murmured to a measure grave,
Scarce thinking of its sense the while.
But as he sat there, with a smile
Came handmaid Asa back, who bare
Heaped in her arms embroidered gear,
Which by his feet did she let fall,
Then gat her gone from out the hall;
John, startled, ceased a while his drone
To gaze upon the gear cast down,
And saw a dark blue cloak and hood
Wrought with strange needlework and rude
That showed the sun and stars and moon;
Then, gazing, John remembered soon
How for Yule sport four years agone
That selfsame raiment he did on,
And thinking on that bygone mirth

His own rich cloak he cast to earth,
And did on him half wittingly
That long-forgotten bravery;
And though the sun was warm that day
He hugged himself in his old way
Within the warmth of fold on fold
As though he came from out the cold,
And 'gan the hall to pace about;
And at the last must needs break out
Into a song remembered well,
That of the Christmas joy did tell.

Outlanders, whence come ye last?
The snow in the street and the wind on the door.
Through what green seas and great have ye past?
Minstrels and maids, stand forth on the floor.

From far away, O masters mine,
The snow in the street and the wind on the door.
We come to bear you goodly wine,
Minstrels and maids, stand forth on the floor.

From far away we come to you,
The snow in the street and the wind on the door.
To tell of great tidings strange and true.
Minstrels and maids, stand forth on the floor.

News, news of the Trinity,
The snow in the street and the wind on the door.
And Mary and Joseph from over the sea!
Minstrels and maids, stand forth on the floor.

For as we wandered far and wide,
The snow in the street and the wind on the door.
What hap do ye deem there should us betide!
Minstrels and maids, stand forth on the floor.

Under a bent when the night was deep,
The snow in the street and the wind on the door.
There lay three shepherds tending their sheep.
Minstrels and maids, stand forth on the floor.

"O ye shepherds, what have ye seen,
The snow in the street and the wind on the door.
To slay your sorrow, and heal your teen?"
Minstrels and maids, stand forth on the floor.

"In an ox-stall this night we saw,
The snow in the street and the wind on the door.
A babe and a maid without a flaw.
Minstrels and maids, stand forth on the floor.

"There was an old man there beside,
The snow in the street and the wind on the door.
His hair was white and his hood was wide.
Minstrels and maids, stand forth on the floor.

"And as we gazed this thing upon,
The snow in the street and the wind on the door.
Those twain knelt down to the Little One.
Minstrels and maids, stand forth on the floor.

"And a marvellous song we straight did hear,
The snow in the street and the wind on the door.
That slew our sorrow and healed our care."
Minstrels and maids, stand forth on the floor.

News of a fair and a marvellous thing,
The snow in the street and the wind on the door,
Nowell, nowell, nowell, we sing!
Minstrels and maids, stand forth on the floor.

So sang he, and in pensive wise
He sighed, but lifting up his eyes
Beheld his mother standing nigh,
Looking upon him pitifully.
He ran to her, for now he knew
Her yearning love, round her he threw
Strong arms, and cried out:
"So it is,
O mother, that some days of bliss
I still may give thee; yet since I
To thee at least will never lie
Of what I am, and what I hope,
And what with ill things I must cope,
Sit thou aside, and look not strange
When of my glory and great change
I shall tell even such a tale
As best for all things may avail.
And if thou wouldst know verily
Meanwhile, how matters fare with me,
This thing of all things may I tell;
I have been happy and fared well,
But now with blind eyes must await
Some unseen, half-guessed turn of fate,
Before the dropping of the scale
Shall make an ending to the tale,
Or blithe or sad: think not meanwhile
That fear my heart shall now beguile
Of all the joy I have in thee."

She wept about him tenderly

A long while, ere she might say aught;
Then she drew back, and some strange thought
Stirred in her heart belike, for she
Gazed at his splendour timidly,
For the rude cloak to earth was cast,
And whispered trembling at the last.

"Fair art thou come again, sweet son,
And sure a long way hast thou gone,
I durst not ask thee where: but this
I ask thee by the first sweet kiss,
Wherewith I kissed thy new-born face
Long since within the groaning place—
If thou hast been so far, that thou
Canst tell to me—grown old, son, now,
Through weary life, unsatisfied
Desires, and lingering hope untried—
If thou canst tell me of thy ruth,
What thing there is of lies or truth,
In what the new faith saith of those
Great glories of the heavenly close,
And how that poor folk twinned on earth
Shall meet therein in joy and mirth."

Smiling with pity and surprise,
He looked into her wistful eyes,
And kissed her brow therewith, and said:

"Nought know I, mother, of the dead,
More than thou dost—let be—we live
This day at least, great joy to give
Each unto other: but the tale
Must come from thee about the dale,
And what has happed therein, since I
That summer eve went off to try
What thing by folly might be wrought
When strength and wisdom came to nought."

She smiled amid her tears, and there
She told him all he fain would hear,
And happily they talked till eve,
When the men-folk the field did leave
And gat them to the hall, and then
Was great rejoicing of all men
Within a while, for, cloak and hood
Thrown off, in glittering gear John stood
And named himself; yet scarcely now
His father durst his arms to throw
Round his son's neck, remembering
How he had thought him such a thing
As scarce was meet his bread to win.

Small thought had John of that old sin,
Yea, scarce had heart to think of aught,
But when again he should be brought
Face to face with his love; and slow
The leaden minutes lingered now;
Nor could he fail to hope that he
That very hour her face would see;
Needs must he hope that his strong love,
So sore the heart in her must move,
That she no more might bear his pain.

That very hour, he thought again—
That very hour; woe worth the while,
Why should his heart not feel her smile
Now, now?—O weary time, O life,
Consumed in endless, useless strife,
To wash from out the hopeless clay
Of heavy day and heavy day
Some specks of golden love, to keep
Our hearts from madness ere we sleep!

Good welcome if of clownish kind
Did John from both his brethren find,
And from the homemen; Thorgerd seemed
As somewhat less of him she deemed
Than heretofore, and smiled, as she
Put up her fair cheek daintily
To take his kiss. So went the night
Midst mirth and manifold delight,
Till John at last was left alone
To think upon the strange day gone,
Scarce knowing yet, if nearer drew
His bliss because it was gone through.

Now in such wise, day passed by day,
Till heavier on him longing lay,
As still less strange it was to wake
And no kind kiss of welcome take,
And welcome with no loving kiss,
Kind eyes to a new day of bliss;
And as the days passed o'er his head
Sometimes he needs must wake in dread,
That all the welfare, that did seem
To be his life, was but a dream,
Or all at least slipped swiftly by
Into a wretched memory.
Yet would hope leave him not, yea, whiles
Wrapped round about by her strange guiles
All seemed to go right well, and oft
Would memory grow so sweet and soft,
That scarce the thing it imaged had

More might in it to make him glad.

Well may ye deem that mid all this
His brooding face would cloud the bliss
Of many a boisterous night; his sire
Would mutter, "He has clomb up higher.
But still is moonstruck as before;"
His brethren ill his silence bore,
Yet feared him; such a tale he told
That in that mead he did behold
Strange outland people come that morn,
'By whom afar he had been borne
Into a fair land, where, he said,
Thriving, the king's child did he wed
Within a while; "Now, when once more
Their keels shall leave their noble shore,
At Norway will they touch, and then
Back go I with those goodly men,
Now I have seen my land and kin."

Fair Thorgerd ever sought to win
Kind looks of him, and many a day
She from the hall would go away
To rage within some secret place,
That all the sweetness of her face,
Her lingering fingers, her soft word,
'Twixt red half-opened lips scarce heard,
Had bought for her so little ruth;
Although there seemed some times, in sooth,
When John, grown weary of the strife
Within him between dreams and life,
Must think it not so over ill
To watch her hand the shuttle fill,
While on her cheek the red and white
Flickered and changed with new delight,
And hope of being a thing to move
That dreamy man to earthly love.

So autumn fell to winter-tide,
And ever there did John abide,
'Mid hope deferred and longing fierce,
That strove the heavy veil to pierce;
And howso strong his love might be,
Yet were there tides of misery,
When, in his helpless, hopeless rage,
He felt himself as in a cage
Shown to the gaping world; again
Would heavy languor dull his pain,
And make it possible to live,
And wait to see if fate would give
Some pleasure yet ere all was done.

Meantime, with every setting sun,
Unto the meadow as she bade
He went, and often, half afraid
Half hopeful, did he watch the night
Suck slowly in the lingering light;
But of the homefolk, though all knew
Whither his feet at evening drew,
Yet now so great a man he was,
None asked him why he needs must pass
Each eve along the self-same way,
Save Thorgerd, who would oft waylay
His feet returning, and would watch
Some gesture or some word to catch
From his unwariness; and whiles
Her tender looks and words and smiles
Would seem to move him now, and she
Laughed to herself delightedly;
And as the days grew heavier
To John, he oft would gaze on her,
At such times as she tripped along,
And wonder where would be the wrong
If he should tell her of his tale;
Withal he deemed her cheek grew pale,
As unto Yule-tide drew the days,
And oft into her eyes would gaze
In such kind wise, that she awhile
Forgot her foolishness and guile
Surprised by sparks of inner love.

Yet nothing a long while did move
His mouth to fatal speech, until
When the snow lay on moor and hill
And it was Yule-day, he did go
'Twixt the high drift o'er beaten snow
Unto the meadow, as the day
Short, wind-bewildered, died away.
And so, being come unto the thorn
Where first that bitter love was born,
He gazed around, but nothing saw
But endless waste of grey clouds draw
O'er the white waste, while cold and blind
The earth looked; e'en the north-west wind
Found there no long abiding place,
But ever the low clouds did chase
Nor let them weep their frozen tears.

Strange is it how the grieved heart bears
Long hours and days and months of woe,
As dull and leaden as they go,
And makes no sign, yea, and knows not

How great a burden it bath got
Upon it, till all suddenly
Some thought scarce heeded shall flit by,
That tears the veil as by it goes
With seeming careless hand, and shows
The shrinking soul that deep abyss
Of days to come all bare of bliss.
And now with John e'en so it fared.
He saw his woe and longing bared
Before his eyes, as slow and slow
The twilight crept across the snow,
Like to the dying out of hope;
And suddenly he needs must cope
With that in-rushing of despair
Long held aback, till all things there
Seemed grown his foes, his prison-wall;
And, whatso good things might befall
To others of the wide world, he
Was left alone with misery.
Why should he hold his peace or strive
Amid these men as man to live
Who recked not of him? Then he cried:

"Would God, would God, that I had died
Before the accursed name of Love
My miserable heart did move!
Why did I leave thee in such wise,
False heart, with lovesome, patient eyes,
And soul intent to do thy will?
And why, why must I love thee still,
And long for thee, and cast on thee
Blessings wrung out of misery,
That will not bless thee, if in sooth
On my wrecked heart thou hast no ruth?
O come, come, come to me, my love,
If aught my heart thy heart may move,
For I am wretched and alone,
With head grown wild, heart turned to stone,
Come, if there yet be truth in thee!"

He gazed about him timorously
While thus he spake, as though he thought
To see some sudden marvel wrought
In earth and heaven; some dreadful death,
Some sight, as when God threateneth
The world with speedy end; but still
Unchanged, o'er mead and wold and hill
Drave on the dull low twilight rack,
Till all light seemed the sky to lack,
And the snow-shrouded earth to gain
What it had lost.

"In vain, in vain!"
He cried, "and I was well bewrayed;
She wept o'er me when I was laid
Upon the grass beside her feet,
Because a pleasure somewhat sweet
She needs must lay aside, while I—
What tears shall help my misery?"

Then back he turned in e'en such mood
As when one thing seems no more good
Than is another, and will seems
To move the body but by dreams
Of ancient life and energy.
But as he wandered listlessly
Midst the wind's howling, and the drift
Of light snow that its force did lift,
And gained at last the garth's great gate,
He started back, for there did wait
A grey form in the dull grey night,
Yea, and a woman's; strange affright,
Strange hope possessed him, and he strove
To cry aloud some word of love,
But his voice failed him; she came nigh
And drew up to him quietly,
Not speaking; when she reached his side
Her hand unto his hand did glide
And thrilled him with its soft warm touch,
He stammered:
"Have I loved too much,
Have I done wrong? I called thee, dear;
Speak, love, and take away my fear!"

A soft voice answered, "O speak not!
I cannot bear my joy, o'er hot
Waxeth my heart, when in such wise
Thou art changed to me—O thine eyes,
I see them through the darksome night
Gazing upon me! sweet delight,
How shall I deal with all my bliss
So that the world know nought of this,
When scarce now I may breathe or stand
Holding thy lovesome clinging hand."

Now therewith Thorgerd's voice he knew,
And from her hand his hand he drew,
While o'er his heart there swept again
The bitter blast of doubting pain,
And scarce he knew who by his side
Was going, as aloud he cried:

"In vain I call; thou comest not

And all our love is quite forgot;
What new world hast thou got to rule?
What mockeries mak'st thou of the fool
Who trusted thee? Alas, alas!
Whatever ill may come to pass
Still must I love thee."
Now by him
Went Thorgerd silent, every limb
Tingling with madness and desire;
Love lit within her such a fire
As e'en that eve in nowise cooled,
As of her sweet, fresh hope befooled
She strove to speak, and found no word
To tell wherewith her heart was stirred.
So on they went, she knowing nought
The bitterness of his ill thought,
He heeding not in any wise
The wretchedness of her surprise,
Until, thus far estranged, they carne
To where the hall's bright light did flame
Over a space of trodden snow.
Faster a space then did she go,
But, as they drew anigh the door,
Stopped suddenly, and stood before
The musing, downcast man, and laid
A hand upon his breast, and said,
In a low smothered voice:
"Wait now,
And tell me straightly what didst thou
To call me love, and then to cry
Thy love came not? I am anigh,
What wouldst thou have, did I not move
Thy cold heart? am I not thy love?"

Then, trembling as those words she spoke,
She cast to earth her heavy cloak;
From head to foot clad daintily,
Meet for that merry tide was she;
A silver girdle clasped around
Her well-wrought loins, her fair hair crowned
With silver, and her gown enwrought
With flowers whereof that tide knows nought;
Nor needed she that rich attire
To set a young man's heart afire,
For she was delicately made
As is the lily; there she swayed,
Leaned forward to the strenuous wind
That her gay raiment intertwined
About her light limbs. Gazing there,
Bewildered with a strange despair,
John saw her beauty, yet in sooth

Something within him slew all ruth
If for a moment:
"Ah, what love,
What love," he cried, "my heart should move,
But mine own love, my worshipped sweet?
Would God that her beloved feet
Would bless our threshold this same night!"

Then, even as a sudden light
Shows to some wretch the murderer's knife
Drawing anear his outworn life,
Knowledge rushed o'er him, and too late
Did he bethink him of the fate
That threatened, and, grown wild and blind,
He turned to meet the western wind
That hurried past him, thinking, "Now
At least the formless sky will show
Some sign of my undoing swift;
Surely the sightless rack will lift
To show some dreadful misery,
Some image of the summer sky
Defaced by the red lightning's sword."
So spake he, and the fierce wind roared
Amid the firs in sullen wise,
But nothing met his fearful eyes
Save the grey waste of night. Withal
He turned round slowly to the hall,
Trembling, yet doubtful of his heart,
Doubtful of love. But for her part
Thorgerd, half mad with love, had turned
And fled from him; a red spot burned
Amidst each smooth cheek, and her eyes
Afire with furious jealousies,
Followed him down the hall, as he
Went toward the dais listlessly,
And the loud horns blew up to meat,
And restless were her fevered feet
Throughout the feast that now befell.

Now thereat men were served right well,
And most were merry, and the horn
Full oft from board to beard was borne;
But no mead brewed of mortal man
Could make John's face less wild and wan;
For a long while he trembled sore
Whene'er the west-wind shook the door
More than its wont; nor heeded he
The curse of Thorgerd's misery
Wild-gleaming from her eyes; and when
She fell to talk with the young men
With hapless, haggard merriment,

No pang throughout his heart there went:
For clear across it were there borne
Pictures of all the life forlorn
That should be, yea, his life he saw,
Unhelped and heavy-burdened, draw
Through the dull joyless years, until
The bitter measure they should fill,
And he, unloved, unsatisfied,
Unkissed, from foolish hope should hide
In some dark corner of death's house.

Yet, as the feast grew clamorous
About him, and the night went past,
The respite wrought on him at last,
And from its midst did he begin
A little rest from fear to win,
And in the feast he joined and seemed
No more as in their midst he dreamed.

So passed a space, till presently
As with a beaker raised on high
He stood, and called on some great name
Writ in the book of northern fame,
Across the wind there came a sound
As though afar a horn were wound,
A dreadful sound to him; the men
Sat hearkening, till it came again
Nigher and sharper now, and John,
Grown white, laid his left hand upon
His beating heart; and then once more
Loud rang the horn close by the door,
And men began in haste to take
Their weapons for their safety's sake;
But John, the cup in his right hand,
His left upon his heart, did stand,
And might not either move nor speak.

Then cried the goodman, "Not so weak
Are we, but these may well come in
Unmet with weapons; they shall win
All good things on this stormy night;
Go welcome them to our delight;
For on this merry tide of Yule
Shall Christ the Lord all matters rule."

Then opened they the door, and strong
The wild wind swept the hall along,
Driving the hangings here and there,
Making the torches ruddier,
Darkening the fires. But therewithal
An utter hush came o'er the hall,

And no man spake of bad or good;
For in the midst of them there stood
A white-clad woman, white as though
A piece of fair moonlitten snow
Had entered the red smoky hall.
Then sweet speech on their ears did fall
Thrilling all hearts through:
"Joy and peace
Be on this house, and all increase
Of all good things! and thou, my love,
I knew how sore desire must move
Thy longing heart, and I am come
To look upon thee in thy home:
Come to me, give me welcome here!"

He stepped adown, and shame and fear
Mixed with the joyful agony
Of love and longing, as anigh
He drew unto her loveliness.
A moment, and his arms did press
His own love to his heaving breast,
And for an instant of sweet rest
Midst clinging hands and trembling kiss
Did he forget all things but bliss;
And still she murmured:
"Now rejoice
That far away I heard thy voice
And came! rejoice this night at least,
And make good ending to the feast!"

Therewith from out his arms she drew,
Yet held his hand still; scarce he knew
Of where he was, and who were round,
And strange and flat his voice did sound
Unto himself, as now he spake:

"Kinsmen, see her, who for my sake
Has left her mighty state and home,
Fair beyond words, that she might come
With you a little to abide!
How say ye, are ye satisfied
Her sweet face in your midst to see?"

Therewith, though somewhat timidly,
Folk shouted; sooth, they deemed her such
As mortal man might scarcely touch
Or dare to love; with fear fulfilled,
With shame of their rough joyance chilled,
They sat, scarce moving: but to John
Some sweet familiar thing seemed won
Despite his fear, as down the hall

He led her: if his eyes did fall
On Thorgerd's face, how might he heed
The anguish of unholpen need,
That filled her heart with all despair,
As on the twain her eyes did glare?

Now softly to the fair high-seat
With trembling hand he led his sweet,
Who kissed the goodman and goodwife,
And wished them fair and happy life,
Then like the earth's and heaven's queen,
She sat there beauteous and serene,
Till, as men gazed upon her there,
Joy of her beauty slew their fear;
Hot grew their hearts now, as they turned
Eyes on her that with strange light burned:
And wild and eager grew the speech
Wherewith they praised her each to each,
As 'neath her eyes they sat.

If he
Who knew the full felicity
Of all they longed for, hushed at whiles,
Might answer not her healing smiles
With aught but sad imploring eyes,
When he bethought him in what wise
She there was come—yet none the less
Amid bewildered happiness
The time went by; until at last
Night waned, and slowly all folk passed
From out the hall, and the soft sleep
O'er all the marvelling house did creep,
Bearing to folk that night such dreams,
As showed, through wild things, very gleams
Of heaven and perfect love, to last
Till grey light o'er the world was cast.

But, midst the other folk, she too
His mazed and doubtful footsteps drew
Unto the chamber; when alone
They were, and his warm heart seemed one
With her and bliss, without a word
She gazed on him, and like a sword,
Cleaving the very heart atwain
That look was, laden with all pain,
All love and ruth that she might feel.

So through the dark the hours did steal
Slow toward the rising of the sun;
But long or ere the night was done
He slept within her arms, nor heard

The sobs wherewith her breast was stirred,
Nor felt the tears and kisses sweet
That round his set calm face did beat,
As round its dead mate beats a bird
With useless flutter no more heard:
Nor did he move when she unwound
The arms that clasped her breast around,
And, weeping sore, the gold ring drew
From off his hand: and nought he knew
When from the bed at last she slid,
And, with her body all unhid,
Stood gazing on him till a sigh
Burst from her heart; and wearily
From her sad tear-stained troubled face
She swept her hair back:
"O the days,
Thy weary days, love! Dream not then
Of named lands, and abodes of men!
Alas, alas, the loneliest
Of all such were a land of rest
When set against the land where I
Unhelped must note the hours go by!
Ah, that my hope thy dream might pierce!
That mid the dreadful grief and tears,
Which presently shall rend thine heart,
This word the cloud might draw apart—
My feet, lost Love, shall wander soon
East of the Sun, West of the Moon!
Tell not old tales of love, so strong,
That all the world with all its wrong
And heedlessness was weak to part
The loving heart from loving heart?"

Therewith she turned about, and now
She wept no more; her cheeks 'gan glow,
And her eyes glittered, and no more
Sorrow her kind mouth brooded o'er,
And strange, unearthly beauty shone
O'er all her face, whence ruth was gone,
Till the dim-litten place was glad
That in the midst thereof it had
Her loveliness grown dangerous;
Softly she gat her through the house
Where here and there a dying light
Shone on her wondrous limbs and white
As through the rough place dreamily
She moved: yet was the night wind high
And its rude hand, as it did shake
Window and door, served but to make
The inner stillness yet more still.
The clouds were riven; o'er the hill

The white moon shone out, yet its light
Made the deep night so much more night,
That now it seemed as ne'er again
The sun would bless the eyes of men;
That all the world had fallen to death.

So on she passed, her odorous breath
Seen now amidst the moonlit hall,
Her unshod foot's light steady fall,
The waving of her gust-moved hair,
Well-nigh the lonely place might hear
Despite the rush and stir without,
As, slowly, yet all void of doubt
She raised the latchet of the door,
And let the wind and moonlight pour
Wild clamour and strange light there through.
She paused not; the wild west wind blew
Her hair straight out from her; her feet
The bitter, beaten snow did meet
And shrank not; slowly forth she passed
Nor backward any look she cast,
Nor gazed to right or left, but went
With eyes on the far sky intent
Into the howling, doubtful night,
Until at last her body white
And its black shadow on the snow,
No more the drift-edged way did know.

Again the thread snapped; Gregory lay
Awake; nor what had passed away
Of the short night could tell, till he
Through the tent's opening seemed to see
A change creep o'er the moonlit sky;
So there a short while did he lie
Striving to think what he had dreamed,
Till utterly awake he seemed;
And then, since no more on that night
He thought to sleep, and lost delight
Of the past dream grown more than dim,
With causeless longing wearied him,
He rose and left the tent once more,
And passed down slowly toward the shore
Until the boat he came unto:
And there he set himself to do
What things were needed to the gear,
Until he saw the dawn draw near
Across the sea: then, e'en as one
Who through a marvellous land hath gone
In sleep, and knowing nought thereof
To tell, yet knows strange things did move
About his sightless journeying,

So felt he; and yet seemed to bring,
Now and again, some things anigh
Unto the wavering boundary
'Twixt sight and blindness that awhile
Our troubled waking will beguile
When happy dreams have just gone by,
And left us without remedy
Within the unpitying hands of life.

At last, amid perplexing strife
With things half seen, drowsy he grew
Once more, and ever slower drew
The tough brown lines from hand to hand,
Until he sank upon the sand
Beside the boat, and, staring out
O'er the grey sea, lost hope and doubt
In little while, nor noted now
The dawn's line wide and wider grow,
Nor waning of the shadow deep
The moon cast from the boat; till sleep
Had closed his eyes, and in the cold
Of the first dawn the ending told
that sweet tale. Yet so it was,
That the King's hall and feast did pass
Clean from his mind; and now it seemed
That of no tale-telling he dreamed,
But of his own life grown to be
A new and marvellous history.

Midst hope and fear and wretchedness,
And Love, that all things doth redress,
Adown the stream of fate he moved
As the carle's son, the well-beloved,
The fool of longing; in such wise
He dealt with his own miseries.

The winter night was on the wane
When the poor wretch woke up again;
The lone strange sound of cock-crow moved
His heart to dream of his beloved
'Twixt sleep and waking, and he turned
A face with utmost love that yearned
And sighed, as his hot hand stole forth
To touch a body of more worth
To him than Heaven's unmeasured years;
Upon his face were undried tears
Left by some dream, and yet he smiled
To think of deep joy so beguiled
By sadness dreamed; his lips began
To speak a name unknown to man.
A little while in bliss he lay

And gathered thoughts of day on day
More joyful each than each, until
Sweet thankful love his soul did fill
With utter ecstasy of bliss,
And low he murmured:
"Kind she is
Beyond all kindness ever told!
Thou wilt not leave me more, a-cold
In the rough world; thou knowest how
My weak and clinging heart will grow
Unto the strength of thy great heart.
O surely no more shall we part,
And never canst thou hurt me more
Till all the world and time is o'er!"

The moonlight waned, on drew the morn,
The lessened west wind moaned forlorn
In the garth nooks; the eaves dripped now
Beneath the thaw, the faint cock-crow
Through the dull dawn, and no sound more
He heard. Awake, and yearning sore,
He turned about and cried:
"Wake, wake!
Day cometh, and my heart doth ache
To think how sleep still takes from me
Some minutes of felicity,
From me and thee, my love, my sweet!
O think of Death's forgotten feet,
That somewhere surely drawn anigh,
And let no minute more pass by
With our lips parted each from each!"

Wildly the ending of his speech
Rang from his lips, all strange, as though
The thought once thought needs thence must go
In words, though all the world were changed.
Wildly his opened eyes now ranged
The twilight chamber void of her,
And through his heart shot such a fear
As words may tell not—nay indeed
No fear—for now he knew the meed
Of his fool's word, and for a while
No hope was left that might beguile
His misery and his loneliness,
No eager sight, born of distress,
Might pierce the cloud that o'er him spread.
Such wild thoughts filled his 'wildered head,
As once or twice may men endure
Yet live; for the earth seemed not sure,
Or the air fleeting; fire burned not,
Nor water moyed; the snow was hot,

The dark hid nought; the coming day
No longer sober seemed and grey,
But full of flashing light and blue.
Yet all things round him well he knew,
More real they seemed than e'er before,
They would not change, nor would pass o'er
One instant of his agony.
It was as he had seen time die,
And good turn evil 'neath his eyes,
And God live to forge miseries
For him alone, for him alone,
For all the world beside seemed gone.

A short while, risen in his bed,
He hung his wretched brooding head
Above the place her limbs had warmed,
And shrieked not, though strange curses swarmed
About his heart, and wild and fierce
Strove hard his dead despair to pierce,
And might not: nought his heart might ease
Or for a moment gain him peace.
Yet in that time of utter ill,
Some reflex of the guiding will
That moved his limbs in happier days
Still wrought in him; round did he gaze
With set eyes, and arose withal;
And e'en therewith a thought did fall
Upon him that some succour brought,
"How can I meet their eyes?" he thought,
"How can I bear to hear again
The voices of the sons of men?"

And, nigh unwitting, at that word,
Hearkening the while if any stirred,
He clad himself and gazed around
The place once more, and on the ground
There lay her raiment: then he turned
His head away, for wild-fire burned
Within it, and he strove to speak;
But, lest his wretched heart should break
And torment end on that first day
A new pain did his pain allay,
And bitter tears and wailing came
To dull the fierceness of the flame
That so consumed him; and withal
Desire of wandering forth 'gan fall
Upon him, though he knew not where
In all the world to seek for her.

So, ere his burning tears were spent,
Through the unwakened hall he went,

And kissed the threshold of the door
Her well-loved feet had touched before,
Yet saw no signs upon the snow
Of those departing feet to show.
Cold blew the wind upon his face,
As now he left behind the place
Where he was born, nor turned again
To look farewell; for nought and vain
Seemed all things but his misery,
That now had grown his life to be,
Not to be given away for aught
That earth might hold; nor had he thought
That anything his lot could change,
That anything could more be strange,
Lovesome or fearful to his heart,
Or in his life have any part.

So he went on from that abode,
Along a well-known, oft-trod road,
He knew not why or where, until
Clean hidden by a bare waste hill,
Were the snow-covered roofs wherein
His outward life did first begin.
Then as he wandered on forlorn,
From out his unrest was there born
Some faint half-memory, that did seem
To be the remnant of a dream;
Some image to his mind there clung,
Some speech upon his lips yet hung
He might not utter.
And now he
Had gone so long that the wide sea
He saw afar, when the dull day
Toward eve again had passed away,
Amidst the utter solitude
Of his time-slaying weary mood.
But weak and way-worn was he now,
Though greater did his longing grow
To wander ever on and on,
Until the unknown rest were won.
And when he gazed from the hill-side,
And saw the great sea spreading wide,
All black and empty from the shore,
So sharp a longing then came o'er
His dull despair, such wild desire,
That stung, as when a coal of fire
Is laid upon an aching wound,
He cast himself upon the ground,
And in the cold snow writhed and wailed,
While over him the sea-mew sailed,
Not silent, and the wind wailed too,

As though his bitter grief they knew,
And mocked him.
            Yet or fell the night
He rose, and on the waste of white
Stood a black speck, then went until
The black night mingled sea and hill
And hurrying rack in nothingness.
Yet, kept alive by his distress,
He fainted not, nor went astray,
For as in dreams he knew the way
At last, and whitherward he went,
Since round the heart of strong intent
His woe was wrapped.

            So o'er the down
He went, until a haven-town
Shone like a patch of stars on earth,
And something like a hope had birth
Within him, and somewhat he knew
His will, now that his body grew
Well-nigh too weak to bear him on.
Yet to the town at last he won,
So heartened now unto the task
That he for food and rest might ask;
And, since no lack of wealth he had,
Soon did he make a goodman glad
With gift of gold, and, all outworn,
Forgot his grief, and life forlorn
In long deep sleep most like to death.

Now at that town, my story saith,
Long must he bide, for so it was
That then no good ship well might pass
From land to land, for winter-tide
Still made the narrow seas full wide.
Each morn did John wake there, to gaze
With dead eyes on the waste of days,
Each eve he laid him down to sleep,
Much marvelling what his life did keep
From passing: still the memory
Of some faint, dreamlike thing gone by
Perplexed his heart, and still he strove,
Amid the anguish of his love,
To speak that half-remembered word,
Amidst a dream, belike, once heard.

This helped him through his dull-eyed woe,
That the time passed, and he should go
To other lands ere many days,
Seeming to seek for that lost face.

At last the day desired came
When o'er the land the Spring did flame
With love and flowers; and on an eve
John's good ship did the haven leave,
And pale he stood upon the prow,
And to the weary place, left now
Behind with all its patience dead,
No more had will to turn his head,
But thinking of the future still,
Amid the shipman's tangled skill,
Stood looking toward the flaming West,
With eyes made strange by love's unrest.

Upon the deck that night he lay,
And nought he slept until the day
Began to dawn, and woke again
In short space, feeling little pain,
And with his pale lips murmuring
Some word half-dreamed, some fleeting thing.
Then on his arm he rose, and saw
The waste of waters seem to draw
Unto him as the black prow clave
With steady heart green wave on wave;
None save the watch were on the deck,
Who, sleepy-eyed, no whit did reck
Of him and all his woe and love,
But 'twixt the bulwarks slow did move,
With little purpose, as it seemed;
The helmsman steered as though he dreamed,
Of seafolk's marvels vaguely told
By firesides in the days of old;
The light wind waxed and waned; the ship
Still through the babbling waves did slip
As though their talk she hearkened to:
And 'midst it all John scarcely knew
Whether he lived still, or was dead:
Well-nigh it came into his head,
That he by ghosts of men was borne
From out his wasted life forlorn
O'er a strange sea to some strange place
Of unknown punishment or grace.
Skyward he looked, and o'er the mast
He saw the moon with all light passed
From out of her, and as he gazed
The great sun o'er the green sea blazed,
And smote his head with sudden light.

Then in his heart the flame burned bright
That long had smouldered there, he cried;
"Ah, woe betide, ah, woe betide,
East of the Sun, West of the Moon!

A land that no man findeth soon,
The grave of greedy love that cries
To all folk of its agonies:
The prison of untrustful love,
That thinketh a light word can move
The heart of kindness, deep and wise.
O love, love, would thy once-kissed eyes
Were glad to-day, that thy sweet smile
Forgat a wretch so base and vile,
That he but lived to make thee sad,
To weep the days that once were glad!"

But now the dreamlike sight that wrapped
His soul all suddenly was snapped.
He heard the watch cry out their cry,
The helmsman answer cheerily,
And mid the homely noise of these
Freshened awhile the morning breeze,
The ship leaned o'er the highway green,
That led to England's meads unseen.

At Dunwich, in the east country,
John landed from the weary sea,
Not recking where on earth he was;
But quickly therefrom did he pass,
Driven by growing hope; that word
In some old dream belike half heard,
East of the Sun, West of the Moon,
Seemed unto him a heaven-sent boon,
Yet made the merry world around
A dreary cage, a narrow round
Of dreamlike pain, a hollow place,
Filled with a blind and dying race.

That town and country-side, indeed,
Seemed all the less to help his need,
Whereas for common homely things
That well he knew, with Easterlings
And his own country-folk they dealt,
And scarce knew aught of what folk dwelt
Southward beyond the narrow seas;
So giving few farewells to these,
Towards London did he take his way,
And, journeying on, at hostels lay
Benights, or whiles at abbeys fair;
And as his hope grew, would he dare,
In manner of a tale, to tell
In what wise woe upon him fell;
And most men praised the tale enow,
And said no minstrel-wight might show
A merrier tale to feasting hall.

And so at last it did befall
That at a holy house he lay,
A noble house, forsooth, to-day,
Men call St. Alban's; there he told
Once more, as a thing known of old,
The story of his hapless love:
Such passion there his tongue did move,
That in that Abbey's guest-chamber
It was a better thing to hear
Than many a history nobly writ,
And much were all folk moved by it.
But when his speech was fully done,
From the board's end there rose up one,
A little dry old monk, right wise
Of semblance, with small glittering eyes,
Who came to John, and said:
"Thy tale,
Fair son, shall much my need avail,
For I have many such-like things
Writ out for sport of lords and kings;
Bide thou with us to-morn, I pray,
And hearken some for half a day;
For certes shall their memory
Help thee to pass the dull days by,
When thou growest old."
Wide-eyed John stared,
For scarce the old man's speech he heard,
Or any speech of men, for still
One thought his whole sad heart did fill.
Howbeit constrained, he knew not why,
He heard full many a history
Like to his own next morn, and went
Yet more upon his love intent;
Yet more the world seemed nought but this,
Longing for bliss and losing bliss.
And yet, of those fresh tales withal
Some endings on his heart did fall
As scarcely new; he 'gan to make
Tales to himself, how for his sake
She wept and waited; how some way
To Love fulfilled yet open lay;
The grey morn often would beguile
With dreams his sad lips to a smile,
While still his shut eyes did behold
Once more her sweetness manifold;
And if the waking from delight
Unto the real day void and white,
Were well-nigh more than man could bear,
Yet his own sad voice would he hear
Muttering as o'erword to the tune,
East of the Sun, West of the Moon.

Now come to London at the last,
Among the chapmen there he passed,
And many a tale of them he had
Concerning outlands good and bad
That they had journeyed through, but still
He heard none speak for good or ill
Of any way unto the place
Whereto for him still led all ways.
But his hope lived, nor might his heart
In any life of man have part,
And forth he wandered once again
As merchant among chaffering men,
And strange he seemed among them all;
His face changed not, whate'er might fall
Of good or ill; he won, he lost,
He gave, as counting not the cost;
Fell sick, grew well, and heeded nought
What the days took or what they brought;
Nowhere he strove great deeds to do,
Scarce spoke he save when spoken to;
Hither and thither still he went
As the winds blow, never content,
Never complaining; resting nought,
And yet scarce asking what he sought.
A strange waif in the tide of life,
With nought he seemed to be at strife,
To nothing earthly to belong.
Still burned his longing bright and strong,
As when upon that bitter morn
He hung with his white face forlorn,
Over the bed yet scarcely cold,
That erst her loveliness did hold.

So chasing dreams, so dreamlike chased,
Through lapse of years his life did waste;
His body changed, and old he grew
Before his time: his face none knew,
When, on a time, from journeyings vain
In southlands, wandering back again,
He heard his father welcome call
Across the smoke-wreaths of his hall.
O lonely heart! the yearning shame
That erst, when back thereto he came,
He felt at being so all alone
Among his own folk, was clean gone;
No lingering kindness of old days
Clung now to the familiar place;
With unmoved mouth he wandered there,
And saw his mother's empty chair,
For she was dead: with unchanged eyes

Thorgerd he saw from spinning rise,
Fair still and young, though he was old.
His father's face he did behold
With no faint smile of memory,
No pang for wasted youth gone by;
Betwixt his brethren twain he sat,
And heard them talk of this and that
Mid stories of a bygone day,
Scarce thinking how they used to play
Fair children once, and innocent,
With the next minute well content.

No goodwill from his kith and kin,
And things kind once, he now might win
From out the well-loved wasting fire
Of unfulfilled scarce-touched desire.
One place was as another place,
Haunted by memories of one face,
Vocal with one remembered voice,
Sad with one time's swift fleeting joys.
Yet as he passed the time-worn door
The last time, said farewell once more,
Scarce mid his outward calm could he
Stay quivering lip and trembling knee,
That on the threshold longed to lie,
Where surely had her feet gone by.

Through what wild lands he wandered wide,
Among what folk he did abide
Thereafter, nought my story saith.
Suffice it, that no outbraved death
Might end him; no chain of delay
His feet from his wild wanderings stay;
That every help he strove to gain
From wise or fools was still but vain;
Until, my story saith, at last
The second time in ship he passed
The wild waves of the Indian Sea,
And with a chaffering company
Long time abode, and ever heard
And saw great marvels, but no word,
No sight of what alone might give
A heart unto the dead-alive.
At last from the strange city there
He set sail in a dromond fair,
With chapmen for his fellows, bound
To such a land, that there the ground
Bears gems and gold, but nourisheth
Little besides save fear and death.
So long they sailed, that at the last
The skipper's face grew overcast,

And the stout chapmen 'gan to fear,
Because no signs of land drew near,
And all the days were fully done
When with fair wind they should have won
Unto the shore for which they made;
But of no death was John afraid
While o'er some space as yet untried
He bore his love unsatisfied;
With hate they eyed his calm face now,
For greater still their fear did grow.

Anigh the prow one eve he stood,
And something new so stirred his blood
With hope, that he at last might say,
A thing unsaid for many a day,
That he was happy; round about
The shipmen stood, and gazed in doubt
' Upon a long grey bank of cloud
The eastern sky-line that did shroud.
He saw it not, grown soft with rest
His face was turned unto the west;
The low sun lit his golden hair
Changed now with years of toil and care,
The light wind stirred it as the prow
The babbling ripple soft did throw
From its black shining side; the sail
Flapped o'erhead as the wind did fail
Fitful that eve; the western sky
Was bright and clear as night drew nigh
Beyond all words to tell; at last
He shivered; to the tall white mast
He raised his eyes just as the sun
Blazed at his lowest: day was done,
But yet night lingered, as o'erhead,
With a new-kindled hope and dread,
The thin-curved moon, all white and cold,
'Twixt day and night did he behold.

No need now of that word to think,
Or where he heard it; he did shrink
Back mid his fellows, for he strove
This first time to forget his love
Lest hope should slay him; therewith now
He heard the shipmen speaking low
With anxious puckered brows, and saw
The merchants each to other draw
As men who feared to be alone;
And knew that a fresh fear had grown
Beside their old fear, nathless nought
To such things might he turn his thought.
All watched that night but he, who slept

While lovesome visions o'er him crept,
Making night happy with the sight
Of kind hands, and soft eyes and bright.
At last within a flowery mead
He seemed to be, clad in such weed
As fellows of the angels wear:
Alone a while he wandered there
Right glad at heart, until at last
By a fair-blossomed brake he passed,
And o'er his shoulder gazed as he
Went by it; and lo, suddenly,
The odorous boughs were thrust apart,
And with all heaven within his heart
He turned, and saw his love, his sweet,
Clad in green raiment to the feet,
Her feet upon the blossoms bare,
A rose-wreath round her golden hair;
Her arms reached out to him, her mouth
Trembling to quench his life-long drouth,
Yet smiling 'neath her deep kind eyes
Upon his trembling glad surprise.
But when he would have gone to her
Him seemed a cry of deadly fear
Rang through the fair and lonely close,
A cold thick mist betwixt them rose,
And then all sight from him did pass,
And darkness a long while there was.

Then all at once he woke up, cast
With mighty force against the mast,
Whereto with desperate hands he clung
Unwitting, while the storm-wind sung
Its song of death about his ears.
But he, though grief had long slain fears,
Shouted midst clash of wind and sea,
Unheard shrieks, unseen misery
Of the black night:
"All come to nought!
Yestreen I deemed that rest was brought
Anigh me, and I thought I knew
That toward my Love at last I drew.
The loveless rest comes, all deceit
Death treads to nothing with his feet!
O idle Maker of the world,
Art thou content to see me hurled
To nought, from longing and from tears,
When thou through all these weary years
With love my helpless soul hast bound,
And fed me in that narrow round
With no delight thy fair world knows?
Come close, my love, come close, come close,

Why wilt thou let me die alone?"

Howso he deemed his days were done,
Yet there still clung he desperately,
Mid wash of the in-rushing sea,
Mid the storm's night, for no least whit
Might he see through the rage of it,
Nor know which unseen hill of wave
The rash frail wooden toy would stave,
Or if another man did cling
Unto the hopeless shivering thing;
Yea, or if day had dawned, and light
High up serene now mocked the night
Of waves and winds. How long he drave
From windless trough to wind-sheared wave,
No whit he knew, although it seemed
So long, that all before was dreamed,
That there was neither heaven nor earth
Before that turmoil had its birth.

And yet at last, as on and on
He swept, and still death was not won;
A pleasure in his heart 'gan rise;
Love blossomed fresh mid fantasies,
Mid dreams born of the overthrow
Of sense and sight; he did not know
If yet he lived, yet wrong and pain
Were words, that hindered not the gain,
Of sweet peace, whatso wild unrest
Were round about; and all the best
Seemed won, nor was one day of bliss
Forgotten; all was once more his,
That while agone he deemed so lost.
How long in sooth the ship was tost
From hill to hill of unseen sea
The tale tells not; but suddenly,
Amid the sweetest dream of all,
A long way down John seemed to fall,
Losing all sense of sight and sound;
Then brake a sudden light around,
Wherethrough he none the less saw nought,
And as it waned, waned sense and thought,
The peace of dull unconsciousness
His wild torn heart at last did bless.

He woke again upon the sand
Of a wide bay's curved shell-strewn strand,
And long belike had he lain there;
For morn it was, and fresh and fair,
And no least sign was on the sea
Of storm or wrack, but peacefully

On the low strand its last wave broke.

Scarce might John dream when thus he woke
Of what had happed or where he was;
Soft thoughts of bygone days did pass
Across his mind at first, and when
His later memory came again,
It was but with great toil that he
Could think about his misery
And all his latter wretched years;
And if the thought to unused tears
Did move him now, yet none the less
A strange content and happiness
Wrapped him around.
So to his feet
He rose now, and most fresh and sweet
The air was round him, and the sun
As of the time when morn begun
In early summer of the north,
Maketh the world seem wondrous worth,
And death and pain awhile doth hide.
He gazed across the ocean wide
With puzzled look; then up and down
Sought curiously the sea-sand brown
And at the last 'gan marvel how
No sign the smooth sea-strand might show
Of his lost ship and company;
Then closer to that summer sea
He went, and surely now it seemed
That he of India had but dreamed,
Because the sand beneath his feet
Washed smooth and flat by the sea's beat,
Or wrinkled by the ripple low,
Such shells and creeping things did show
As in the northland well he knew,
And round about o'erhead there flew
Such sea-fowl as in days of old;
Their unknown tales unto him told.
He gave a deep sigh, yet his heart
From that new bliss would nowise part,
Or battle with its strange content;
And no more midst his wonderment,
Rather for more of pain, he yearned,
Than any rest save one: he turned
From the green sea his dreamy eyes,
And saw soft slopes and lowly, rise
Green and unburnt from the smooth strand,
And further in, the rising land,
Besprent with trees of no such clime
As he had known for weary time;
From slope and thicket then there grew

High grassy, treeless hillsides, blue
With the light haze of that fair tide.

A little while did he abide
Gazing upon that pleasant place,
Then o'er his shoulder turned his face
Seaward, yet once more 'gan to go
Unto the hills, and felt as though
He bade unto the weltering flood
A last farewell; and sweet and good
His life seemed grown, e'en when he said,
"It may be that my love is dead;
Or living, still more like that I
Shall see her not before I die;
Fool am I then to feel my feet
Drawn on some happiness to meet!"

So went his words, but e'en as erst
When most he felt forlorn and cursed,
The words of hope seemed words and air,
So now seemed all his words of care
Empty of meaning. Forth he went
Light-hearted, till his firm feet bent
The daisies of the flowery grass,
And swiftly onward did he pass
From slope to slope: the land was fair,
Yet saw he no house anywhere,
No hedge or garden-close or corn;
Nor heard he halloo there or horn,
To make the dappled deer afraid,
That here and there about him strayed
Scarce heeding him: no arms he bare,
His raiment that had once been fair,
Was sorely stained, and worn, and rent,
And thirst and hunger as he went
Pressed on him; till he came at last
To where a spreading fruit-tree cast
Its shadows round deliciously;
John stayed there, for that friendly tree
Had load of apples; so he ate
And found them sweet and delicate,
As ever monk in garden grew,
Though little care belike they knew.
But now, when he had had his fill
Thereof, there marvelling stood he still,
Because to one bough blossoms clung
As it were May, but ripe fruit hung
Upon the other: then he smiled,
As one by a strange dream beguiled,
Then slowly on the grass sank down,
For sorely sweet had longing grown

With gathering languor of the day.
But looking round, as there he lay,
Upon the flowers besprent about,
Still more was love confused with doubt
If still he lived:
"Red roses fair
To wreathe my love that wanders here,
Gold-hearted lilies for her hand!
And yet withal that she may stand
On something other folk think sweet,
March violets for her rosy feet;
The black-heart amorous poppy, fain
Death from her passing knee to gain,
Bows to the gilliflower there:
The fiery tulip stands to stare
Upon her perfect loveliness,
That 'gainst the corn-cockle will press
Its fainting leaves: further afield
The untended vine black fruit doth yield,
That bore long torment of the heat,
At last in bliss her lips to meet;
The wind-flowers wotting of the thing
Must gather round there in the Spring,
And live and die and live again,
That they might feel the joyous pain
At last, of lying crushed and rent
Beneath her feet, while well content
Above their soft leaves she doth sing.
What marvel, love, that everything
That far apart the troubled year,
Midst toil and doubt, gives otherwhere,
Must gather in this land round thee,
Living and dying, still to see
A wonder God shall not make twice.
Come swiftly, love, because mine eyes
Grow dim with love; a little while
Shall hope my fainting heart beguile
To think me strong; yet well I know
That nought of strength is in me now,
Save wasting fire of love alone—
Come to me then, ere all is gone!
And let it not be all for nought
That ever one heart have I sought
Of all the world, and cast aside
All thought that any bliss might hide
In aught save in thy love; thy love
That even yet perchance might move
The Great God not all utterly
To slay me, casting my soul by
As void henceforth for evermore,
What love soever once it bore,

That nothing mortal satisfied!"

He sprang up, o'er the countryside
He gazed long, and down ran the tears,
At thought of all the pain of years,
When he beheld its emptiness;
Yet presently on did he press,
With longing grown not all a pain.

The higher slopes now did he gain,
Through flowers and blooming trees, until
He 'gan to breast a steeper hill,
And coming out of a close wood,
High up above the lowlands stood,
And far away beheld the sea
Guarding the sweet land patiently,
Then turning, clomb on, till the sun
Sank low adown and day was done,
Before the hill's top he might gain;
Then e'en his restlessness was fain
There to abide the next day's light.
So down he lay, aid the short night
Went by in dreams of that past day
When in the hawthorn-brake he lay;
How many lifetimes now agone
That day seemed, when once more alone
In the dawn's shiver he awoke!
Nathless with sturdy heart he broke
Through the morn's hopelessness, and still
Pressed up the last steep of the hill,
Until together with the sun
Its grey and rugged brow he won.

Then down into the vale he gazed,
And held his breath, as if amazed
By all its wondrous loveliness;
For as the sun its depths did bless,
It lighted up from side to side,
A close-shut valley, nothing wide,
But ever full of all things fair.
A little way the hill was bare,
Then clung to it a deep green wood
That guarded many a fertile rood
Of terraced vine and slopes of wheat;
A white way wound about its feet,
Beset with heavy-fruited trees
And cleaving orchards through; midst these,
Each hemmed round with its flowery close,
The cottages and homesteads rose;
But the hill-side sprang suddenly
From level meadows that did lie

On either side a noble stream,
O'er which the morning haze did steam,
Made golden now; then rose again
The further hill-sides, bright with grain,
And fair with orchard and close wood,
From whence at last the scarped cliffs stood,
And clear now, golden in the morn,
Against the western sky upborne,
Seemed like a guarded wall, lest care
Or unrest yet should creep in there.

At John's back now bright the sun shone
Once more, once more with all light gone,
Above the further hills hung high,
The pale thin moon was in the sky;
Then he cried out:
"Ah, end the strife
Twin lights of God; give death or life!
Surely shall I be lying soon
East of the Sun, West of the Moon;
What matter if alive or dead,
If so once more our lips are wed!"

And now he 'gan to look around,
To see how he the lower ground
Might gain, for there the hill had end
In shear rocks, so he needs must wend
Along its rugged brow; at last,
When he a little way had passed,
The hill's crest lowered, and 'gan draw
Back from the vale, and then he saw
How it grew wide, and 'neath his eyes
The river wound now circle-wise,
And at the furthest curve thereof
There lay, half hid by close and grove,
A marvellous house, that jewel-like
Gleamed, where the sun its roofs did strike,
Or strange-wrought walls; down-gazing now
With fluttering heart, he wondered how
Its white walls, and its roofs that burned,
Should seem e'en like a dream returned
From the forgotten land; then down
The hill-side, soft and easy grown,
He slipped, and when he reached the way
Folk stirred about the morn of day
In field and house: fair folk were all
He saw, and yet a chill did fall
Upon him when he noted them;
White linen, well-embroidered hem,
Round clean-made limbs he saw, above
Were faces sweet, well wrought for love;

Yet man and maid, young folk and old,
With sad eyes, lonely, strange, and cold,
Still seemed to go upon their ways.
Moreover, none on him did gaze;
And if their eyes met his, as though
They saw him not, past did they go;
Nor heard he any spoken word
Amongst them, nor saw any stirred
To laugh or smile by anything.
But fearful, yet his hope did cling
Unto his heart, nay more, he thought
Once more that surely not for nought
Among such marvels he was come.

So forth he passed by house and home
E'en like a ghost; the open door
Of one fair house he stood before,
Where folk got ready for their meal,
With little sign of woe or weal;
And as he stood before their eyes,
They looked his way with no surprise,
Nor seemed to see him: nought they spake,
Neither durst he the silence break,
But went his ways.

A tall man stood
By the wayside a-hewing wood,
And close by was a fair-haired child,
Who watched him, but spake not nor smiled,
Nor looked up at the wayfarer;
John strove to make this goodman hear,
Crying out to him cheerily
What land of all lands this might be;
But nowise did he turn him round,
Nor did the youngling heed the sound.
Next, as he turned therefrom, there came
Along the road an ancient dame,
High-perched upon a mule, a lad
Of fifteen springs his left hand had
Upon the bell-hung bridle-rein—
And still with these were all words vain.
So on he went, and no more speech
Had heart to try till he did reach
The delicate house; and in the square
Before it was a conduit fair,
Where to and fro the girls did pass,
Bearing their jars of earth or brass;
Shrill sounded there the grey doves' wings,
The steep roof knew their murmurings,
The sparrows chirped, the brass did clash,
The water on the stones did plash,

The damsels' wind-blown raiment fair
And tinkling gold toys sounded there,
But not their voices: unto one
Who stood and watched the water run
Over her jar's lip pensively
John turned, for kind she seemed to be:
But when with soft beseeching eyes
He spake, still in no other wise
She dealt with him than had the rest;
So when with growing fear oppressed
He spake more earnestly, and she
Still answered nought, then timidly
Upon her hand his hand he laid;
Warm was it, but no heed she paid
Unto the touch, and he fell back,
Wondering what thing those folk did lack
That yet they died not: but still burned
Hope amid great fear, and he turned
Unto the palace door, wherethrough
Passed fair-clad people to and fro.

When he essayed to enter in
None stayed or heeded; he did win
Into a fair porch, set around
With images of maidens crowned
And kings all-armed; through this he gained
A pillared court, where waxed and waned
A babbling fountain, maidens fair
And slim youths saw he loitering there
As lovers loiter; but their eyes,
Listless and sad, changed in nowise
As past he brushed with hurrying feet
And glittering eyes: then did he meet
The all-armed clashing guard, and then
The long line of the serving-men
Bearing up victuals to the hall,
And, without bell or trumpet-call,
Thither folk streamed. He went with them,
And many a wrought cloak and rich hem
Brushed past him, many a jewelled sword
Clinked at the side of knight or lord,
And no word spoken yet—at last
Into the mighty hall he passed,
And thought no greatest king on earth,
E'en were it he of Micklegarth,
Or the great lord of Babylon,
So fair a place as that had won.

Now there he stood, till every place
Was filled, save midmost of the dais
The high-seat lacked a man; so then

He laughed loud mid those silent men,
Grown reckless in that kingdom cold,
And clad in rags mid silk and gold,
Barefooted in that dainty hall,
He strode up to the ivory stall,
And sat him down, and laughed once more
Unheeded, while the servers bore
Unto the guests rich meats and drink;
Nor from the victuals did he shrink,
But well his hunger satisfied
Though not long there might he abide,
For still his lovesome restlessness
Midst all upon his heart did press.

So rising ere the feast was done,
He paced the echoing hall alone,
And passed the door, and wandered now,
Unchecked by any, high and low,
And saw strange things and fair; at last
A silent maid his side brushed past,
And to a carven door did wend,
At a long cloister's nether end,
Passed in and shut it to again.
Then John stood still and strove in vain,
With a new hope and gathering fear,
And weakly drew the door anear,
And laid his hand upon the latch,
And with a sob his breath must catch
Because of thronging memories.
He opened the door now, with eyes
Cast down for fear, and therewith heard,
As heretofore, no spoken word;
But rustling as of women's gear
And gentle breathing did he hear
And the dull noise upon the ground
Of restless spindles; all around
Floated a delicate sweet scent,
As though the wind o'er blossoms went.

His breath came fast, his fevered blood
Tingled and changed, as there he stood,
And each 'gainst each now smote his knees;
E'en as a world of images
The past was grown to him; he knew
What in those days he used to do,
But knew not what it meant; and yet
Would she the past days quite forget,
And was she like these dead-alive?

None came, sore trembling did he strive
To search the strange place through, but still

His hope, fear-tangled, and the ill
That might be, bound his eyes full fast
A long while—crying out at last
E'en ere his eyes had left the ground,
As one who some lost thing has found,
He stepped forth, and with all surprise
Made nought by love, his mortal eyes,
His weary eyes, beheld indeed,
His heart's desire, his life, his need,
Still on the earth, still there for him;
And as he gazed, most weak and dim,
Seemed all the visions wherewith he
Was wont to feed his misery,
To dull the pain unsatisfied,
That still for death or presence cried.

Round the World's Love, the glorious one,
My tale says, many maidens spun,
Howso John's eyes beheld them not,
And she upon her knees had got
Some broidery fair, and whiles her hand
Moved by her half-dead will's command
Would raise it up, and whiles again,
As too much all in all grew pain,
Would let it fall adown: her face
Was altered nothing from the grace
That he remembered, save that erst
A sad smile even at the worst
Would gleam across her pity, but now
Betwixt her round chin and smooth brow
Lay bound the sorrow of the years,
Too sharp for smiles, too hard for tears:
Sometimes as some sweet memory
Pierced the dull present, wearily
She writhed her neck, and raised her head;
Sometimes her hands, as feebly led
By ghosts of her old longings, moved
As though toward some one long time loved,
And long time lost; then from her seat
Whiles she half rose as if to meet
Loved footfalls half-remembered; then
The dull pain swallowed all again,
Its child, dull patience, death-in-life,
Choked down the rising rest of strife.

Scarcely his feet might bear him o'er
The smoothness of the marble floor
Unto her feet; scarce might he raise
His wild eyes to her weary face,
Scarcely his hand had strength to touch
The open hand he loved so much;

And yet his thirsting lips love drew
Unto dear eyes that nothing knew
What closed their lids, to lips still warm,
But all forgetful of the harm
Their fruitful sweetness erst had wrought,
To feet desired, that erewhile brought
Love's grief on the sad moaning man,
Who fawned on them with lips grown wan,
And cheeks grown thin for lack of love.

How might he tell if aught could move
Her grief-chilled heart; yet love slew fear,
Lulled speech to sleep—sweet to be near;
Yea, even if all were changed, if all
Into this dumb, strange life must fall,
And all the longing and the pain
For signs of love were spent in vain;
If, in strange wise together brought,
They were apart still, and still nought
Might tell of better hope! O sweet
Beyond all words, there at her feet
To lie and watch her! By what word
Might his deep love be better heard
Than by that silence.
Nought he said
A long while, and her weary head
Hung low, and still she saw him not.
At last the heart in him waxed hot,
And he cried out:
"Time long ago,
How long, how long, I know not now,
I sinned and lost thee: scarce a hope
Was left with the dull years to cope;
Yet this my hand now touches thee,
My cheek is laid upon thy knee;
I am thy love, beloved, come,
I know not how, to thy new home!"

She moved not, but a rush of tears
Blinded his eyes, as all the years
With all their pain rose up to him;
Her head moved then, through foot and limb
A tremor ran, as the tears fell.
Upon her hands:
"O Love, scarce well,"
He sobbed, "that we should be apart,
My sorrow laid upon thy heart,
And my heart worn with thine, my love—
No word 'twixt lips and lips, to move
The double burden—found at last,
What chain is it that binds thee fast?

Was my great grief so hard to bear
That thou art grown cold? Sweet and dear
I bore thy grief yet love and live!"

He trembled, for she seemed to strive
To grasp strange thoughts that flitted round,
She clenched her delicate hands, and frowned,
And her feet moved uncertainly,
The while the maidens sitting by
Spun and spun on, nor changed at all.

Then a strange thought on him did fall,
To choke his tears back and tell o'er
The story of his longing sore,
E'en from that well-remembered day
When in the hawthorn-brake he lay.
God wot, if his hand trembled oft
As he recalled words sweet and soft,
And tender touches, all the bliss
Of clinging hand and lingering kiss!
God wot if he stayed tremblingly
As from her breast brake forth a sigh
And she fell trembling! And at last,
Amid his tale of how she passed
Away from him, and left him bare
In the rough world of hate and care,
Her fingers tightened round his own,
And a sound like a tender moan
Parted her lips; he stayed awhile,
And on his face a quivering smile
Masked the unshed tears, as he told
How in that morning drear and cold
He found her gone: and therewith she
Raised up her head, and eagerly
Gazed round, and yet looked not on him:

"No hope," he said, "however dim,
At first, sweet love, abode with me;
I know not how I lived; the sea,
The earth, and sky, that day had grown
A heavy burden all mine own;
As if mine hand all things had wrought
To find their strength come all to nought,
Their beauty perished, all made vain,
Unnoticed parts of the huge pain
That filled the world and crushed my heart.
Then first, the heavy veil to part,
Came memory of thy mouth divine,
Some image of a word of thine—
—Is it not so that thou saidst this,
That morn that parted me and bliss,

'Ah, couldst thou know, I go too soon
East of the Sun, West of the Moon?'"

With a great sigh, as one who throws
A burden off, that sweet arose,
And stood before him, trembling sore
With love and joy; ah, me! once more
Fulfilled of love their kind eyes met,
Although apart they stood as yet,
Helpless with pain of ecstasy;
Till from her lips a joyful cry,
Ringing and sweet, burst forth, and he,
Strong no more with love's misery,
Faint, changed with this new joyful love,
His wandering hands toward her did move
E'en but a little way. But round
His fluttering heart her arms she wound,
And kissed his pale cheeks red again,
And hung above his lovesome pain,
Desiring him as the spring yearns
For the young summer sun, that burns
His soft heart into fruitful death.
His parched mouth felt her odorous breath,
His weary burning head did rest
Upon the heaven of her sweet breast,
His mazed ears heard her tender speech;
His eyes, his silence did beseech
For more and more and more of love.

How this their joy fulfilled might move
The world around I know not well;
But yet this idle dream doth tell
That no more silent was the place,
That new joy lit up every face,
That joyous lovers kissed and clung,
E'en as these twain, that songs were sung
From mouth to mouth in rose-bowers,
Where, hand in hand and crowned with flowers,
Folk praised the Lover and Beloved
That such long years, such pain had proved.
But soft, they say, their joyance was
When midst them soon the twain did pass,
Hand locked in hand, heart kissing heart,
No more this side of death to part—
No more, no more—Full soft I say
Their greetings were that happy day,
As though in pensive semblance clad;
For fear their faces over-glad
This certain thing should seem to hide,
That love can ne'er be satisfied.

O'er Gregory's eyes the pain of morn
Flashed suddenly, and all forlorn
Of late-gained clean forgot delight,
He sat up, scowling on the bright
Broad day that lit the hurrying crowd
Of white-head waves, while shrill and loud
About him cried the gulls; but he
Lay still with eyes turned toward the sea,
And yet beholding nought at all,
Till into ill thoughts did he fall,
Of what a rude and friendless place
The world was, through what empty days
Men were pushed slowly down to death.
Then o'er the fresh morn's breezy breath
Was borne his fellows' cheery cry;
He rose up, sighing heavily,
And turned round to the steep grey bent,
Whereunder had been pitched their tent
Upon the odorous thymy grass.
And down the slope he saw them pass,
And heard their voices blithe enough:
But loathsome unto him, and rough
Must all men seem urn that morn,
Their speech a hard thing to be borne.

He stood by as they launched the boat,
And little did their labour note.
And set no hand thereto at all;
Until an awe on these did fall;
They muttered, "Ah, the Stargazer
Beholdeth strange things drawing near!"
So somewhat silently they sailed
In up the firth, till the wind failed,
Betwixt the high cliffs, and with oars
They swept midmost the rocky shores
And spake few words.

But smoother now
Was grown the worn Stargazer's brow,
And his thin lips were less close-set,
For well-nigh now did he forget
Fellows and boat and land and sea,
And, waking, seemed no less to be
East of the Sun, West of the Moon,
And when they landed at high-noon,
From all men would he go apart
In woods and meads, and deal by art
With his returning memory;
And, some things gained, and some slipped by,
His weary heart a while to soothe,
He wove all into verses smooth,

As tells the tale: that wotteth not
Hoer much within it it hath got
That his hand writ: for soothly he
Was deemed a craftsmaster to be
In those most noble days of old,
Whose words were e'en as kingly gold
To our thin brass, or drossy lead:
Well, e'en so all the tale is said
How twain grew one and came to bliss—
Woe's me an idle dream it is!

The autumn day, the strange and dreamy tale
Were soft as far-off bells adown a vale,
Borne to the hill-top on the fitful wind;
And like their music past, they left behind
Sad thoughts of old desires unsatisfied,
And pain and joy that long ago had died,
Yea, long been buried 'neath the strife of days,
Too hard and hapless any woe to raise
And crown it with the flowery, fleeting crown
Of that strange rest, whose seed is all unknown,
That withereth while reproachfully we say;
"Why grow'st thou unsought 'neath my hand to-day,
Whose longed-for scent through many an ill day sought,
Swift healing to my sickening soul had brought
And kept me young. Fair rest, what dost thou here?"

The wind dealt with the autumn haze, and clear
The afternoon was, though the great clouds drew
In piled-up hills across the faint-streaked blue,
And 'gainst them showed the wind-hover's dark spot,
Nor yet midst trembling peace was change forgot.

OCTOBER

O love, turn from the unchanging sea, and gaze
Down these grey slopes upon the year grown old,
A-dying mid the autumn-scented haze,
That hangeth o'er the hollow in the wold,
Where the wind-bitten ancient elms infold
Grey church, long barn, orchard, and red-roofed stead,
Wrought in dead days for men a long while dead.

Come down, O love; may not our hands still meet,
Since still we live to-day, forgetting June,
Forgetting May, deeming October sweet—
O hearken, hearken! through the afternoon,
The grey tower sings a strange old tinkling tune!
Sweet, sweet, and sad, the toiling year's last breath,

Too satiate of life to strive with death.

And we too—will it not be soft and kind,
That rest from life, from patience and from pain,
That rest from bliss we know not when we find,
That rest from Love which ne'er the end can gain?—
Hark, how the tune swells, that erewhile did wane!
Look up, love!—ah, cling close and never move!
How can I have enough of life and love?

October drew our elders to a house,
That mid the tangled vines, and clamorous
Glad vintagers, stood calm, slim-pillared, white,
As though it fain would hide away from sight
The joy that through the sad lost autumn rung.
As hot the day was, as when summer hung,
With worn feet, on the last step of July,
Ashamed to cast its flowery raiment by:
Round the old men the white porch-pillars stood,
Gold-stained, as with the sun, streaked as with blood,
Blood of the earth, at least, and to and fro
Before them did the high-girt maidens go,
Eager, bright-eyed, and careless of tomorn;
And young men with them, nowise made forlorn
By love and autumn tide; and in nowise
Content to pray for love with hopeless eyes,
Close lips, and timid hands; rather, indeed,
Lest youth and life should fail them at their need,
At what light joyous semblance of him ran
Amidst the vines, 'twixt eyes of maid and man,
Wilfully blind they caught.

But now at last,
As in the apple-gathering tide late past,
So would the elders do now; in a while,
He who should tell the tale, with a grave smile,
And eyes fixed on the fairest damsel there,
Began to say: "Ye blithe folk well might bear
To hearken to a sad tale, yet to-day
No heart I have to cast all hope away
From out my history: so be warned hereby,
Nor wait unto the end, deliciously
To nurse your pity; for the end is good
And peaceful, howso buffeting and rude
Winds, waves, and men were, ere the end was done."

The sweet eyes that his eyes were set upon
Were hid by shamefast lids as he did speak,
And redder colour burned on her fresh cheek,
And her lips smiled, as, with a half-sad sigh,
He 'gan to tell this lovesome history.

THE STORY OF ACCONTIUS AND CYDIPPE

ARGUMENT

A certain man coming to Delos beheld a noble damsel there, and was smitten with the love of her, and made all things of no account but the winning of her, which at last he brought about in strange wise.

A certain island-man of old,
Well fashioned, young, and wise and bold,
Voyaged awhile in Greekish seas,
Till Delos of the Cyclades
His keel made, and ashore he went;
And, wandering with no fixed intent,
With others of the shipmen there,
They came into a garden fair,
Too sweet for sea-tossed men, I deem,
If they would scape the lovesome dream
That youth and May cast o'er the earth,
If they would keep their careless mirth
For hands of eld to deal withal.

So in that close did it befall
That 'neath the trees well wrought of May
These sat amidmost of the day
Not dry-lipped, and belike a-strain,
All gifts of that sweet time to gain,
And yet not finding all enow
That at their feet the May did throw,
But longing, half-expecting still
Some new delight their cup to fill—
Yea, overfill, to make all strange
Their lazy joy with piercing change.
Therewith their youngest, even he
I told of first, all suddenly
'Gan sing a song that fitted well
The thoughts that each man's heart did tell
Unto itself, and as his throat
Moved with the music, did he note
Through half-shut eyes a company
Of white-armed maidens drawing nigh,
Well marshalled, as if there they went
Upon some serious work intent.

SONG.

Fair is the night and fair the day,
Now April is forgot of May,

Now into June May falls away;
Fair day, fair night, O give me back
The tide that all fair things did lack
Except my love, except my sweet!

Blow back, O wind! thou art not kind,
Though thou art sweet; thou hast no mind
Her hair about my sweet to wind;
O flowery sward, though thou art bright,
I praise thee not for thy delight,
Thou hast not kissed her silver feet.

Thou know'st her not, O rustling tree,
What dost thou then to shadow me,
Whose shade her breast did never see?
O flowers, in vain ye bow adown!
Ye have not felt her odorous gown
Brush past your heads my lips to meet.

Flow on, great river—thou mayst deem
That far away, a summer stream,
Thou sawest her limbs amidst thee gleam,
And kissed her foot, and kissed her knee,
Yet get thee swift unto the sea!
With nought of true thou wilt me greet.

And thou that men call by my name,
O helpless one, hast thou no shame
That thou must even look the same,
As while agone, as while agone,
When thou and she were left alone,
And hands, and lips, and tears did meet?

Grow weak and pine, lie down to die,
O body in thy misery,,
Because short time and sweet goes by;
O foolish heart, how weak thou art!
Break, break, because thou needs must part
From thine own love, from thine own sweet!

What was it that through half-shut eyes
Pierced to his heart, and made him rise
As one the July storm awakes
When through the dawn the thunder breaks?
What was it that the languor clove,
Wherewith unhurt he sang of love?
How was it that his eyes had caught
Her eyes alone of all; that nought
The others were but images,
While she, while she amidst of these
Not first or last—when she was gone,

Why must he feel so left alone?
An image in his heart there was
Of how amidst them one did pass
Kind-eyed and soft, and looked at him;
And now the world was waxen dim
About him, and of little worth,
Seemed all the wondrous things of earth,
And fain would he be all alone,
To wonder why his mirth was gone;
To wonder why it seemed so strange
That in nought else was any change,
When his old life seemed passed away,
And joy in narrow compass lay,
He scarce knew where. With laugh and song
His fellows mocked the dim world's wrong,
Nor noted him as changed o'ermuch;
Or if their jests his mood did touch,
To his great wonder lightly they
By stammering word were turned away.

Well, from the close they went at last,
And through the noble town they passed,
And saw the wonders wrought of old
Therein, and heard famed stories told
Of many a thing; and as a dream
Did all things to Accontius seem.
But when night's wings came o'er that place,
And men slept, piteous seemed his case
And wonderful, that therewithal
Night helped him not. From wall to wall
Night-long his weary eyes he turned,
Till in the east the daylight burned.
And then the pang he would not name,
Stung by the world's change, fiercer came
Across him, and in haste he rose,
Driven unto that flowery close
By restless longing, knowing not
What part therein his heart had got,
Nor why he thitherward must wend.

And now had night's last hope an end,
When to the garden-gate he came.
In grey light did the tulip flame
Over the sward made grey with dew,
And as unto the place he drew
Where yesterday he sang that song
The ousel-cock sang sweet and strong,
Though almost ere the sky grew grey
Had he begun to greet the day.
There now, as by some strong spell bound,
Accontius paced that spot of ground,

Restless, with wild thoughts in his head;
While round about the white-thorn shed
Sweet fragrance, and the lovely place,
Lonely of mankind, lacked no grace
That love for his own home would have.
Well sang the birds, the light wind drave
Through the fresh leaves, untouched as yet
By summer and its vain regret;
Well piped the wind, and as it swept
The garden through, no sweet thing slept,
Nor might the scent of blossoms hide
The fresh smell of the country side
It bore with it; and the green bay,
Whose breast it kissed so far away,
Spake sometimes yet amid the noise
Of rustling leaves and song-birds' voice.

So there awhile our man did pace,
Still wondering at his piteous case
That, certes, not to anyone
Had happed before—awhile agone
So pleased to watch the world pass by
With all its changing imagery;
So hot to play his part therein,
From each day's death good life to win;
And now, with a great sigh, he saw
The yellow level sunbeams draw
Across the wet grass, as the sun
First smote the trees, and day begun
Smiled on the world, whose summer bliss
In nowise seemed to better his.
Then, as he thought thereof, he said:
"Surely all wisdom is clean dead
Within me. Nought I lack that I,
By striving, may not come anigh
Among the things that men desire;
And why, then, like a burnt-out fire,
Is my life grown?"
E'en as he spoke
A throstle-cock beside him broke
Into the sweetest of his song,
Yet with his sweet note seemed to wrong
The unknown trouble of that morn,
And made him feel yet more forlorn.
Then he cried out, "O fool, go forth!
The world is grown of no less worth
Than yester-morn it was; go then
And play thy part among brave men
As thou hadst will to do before
Thy feet first touched this charmed shore
Where all is changed."

But now the bird
Flew from beside him, and he heard
A rustling nigh, although the breeze
Had died out mid the thick-leaved trees.
Therewith he raised his eyes and turned,
And a great fire within him burned,
And his heart stopped awhile, for there,
Against a flowering thorn-bush fair,
Hidden by tulips to the knee,
His heart's desire his eyes did see.
Clad was she e'en as is the dove,
Who makes the summer sad with love;
High-girded as one hastening
In swift search for some longed-for thing;
Her hair drawn by a silken band
From her white neck, and in her hand
A myrtle-spray. Panting she was
As from the daisies of the grass
She raised her eyes, and looked around
Till the astonished eyes she found
That saw not aught but even her.

There in a silence hard to bear,
Impossible to break, they stood,
With faces changed by love, and blood
So stirred, that many a year of life
Had been made eager with that strife
Of minutes; and so nigh she was
He saw the little blue veins pass
Over her heaving breast; and she
The trembling of his lips might see,
The rising tears within his eyes.

Then standing there in mazed wise
He saw the black-heart tulips bow
Before her knees, as wavering now
A half-step unto him she made.
With a glad cry, though half afraid,
He stretched his arms out, and the twain,
E'en at the birth of love's great pain,
Each unto each-so nigh were grown,
That little lacked to make them one—
That little lacked but they should be
Wedded that hour; knee touching knee,
Cheek laid to cheek. So seldom fare
Love's tales, that men are wise to dare;
Rather, dull hours must pass away,
And heavy day succeed to day,
And much be changed by misery,
Ere two that love may draw anigh-
And so with these. What fear or shame

'Twixt longing heart and body came
'T were hard to tell—they lingered yet.
Well-nigh they deemed that they had met,
And that the worst was o'er; e'en then
There drew anigh the sound of men—
Loud laugh, harsh talk. With ill surprise ,
He saw fear change her lovesome eyes;
He knew her heart bethought it now
Of other folk, and ills that grow
From overmuch of love; but he
Cried out amidst his agony,
Yet stood there helpless, and withal
A mist across his eyes did fall,
And all seemed lost indeed, as now
Slim tulip-stem and hawthorn-bough
Slipped rustling back into their place,
And all the glory of her face
Had left the world, at least awhile,
And once more all was base and vile.

And yet, indeed, when that sharp pain
Was something dulled, and once again
Thought helped him, then to him it seemed
That she had dreamed as he had dreamed,
And, hoping not for any sight
Of love, had come made soft by night,
Made kind by longings unconfessed,
To give him good hope of the best.
Then pity came to help his love,
For now, indeed, he knew whereof
He sickened; pity came, and then
The fear of the rough sons of men,
Sore hate of things that needs must part
The loving heart from loving heart;
And at each turn it seemed as though
Fate some huge net round both did throw
To stay their feet and dim their sight
Till they were clutched by endless night;
And then he fain had torn his hair,
And cried aloud in his despair,
But stayed himself as still he thought
How even that should help him nought,
That helpless patience needs must be
His loathed fellow. Wearily
He got him then from out the place,
Made lovely by her scarce-seen face,
And knew that day what longing meant.

But when the restless daylight went
From earth's face, through the weary night
He lay again in just such plight

As on the last night he had lain;
But deemed that he would go again
At daylight to that place of flowers.
So passed the night through all its hours,
But ere the dawn came, weak and worn
He fell asleep, nor woke that morn
Till all the city was astir;
And waking must he think of her
Stolen to that place to find, to find him not—
Her parted lips, her face flushed hot,
Her panting breast and girt-up gown,
Her sleeve ill-fastened, fallen adown
From one white shoulder, her grey eyes
Fixed in their misery of surprise,
As nought they saw but birds and trees;
Her woeful lingering, as the breeze
Died 'neath the growing sun, and folk
Fresh silence of the morning broke;
And then, the death of hope confessed,
The quivering lip and heaving breast,
The burst of tears, the homeward way
Made hateful by joy past away,
The dreary day made dull and long
By hope deferred and gathering wrong.
All this for him!—and thinking thus
Their twinlife seemed so piteous
That all his manhood from him fled,
And cast adown upon the bed
He sobbed and wept full sore, until
When he of grief had had his fill
He 'gan to think that he might see
His love, and cure her misery
If she should be in that same place
At that same hour when first her face
Shone on him.

So time wore away
Till on the world the high noon lay,
And then at the due place he stood,
Wondering amid his love-sick mood
Which blades of grass her foot had bent;
And there, as to and fro he went,
A certain man who seemed to be
A fisher on the troubled sea,
An old man and a poor, came nigh
And greeted him and said:
                        "Hereby
Thou doest well to stand, my son,
Since thy stay here will soon be done,
If of that ship of Crete thou be,
As well I deem. Here shalt thou see

Each day at noon a company
Of all our fairest maids draw nigh;
To such an one each day they go
As best can tell them how to do
In serving of the dreadful queen,
Whose servant long years bath she been,
And dwelleth by her chapel fair
Within this close; they shall be here,
E'en while I speak. Wot well, fair son,
Good need it is this should be done,
For whatso hasty word is said
That day unto the moon-crowned maid,
For such an oath is held, as though
The whole heart into it did go—
Behold, they come! A goodly sight
Shalt thou have seen, e'en if to-night
Thou diest!"
       Grew Accontius wan
As the sea-cliffs, for the old man
Now pointed to the gate, wherethrough
The company of maidens drew
Toward where they stood; Accontius,
With trembling lips, and piteous
Drawn brow, turned toward them, and afar
Beheld her like the morning-star
Amid the weary stars of night.
Midmost the band went his delight,
Clad in a gown of blue, whereon
Were wrought fresh flowers, as newly won
From the May fields; with one hand she
Touched a fair fellow lovingly,
The other, hung adown, did hold
An ivory harp well strung with gold;
Gaily she went, nor seemed as though
One troublous thought her heart did know.
Accontius sickened as she came
Anigh him, and with heart aflame
For very rage of jealousy,
He heard her talking merrily
Unto her fellow—the first word
From those sweet lips he yet had heard,
Nor might he know what thing she said;
Yet presently she turned her head
And saw him, and her talk she stopped
E'en therewith, and her lips down dropped,
And trembling amid love and shame
Over her face a bright flush came;
Nathless without another look
She passed him by, whose whole frame shook
With passion as an aspen leaf.
But she being gone, all blind with grief,

He stood there long, and muttered:
"Why
Would she not note my misery?
Had it been then so hard to turn
And show me that her heart did yearn
For something nigher like mine own?
O well content to leave me lone,
O well content to stand apart,
And nurse a pleasure in thine heart,
The joy of being so well beloved,
Still taking care thou art not moved
By aught like trouble!—yet beware,
For thou mayst fall for all thy care!"

So from the place he turned away;
Some secret spell he deemed there lay,
Some bar unseen athwart that grass,
O'er which his feet might never pass
Whatso his heart bade. Hour by hour
Passed of the day, and ever slower
They seemed to pass, and ever he
Thought of her last look wearily—
Now meant it that, now meant it this;
Now bliss, and now the death of bliss.
'But O, if once again,' he thought,
'Face unto face we might be brought,
Then doubt I not but I should read
What at her hands would be my meed,
And in such wise my life would guide;
Either the weary end to bide
E'en as I might, or strengthen me
To take the sweet felicity,
Casting by thought of fear or death—
But now when I must hold my breath,
Who knows how long, while scale mocks scale
With trembling joy, and trembling bale
O hard to bear! O hard to bear!'

So spake he, knowing bitter fear
And hopeful longing's sharp distress,
But not the weight of hopelessness.

And now there passed by three days more,
And to the flowery place that bore
The sharp and sweet of his desire
Each day he went, his heart afire
With foolish hope. Each day he saw
The band of damsels toward him draw,
And trembling said, "Now, now at last
Surely her white arms will be cast
About my neck before them all;

Or at the worst her eyes will call
My feet to follow. Can it be
That she can bear my misery,
When of my heart she surely knows?"
And every day midmost the close
They met, and on the first day she
Did look upon him furtively
In loving wise; and through his heart
Love sent a pleasure-pointed dart—
A minute, and away she went,
And left him nowise more content
Than erst he had been.

The next day
Needs must she flush and turn away
Before their eyes met, and he stood
When she was gone in wretched mood,
Faint with desire.

The third hope came,
And then his hungry eyes, aflame
With longing wild, beheld her pass
As though amidst a dream she was;
Then e'en ere she had left the place
With his clenched hand he smote his face,
And void of everything but pain,
Through the thronged streets the sea did gain,
Not recking aught, and there at last
His body on the sand he cast,
Nigh the green waves, till in the end
Some thought the crushing cloud did rend,
And down the tears 'rushed from his eyes
For ruth of his own miseries;
And with the tears came thought again
To mingle with his formless pain
And hope withal—but yet more fear,
For he bethought him now that near
The time drew for his ship to sail.
Yet was the thought of some avail
To heal the unreason of his 'heart,
For now he needs must play a part
Wherein was something to be done,
If he would not be left alone
Life-long, with love unsatisfied.

So now he rose, and looking wide
Along the edges of the bay,
Saw where his fellows' tall ship lay
Anigh the haven, and a boat
'Twixt shore and ship-side did there float
With balanced oars; but on the shroud

A shipman stood, and shouted loud
Unto the boat—words lost, in sooth,
But which no less the trembling youth
Deemed certainly of him must be
And where he was; then suddenly
He turned, though none pursued, and fled
Along the sands, nor turned his head
Till round a headland he did reach
A long cove with a sandy beach;
Then looking landward he saw where
A streamlet cleft the sea-cliffs bare,
Making a little valley green,
Beset with thorn-trees; and between
The yellow strand and cliff's grey brow
Was built a cottage white and low
Within a little close, upon
The green slope that the stream had won
From rock and sea; and thereby stood
A fisher, whose grey homespun hood
Covered white locks: so presently
Accontius to that man drew nigh,
Because he seemed the man to be
Who told of that fair company,
Deeming that more might there be learned
About the flame wherewith he burned.

Withal he found it even so,
And that the old man him did know,
And greeted him, and fell to talk,
As such folk will of things that balk
The poor man's fortune, waves and winds,
And changing days and great men's minds;
And at the last it so befell
That this Accontius came to tell
A tale unto the man—how he
Was fain to 'scape the uneasy sea,
And those his fellows, and would give
Gold unto him, that he might live
In hiding there, till they had sailed.
Not strange it was if he prevailed
In few words, though the elder smiled
As not all utterly beguiled,
Nor curious therewithal to know
Such things as he cared not to show.

So there alone a while he dwelt,
And lonely there, all torment felt,
As still his longing grew and grew;
And ever as hot noontide drew
From dewy dawn and sunny morn,
He felt himself the most forlorn;

For then the best he pictured her:

"Now the noon wind, the scent-bearer
Is busy midst her gown," he said,
"The fresh-plucked flowers about her head
Are drooping now with their desire;
The grass with unconsuming fire
Faints 'neath the pressure of her feet;
The honey-bees her lips would meet,
But fail for fear; the swift's bright eyes
Are eager round the mysteries
Of the fair hidden fragrant breast,
Where now alone may I know rest—
Ah pity me, thou pityless!
Bless me who know'st not how to bless;
Fall from thy height, thou highest of all,
On me a very wretch to call!
Thou, to whom all things fate doth give,
Find without me thou canst not live!
Desire me, O thou world's desire,
Light thy pure heart at this base fire!
Save me, save me, thou knowest nought,
Of whom thou never hadst a thought!
O queen of all the world, stoop down,
Before my feet cast thou thy crown!
Speak to me, as I speak to thee!"

He walked beside the summer sea
As thus he spake, at eventide;
Across the waste of waters wide;
The dead sun's light a wonder cast,
That into grey night faded fast;
And ever as the shadows fell,
More formless grew the unbreaking swell
Far out to sea; more strange and white,
More vocal through the hushing night,
The narrow line of changing foam,
That 'twixt the sand and fishes' home
Writhed, driven onward by the tide—
So slowly by the ocean's side
He paced, till dreamy passion grew;
The soft wind o'er the sea that blew,
Dried the cold tears upon his face,
Kindly if sad seemed that lone place,
Yea, in a while it scarce seemed lone,
When now at last the white moon shone
Upon the sea, and showed that still
It quivered, though a moveless hill
A little while ago it seemed.

So, turning homeward now, he dreamed

Of many a help and miracle,
That in the olden time befell
Unto love's servants; e'en when he
Had clomb the hill anigh the sea,
And reached the hut now litten bright,
Not utterly with food and light
And common talk his dream passed by.
Yea, and with all this, presently
'Gan tell the old man when it was
That the great feast should come to pass
Unto Diana: Yea, and then
He, among all the sons of men,
E'en of that very love must speak;
Then grew Accontius faint and weak,
And his mouth twitched, and tears began
To pain his eyes; for the old man,
As one possessed, went on to tell
Of all the loveliness that well
Accontius wotted of, and now
For the first time he came to know
What name among her folk she had,
And, half in cruel pain, half glad,
He heard the old man say:
"Indeed
This sweet Cydippe bath great need
Of one to save her life from woe,
Because or ere the brook shall flow
Narrow with August 'twixt its banks,
Her folk, to win Diana's thanks,
Shall make her hers, and she shall be
Honoured of all folk certainly,
But unwed, shrunk as time goes on
Into a sour-hearted crone."

Accontius 'gan the room to pace
Ere he had done; with curious face
The old man gazed, but uttered nought;
Then in his heart Accontius thought,
"Ah when her image passeth by
Like a sweet breath, the blinded eye
Gains sight, the deaf man heareth well,
The dumb man lovesome tales can tell,
Hopes dead for long rise from their tombs,
The barren like a garden blooms;
And I alone—I sit and wait,
With deedless hands, on black-winged fate."

And so, when men had done with day,
Sleepless upon his bed he lay,
Striving to think if aught might move
Hard fate to give him his own love;

And thought of what would do belike,
And said, "Tomorrow will I strike
Before the iron groweth dull."
And so, with mind of strange things full,
Just at the dawn he fell asleep,
Yet as the shadows 'gan to creep
Up the long slope before the sun,
His blinking, troubled sleep was done;
And with a start he sat upright,
Now deeming that the glowing light
Was autumn's very sun, that all
Of ill had happed that could befall;
Yet fully waked up at the last,
From out the cottage-door he passed,
And saw how the old fisherman
His coble through the low surf ran
And shouted greeting from the sea;
Then 'neath an ancient apple-tree,
That on the little grassy slope
Stood speckled with the autumn's hope
He cast him down, and slept again;
And sleeping dreamed about his pain,
Yet in the same place seemed to be,
Beneath the ancient apple-tree.
So in his dream he heard a sound
Of singing fill the air around,
And yet saw nought; till in a while
The twinkling sea's uncounted smile
Was hidden by a rosy cloud,
That seemed some wondrous thing to shroud,
For in its midst a bright spot grew
Brighter and brighter, and still drew
Unto Accontius, till at last
A woman from amidst it passed,
And, wonderful in nakedness,
With rosy feet the grass did press,
And drew anigh; he durst not move
Or speak, because the Queen of Love
He deemed he knew; she smiled on him,
And, even as his dream waxed dim,
Upon the tree-trunk gnarled and grey
A slim hand for a while did lay;
Then all waxed dark, and then once more
He lay there as he lay before,
But all burnt up the green-sward was,
And songless did the throstle pass
'Twixt dark green leaf and golden fruit,
And at the old tree's knotted root
The basket of the gatherer
Lay, as though autumn-tide were there.
Then in his dream he thought he strove

To speak that sweet name of his love
Late learned, but could not; for away
Sleep passed, and now in sooth he lay
Awake within the shadow sweet,
The sunlight creeping o'er his feet.

Then he arose to think upon
The plans that he from night had won,
And still in each day found a flaw
That night's half-dreaming eyes ne'er saw,
And far away all good hope seemed,
And the strange dream he late had dreamed
Of no account he made, but thought .
That it had come and gone for nought.

And now the time went by till he
Knew that his keel had put to sea,
Yet after that a day or two
He waited, ere he dared to do
The thing he longed for most, and meet
His love within the garden sweet.
He saw her there, he saw a smile
The paleness of her face beguile
Before she saw him; then his heart
With pity and remorse 'gan smart;
But when at last she turned her head,
And he beheld the bright flush spread
Over her face, and once again
The pallor come, 'twixt joy and pain
His heart was torn; he turned away,
Thinking: "Long time ere that worst day
That unto her a misery
Will be, yea even as unto me,
And many a thing ere then may fall,
Or peaceful death may end it all."

The host that night his heart did bless
With praises of her loveliness
Once more, and said: "Fools men are
Who work themselves such bitter care
That they may live when they are dead;
Her mother's stern cold hardihead
Shall make this sweet but dead-alive;
For who in all the world shall strive
With such an oath as she shall make?"

Accontius, for self-pity's sake,
Must steal forth to the night to cry
Some wordless prayer of agony;
And yet, when he was come again,
Of more of such-like speech was fain,

And needs must stammer forth some word,
That once more the old fisher stirred
To speech; who now began to tell
Tales of that oath as things known well,
To wise men from the days of old,
Of how a mere chance-word would hold
Some poor wretch as a life-long slave;
Nay, or the very wind that drave
Some garment's hem, some lock of hair
Against the dreadful altar there,
Had turned a whole sweet life to ill;
So heedfully must all fulfil
Their vows unto the dreadful maid.
Accontius heard the words he said
As through a thin sleep fraught with dreams,
Yet afterward would fleeting gleams
Of what the old man said confuse
His weary heart, that ne'er was loose
A minute from the bonds of love,
And still of all, strange dreams he wove.

So the time passed; a brooding life
That with his love might hold no strife
Accontius led; he did not spare
With torment vain his soul to tear
By meeting her in that same place:
No fickle hope now changed her face,
No hot desire therein did burn,
Rather it seemed her heart did yearn
With constant sorrow, and such love
As surely might the hard world move.
—Ah! shall it? Love shall go its ways,
And sometimes gather useless praise
From joyful hearts, when now at rest
The lover lies, but oftenest
To hate thereby the world is moved,
But oftenest the well-beloved
Shall pay the kiss back with a blow,
Shall smile to see the hot tears flow,
Shall answer with scarce-hidden scorn
The bitter words by anguish torn
From such a heart, as fain would rest
Silent until death brings the best.

So drew the time on to the day
When all hope must be cast away;
Late summer now was come, and still
As heeding neither good or ill
Of living men, the stream ran down
The green slope to the sea-side brown,
Singing its changeless song; still there

Accontius dwelt 'twixt slope-side fair
And changing murmur of the sea.

The night before all misery
Should be accomplished, red-eyed, wan,
He gave unto the ancient man
What wealth he had, and bade farewell
In such a voice as tale doth tell
Unto the wise; then to his bed
He crept, and still his weary head
Tossed on the pillow, till the dawn
The fruitful mist from earth had drawn.
Once more with coming light he slept,
Once more from out his bed he leapt,
Thinking that he had slept too fast,
And that all hope was over-past;
And with that thought he knew indeed
How good is hope to man at need,
Yea, even the least ray thereof.
Then dizzy with the pain of love
He went from out the door, and stood
Silent within the fruitful rood.
Still was the sunny morn and fair,
A scented haze was in the air;
So soft it was, it seemed as spring
Had come once more her arms to fling
About the dying year, and kiss
The lost world into dreams of bliss.

Now 'neath the tree he sank adown,
Parched was the sward thereby and brown,
Save where about the knotted root
A green place spread. The golden fruit
Hung on the boughs, lay on the ground;
The spring-born thrushes lurked around,
But sang not, yet the stream sang well,
And gentle tales the sea could tell.
Ere sunrise was the fisher gone,
And now his brown-sailed boat alone,
Some league or so from off the shore,
Moved slowly 'neath the sweeping oar.
So soothed by sights and sounds that day,
Sore weary, soon Accontius lay
In deep sleep as he erst had done,
And dreamed once more, nor yet had gone
E'en this time from that spot of ground;
And once more dreaming heard the sound
Of unseen singers, and once more
A pink-tinged cloud spread thwart the shore,
And a vague memory touched him now
Amid his sleep; his knitted brow

'Gan to unfold, a happy smile
His long love-languor did beguile
As from the cloud the naked one
Came smiling forth—but not alone;
For now the image of his love,
Clad like the murmuring summer dove,
She held by the slim trembling hand,
And soon he deemed the twain did stand
Anigh his head. Round Venus' feet
Outbroke the changing spring-flowers sweet
From the parched earth of autumn-tide;
The long locks round her naked side
The sea-wind drave; lily and rose,
Plucked from the heart of her own close,
Were girdle to her, and did cling,
Mixed with some marvellous golden thing,
About her neck and bosom white,
Sweeter than they; with eyes that bliss
Changed not, her doves brushed past to kiss
The marvel of her limbs; yet bright,
Fair beyond words as she might be,
So fell it by love's mystery
That open-mouthed Accontius lay
In that sweet dream, nor drew away
His eyes from his love's pitying eyes;
And at the last he strove to rise,
And dreamed that touch of hand in hand
Made his heart faint; alas! the band
Of soft sleep, overstrained therewith,
Snapped short, and left him there to writhe
In helpless woe.

Yet in a while
Strange thoughts anew did him beguile;
Well-nigh he dreamed again, and saw
The naked goddess toward him draw,
Until the sunshine touched his face
And stark awake in that same place
He sighed, and rose unto his knee,
And saw beneath the ancient tree,
Close by his hand, an apple lie,
Great, smooth, and golden. Dreamily
He turned it o'er, and in like mood
A long sharp thorn, as red as blood,
He took into his hand, and then,
In language of the Grecian men,
Slowly upon its side he wrote,
As one who thereof took no note,
Accontius will I wed to-day;
Then stealthily across the bay
He glanced, and trembling gat him down

With hurried steps unto the town,
Where for the high-tide folk were dight,
And all looked joyous there and bright,
As toward the fane their steps they bent.
And thither, too, Accontius went,
Scarce knowing if on earth or air
His feet were set; he coming there,
Gat nigh the altar standing-place,
And there with haggard eyes 'gan gaze
Upon the image of the maid
Whose wrath makes man and beast afraid.

So in a while the rites began,
And many a warrior and great man
Served the hard-hearted one, until
Of everything she had her fill
That Gods desire; and, trembling now,
Accontius heard the curved horns blow
That heralded the damsels' band;
And scarce for faintness might he stand,
When now, the minstrels' gowns of gold
Being past, he could withal behold
White raiment fluttering, and he saw
The fellows of his own love draw
Unto the altar; here and there
The mothers of those maidens fair
Went by them, proud belike, and fain
To note the honour they should gain.

Now scarce with hungry eyes might he
Gaze on those fair folk steadily,
As one by one they passed by him;
His limbs shook, and his eyes did swim,
And if he heard the words they said,
As outstretched hand and humble head
Strengthened the trembling maiden's vow,
Nought of their meaning did he know—
—And still she came not—what was this?
Had the dull death of hope of bliss
Been her death too—ah, was she dead?
Or did she lie upon her bed,
With panting mouth and fixed bright eyes,
Waiting the new life's great surprise,
All longings past, amid the hush
Of life departing?

A great rush
Of fearful pain stopped all his blood
As thus he thought; a while he stood
Blinded and tottering, then the air
A great change on it seemed to bear,

A heavenly scent; and fear was gone,
Hope but a name; as if alone
Mid images of men he was,—
Alone with her who now did pass
With fluttering hem and light footfall
The corner of the precinct wall.
Time passed, she drew nigh to the place,
Where he was standing, and her face
Turned to him, and her steadfast eyes
Met his, with no more of surprise
Than if in words she had been told
That each the other should behold
E'en in such wise—Pale was she grown;
Her sweet breath, that an unheard moan
Seemed to her lover, scarce might win
Through her half-opened lips; most thin
The veil seemed 'twixt her mournful eyes,
And death's long-looked-for mysteries;
Frail were her blue-veined hands; her feet
The pink-tinged marble steps did meet
As though all will were gone from her.
There went a matron, tall and fair,
Noble to look on, by her side,
Like unto her, but for cold pride
And passing by of twenty years,
And all their putting back of tears;
Her mother, certes, and a glow
Of pleasure lit her stern face now
At what that day should see well done.

But now, as the long train swept on,
There on the last step of the fane
She stood, so loved, so loved in vain;
Her mother fallen aback from her,
Yet eager the first word to hear
Of that her dreadful oath—so nigh
Were misery to misery,
That each might hear the other's breath;
That they this side of fair hope's death
Might yet have clung breast unto breast,
And snatched from life a little rest,
And snatched a little joy from pain.

O weary hearts, shall all be vain,
Shall all be nought, this strife and love?
—Once more with slow foot did she move
Unto the last step, with no sound
Unto Accontius turning round,
Who spake not, but, as moved at last
By some kind God, the apple cast
Into her bosom's folds—once more

She stayed, while a great flush came o'er
Her sweet face erst half-dead and wan;
Then went a sound from man to man
So fair she seemed, and some withal
Failed not to note the apple fall
Into her breast.

Now while with fear
And hope Accontius trembled there
And to her side her mother came,
She cast aside both fear and shame
From out her noble heart, and laid
Upon the altar of the maid
Her fair right hand, clasped firm around
The golden fruit, and with no sound
Her lips moved, and her eyes upraised
Upon the marble image gazed,
With such a fervour as if she
Would give the thing humanity
And love and pity—then a space
Unto her love she turned her face
All full of love, as if to say,
"So ends our trouble from to-day,
Either with happy life or death."

Yet anxious still, with held-back breath,
He saw her mother come to her
With troubled eyes. "What hast thou there?"
He heard her say. "Is the vow made?
I heard no word that thou hast said?"

Then through him did her sweet voice thrill:
"No word I spake for good or ill;
But this spake for me; so say ye
What oath in written words may be;
Although, indeed, I wrote them nought;
And in my heart had got no thought,
When first I came hereto this morn,
But here to swear myself forlorn
Of love and hope—because the days
Of life seemed but a weary maze,
Begun without leave asked of me,
Whose ending I might never see,
Or what came after them—but now
Backward my life I will not throw
Into your deep-dug, spice-strewn grave,
But either all things will I save
This day, or make an end of all."

Then silence on the place did fall;
With frowning face, yet hand that shook,

The fated fruit her mother took
From out her hand, and pale she grew,
When the few written words she knew,
And what they meant; but speedily
She brushed the holy altar by,
Unto the wondering priests to tell
What things there in their midst befell.

There, in low words, they spoke awhile,
How they must deal with such a guile,
Cast by the goddess of desire
Into the holy maiden's fire.
And to the priests it seemed withal,
That a full oath they needs must call
That writing on the altar laid:
Then, wroth and fearful, some there bade
To seek a death for these to die,
If even so they might put by
The maid's dread anger; crueller
They grew as still they gathered fear,
And shameful things the dusk fane heard,
As grey beard wagged against grey beard,
And fiercer grew the ancient eyes.

But from the crowd, meanwhile, did rise
Great murmuring, for from man to man
The rumour of the story ran,
I know not how; and therewithal
Some god-sent lovesome joy did fall
On all hearts there, until it seemed
That each one of his own soul dreamed,
Beloved, and loving well; and when
Some cried out that the ancient men
Had mind too slay the lovers there,
A fierce shout rent the autumn air:
"Nay, wed the twain; love willeth it!"
But silent did the elders sit,
With death and fear on either hand,
Till one said, "Fear not, the whole land,
Not we, take back what they did give;
With many scarce can one man strive;
Let be, themselves shall make amends."

"Yea, let be," said the next; "all ends,
Despite the talk of mortal men,
Who deem themselves undying, when,
Urged by some unknown God's commands,
They snatch at love with eager hands,
And gather death that grows thereby,
Yet swear that love shall never die—
Let be—in their own hearts they bear

The seeds of pangs to pierce and tear.
What need, White-armed, to follow them,
With well-strung bow and fluttering hem,
Adown the tangle of life's wood?
Thou knowest what the fates deem good
For wretches that love overmuch—
One mad desire for sight and touch;
One spot alone of all the earth
That seems to them of any worth;
One sound alone that they may bear
Amidst earth's joyful sounds to hear;
And sight, and sound, and dwelling-place,
And soft caressing of one face,
Forbidden, and forbidden still,
Or granted e'en for greater ill,
But for a while, that they may be
Sunk deeper into misery—
Great things are granted unto those
That love not—far-off things brought close,
Things of great seeming brought to nought,
And miracles for them are wrought;
All earth and heaven lie underneath
The hand of him who wastes not breath
In striving for another's love,
In hoping one more heart to move.
A light thing and a little thing,
Ye deem it, that two hearts should cling
Each unto each, till two are one,
And neither now can be alone?
O fools, who know not all has sworn
That those shall ever be forlorn
Who strive to bring this thing to pass—
So is it now, as so it was,
And so it shall be evermore,
Till the world's fashion is passed o'er."

White-bearded was the ancient man
Who spoke, with wrinkled face and wan;
But as unto the porch he turned
A red spot in his cheek there burned,
And his eyes glittered, for, behold! .
Close by the altar's horns of gold,
There stood the weary ones at last,
Their arms about each other cast,
Twain no more now, they said—no more
What things soe'er fate had in store.
Careless of life, careless of death;
Now, when each felt the other's breath
On lip and cheek, and many a word
By all the world beside unheard,
Or heard and little understood,

Each spake to each, and all seemed good;
Yea, though amid the world's great wrong,
Their space of life should not be long;
O bitter sweet if they must die!
O sweet, too sweet, if time passed by;
If time made nought for them, should find
Their arms in such wise intertwined
Years hence, with no change drawing near!

Nor says the tale, nor might I hear,
That aught of evil on them fell.
Few folk there were but thought it well,
When saffron-robed, fair-wreathed, loose-haired
Cydippe through the city fared
Well won at last; when lingering shame
Somewhat upon the lovers came,
Now that all fear was quite bygone,
And yet they were not all alone,
Because, from men the sun was fain
A little more of toil to gain
Awhile in prison of his light,
To hold aback the close-lipped night.

Silence a little when the tale was told,
Soon broken by the merry-voiced and bold
Among the youths, though some belike were fain
For more of silence yet, that their sweet pain
Might be made sweeter still by hope and thought
Amid the words of the old story caught—
Might be made keener by the pensive eyes
That half-confessed love made so kind and wise;
Yet these too, mid the others, went their way,
To get them through the short October day
'Twixt toil and toilsome love, e'en as they might;
If so, perchance, the kind and silent night
Might yet reward their reverent love with dreams
Less full of care.

But round the must's red streams,
'Twixt the stripped vines the elders wandered slow,
And unto them, e'en as a soothing show
Was the hid longing, wild desire, blithe hope,
That seethed there on the tangled sun-worn slope
'Twixt noon and moonrise. Resolute were they
To let no pang of memory mar their day,
And long had fear, before the coming rest,
Been set aside. And so the changed west,
Forgotten of the sun, was grey with haze;
The moon was high and bright, when through the maze
Of draggled tendrils back at last they turned,
And red the lights within the fair house burned

Through the grey night; strained string, and measured voice
Of minstrels, mingled with the varying noise
Of those who through the deep-cut misty roads
Went slowly homeward now to their abodes.
A short space more of that short space was gone,
Wherein each deemed himself not quite alone.

In late October, when the failing year
But little pleasure more for men might bear,
They sat within the city's great guest-hall,
Nigh enow to the sea to hear the fall
Of the low haven-waves when night was still.
But on that day wild wind and rain did fill
The earth and sea with clamour, and the street
Held few who cared the driving scud to meet.
But inside, as a little world it was,
Peaceful amid the hubbub that did pass
Its strong walls in untiring waves of rage,
With the earth's intercourse wild war to wage.
Bright glowed the fires, and cheerier their light
Fell on the gold that made the fair place bright
Of roof and wall, for all the outside din.
Yet of the world's woe somewhat was within
The noble compass of its walls, for there
Were histories of great striving painted fair,
Striving with love and hate, with life and death,
With hope that lies, and fear that threateneth.
And so mid varied talk the day went by,
As such days will, not quite unhappily,
Not quite a burden, till the evening came
With lulling of the storm: and little blame
The dark had for the dull day's death, when now
The good things of the hall were set aglow
By the great tapers. Midmost of the board
Sat Rolf, the captain, who took up the word,
And said:
"Fair fellows, a strange tale is this,
Heard and forgotten midst my childish bliss,
Little remembered midst the change and strife,
Come back again this latter end of life,
I know not why; yet as a picture done
For my delight, I see my father's son,
My father with the white cloth on his knees,
Beaker in hand, amid the orange-trees
At Micklegarth, and the high-hatted man
Over against him, with his visage wan,
Black beard, bright eyes, and thin composed hands,
Telling this story of the fiery lands."

ARGUMENT

A certain man, who from rich had become poor, having been taken by one of his former friends to a fair house, was shown strange things there, and dwelt there awhile among a company of doleful men; but these in the end dying, and he desiring above all things to know their story, so it happened that he at last learned it to his own cost.

A city was there nigh the Indian Sea,
As tells my tale, where folk for many an age
Had lived, perforce, such life as needs must be
Beneath the rule of priestly king and mage,
Bearing with patient hearts the summer's rage,
Yea, even bowing foolish heads in vain
Before the mighty sun, their life and bane.

Now ere the hottest of the summer came,
While yet the rose shed perfume on the earth,
And still the grass was green despite the flame
Of that land's sun—while folk gave up to mirth
A little of their life, so little worth,
And the rich man forgot his fears awhile
Beneath the soft eve's still recurring smile—

Mid those sweet days, when e'en the burning land
Knew somewhat of the green north's summer rest,
A stately house within the town did stand,
When the fresh morn was failing from its best,
Though the street's pavement still the shadow blessed
From whispering trees, that rose, thick-leaved and tall,
Above the well-built marble bounding-wall.

Each side the door therein rose-garlands hung,
And through the doorway you might see within
The glittering robes of minstrel-men that sung,
And resting dancing-girls in raiment thin,
Because the master there did now begin
Another day of ease and revelry,
To make it harder yet for him to die.

And toward the door, perfumed and garlanded,
The guests passed, clad in wonderful attire,
And this and that one through the archway led
Some girl, made languid by the rosy fire
Of that fair time; with love and sweet desire
The air seemed filled, and how could such folk see
In any eyes unspoken misery?

Yet 'gainst the marble wall, anigh the door,
A man leaned, gazing at the passers-by,

Who, young, was clad in wretched clothes and poor,
And whose pale face, grown thin with misery,
Told truthful stories of his end anigh,
For such a one was he as rich men fear,
Friendless and poor, nor taught hard toil to bear;

And some in passing by that woeful man
A little time indeed their loud talk stayed
To gaze upon his haggard face and wan,
Some even, their hands upon their pouches laid,
But all passed on again, as if afraid
That, e'en in giving thanks for unasked gift,
His dolorous voice their veil of joy would lift.

He asked for nought, nor did his weary eyes
Meet theirs at all, until there came at last,
On a white mule, and clad in noble guise,
A lonely man, who by the poor wretch passed,
And, passing, on his face a side-glance cast,
Then o'er his shoulder eyed him, then drew rein
And turned about, and came to him again;

And said, "Thou hast the face of one I knew,
Men called the Golden One, in such a town,
Because they deemed his wealth for ever grew,
E'en in such times as beats the richest down;
What stroke of hapless fate, then, hast thou known
That thou hast come to such a state as this,
To which the poorest peasant's would be bliss?"

The other raised his eyes, and stared awhile
Into the speaker's face, as one who draws
His soul from dreams, then with a bitter smile
He said, "Firuz, thou askest of the cause
Of this my death? I knew not the world's laws,
But 'give today, and take tomorrow-morn,'
I needs must say, holding the wise in scorn.

"For even as with gifts contempt I bought,
So knowledge buys disease, power loneliness,
And honour fear, and pleasure pains unsought,
And friendship anxious days of great distress,
And love the hate of what we used to bless—
Ah, I am wise, and wiser soon shall grow,
And know the most that wise dead men can know.

"What shall I say? thou knowest the old tale;
I gave, I spent, and then I asked in vain,
And when I fell, my hands could scarce avail
For any work; at last, worse woe to gain,
I fled from folk who knew my present pain

And ancient pleasure—'midst strange men I wait,
In this strange town, the last new jest of fate.

"But since we talk of such-like merchandize,
What gift has bought for thee an equal curse?
Because, indeed, I deem by this thy guise
Thou hast not reached the bottom of thy purse;
Therefore, perchance, thy face seems something worse
Than mine, for I shall die, but thou must live,
More laughter yet unto the Gods to give?"

Nor did he speak these words unwarranted,
For in the other's face those signs there were
That mark the soul wherein all hope is dead;
While, with the new-born image of despair
The first man played, and found life even there,
Changeless his old friend's face was grown, and he
Had no more eyes things new or strange to see.

He said, "Then hast thou still a wish on earth;
Come now with me, if thou wouldst know my fate:
Thou yet mayst win again that time of mirth
When every day was as a flowery gate
Through which we passed to joy, importunate
To win us from the thought of yesterday,
In whatso pleasures it had passed away!"

"Great things thou promisest," the other said,
"And yet indeed since I have feared to die,
Though well I know that I were better dead,
The life thou givest me I yet will try;
It will not be so long in passing by,
If it must be such life as thou hast shared—
Yet thanks to thee who thus for me hast cared."

"Friend," said he, "in thine hand thy life thou hast,
If thou hast told me all that grieveth thee,
And unto thee the past may well be past,
And days not wholly bad thou yet mayst see;
And if indeed thy first felicity
Thou winnest not, yet something shalt thou have
Thy soul from death, or loathed life, to save.

"And for thy thanks, something I deem I owe
To our old friendship, could I mind it aught,
And well it is that I should pay it now
While yet I have a little wavering thought
Of things without me: neither have I brought
A poisoned life to give to thee today,
Or such a life as I have cast away."

"Nay," said he, "let all be since I must live,
I will not think of how to play my part:
And now some food to me thou needs must give,
For wretched hunger gnaweth at my heart.
Take heed withal that old desires will start
Up to the light since first I heard thee speak,
Wretched as now I am, and pined and weak."

Firuz thenceforward scarcely seemed to heed
What words he said, but as a man well taught
To do some dull task, set himself to lead
That man unto an hostel, where they brought
Food unto him, and raiment richly wrought;
Then he being mounted on a mule, the twain
Set out therefrom some new abode to gain.

NOW cheered by food, and hope at least of ease,
Perchance of something more, as on they went
Betwixt the thronged streets and the palaces,
No more did Bharam keep his head down bent,
Rather from right to left quick glances sent,
And though his old complaints he murmured still,
He scarcely thought his life so lost and ill.

But for his fellow, worse he seemed to be
Than e'en before, his thin face pinched and grey,
Seemed sunk yet deeper into misery,
Nor did he lift his eyes from off the way,
Nor heed what things his friend to him might say,
But plodded on till they were past the town,
When now the fiery sun was falling down.

Then by the farms and fields they went, until
All tillage and smooth ways were left behind,
And half-way up a bare and rugged hill
They entered a rude forest close and blind,
And many a tale perforce seized Bharam's mind
Of lonely men by fiends bewildered,
So like his fellow looked to one long dead.

But now, as careless what might hap to him,
He 'gan to sing of roses and delight
Some snatch, until the wood that had been dim,
E'en in broad day, grew black with coming night;
Then lower sank his song, and dropped outright,
When on his rein he felt his guide's hand fall,
And still they pierced that blackness like a wall.

Thus on the little-beaten forest-soil
They went, with nought to see, and nought to hear
Except their mules' unceasing, patient toil:

But full the darkness seemed of forms of fear,
And like long histories passed the minutes drear
To Bharam's o'erwrought mind expecting death,
And like a challenge seemed his lowest breath.

How long they went he knew not, but at last
Upon his face he felt a doubtful breeze,
Quickening his soul, and onward as they passed
A feeble glimmer showed betwixt the trees,
And his eyes, used to darkness, by degrees
Could dimly see his fellow, and the way
Whereon they rode to some unearthly day.

Then as the boughs grew thinner overhead,
That glimmer widened into moonlit night,
And 'twixt the trees grown sparse their pathway led
Unto a wide bare plain, that 'neath that light
Against the black trunks showed all stark and white;
Then Bharam, more at ease thereat, began
His fellow's visage in that light to scan.

No change was in his face, and if he knew
Who rode beside him, 'twas but as some hook
Within an engine knows what it must do,
His hand indeed from his friend's rein he took,
But never cast on him one slightest look;
Then, shuddering, Bharam 'gan to sing again
To make him turn, but spent his breath in vain.

But when the trees were wholly past, afar
Across the plain they saw a watch-tower high,
That 'neath the moonlight, like an angry star,
Shone over a white palace, and thereby
Within white walls did black-treed gardens lie:
And Firuz smote his mule and hastened on
To where that distant sign of trouble shone.

And as they went, thereon did Bharam stare,
Nor turned his eyes at all unto the plain,
Nor heeded when from out her form the hare
Started beneath the mule's feet, and in vain
The owl called from the wood, for he drew rein
Within a little while before the gate,
Casting his soul into the hands of fate.

Then Firuz blew the horn, nor waited long
Ere the gate, opened by a man scarce seen,
Gave entry to a garden, where the song
Of May's brown bird had hardly left the green
Sweet-blossomed tree-tops lonely, and between
The whispering glades the fountain leaped on high,

And the rose waited till morn came, to die.

But when the first wave of that soft delight
Swept o'er the spendthrift's sense, he smiled and turned
Unto his guide throughout the wondrous night,
And while his heart with hope and wonder burned,
He said, "Indeed a fair thing have I learned
With thee for master; yet is this the end?
Will they not now bring forth the bride, O friend?"

Drunk with the sweetness of that place he spoke,
And hoped to see the mask fall suddenly
From his friend's face, from whose thin lips there broke
A dreadful cry of helpless misery,
Scaring the birds from flowery bush and tree;
"O fool!" he said; "say such things in the day,
When noise and light take memory more away!"

Bharam shrank back abashed, nor had a word
To say thereto, and 'twixt the trees they rode,
Noted of nothing but some wakeful bird,
Until they reached a fair and great abode
Whereon the red gold e'en in moonlight glowed.
There silently they lighted down before
Smooth marble stairs, and through the open door

They entered a great, dimly-lighted hall;
Yet through the dimness well our man could see
How fair the hangings were that clad the wall,
And what a wealth of beast and flower and tree
Was spent wherever carving there might be,
And what a floor was 'neath his wearied feet,
Not made for men who call death rest and sweet.

Now he, though fain to linger and to ask
What was the manner of their living there,
And what thenceforth should be his proper task,
And who his fellows were, did nowise dare
To meet that cry again that seemed to bare
A wretched life of every softening veil—
A dreadful prelude to a dreadful tale.

So silently whereas the other led
He followed, and through corridors they passed,
Dim lit, but worthy of a king new wed,
Till to a chamber did they come at last,
O'er which a little light a taper cast,
And showed a fair bed by the window-side;
Therewith at last turned round the dreary guide,

And said, "O thou to whom night still is night

And day is day, bide here until the morn,
And take some little of that dear delight,
That we for many a long day have outworn.
Sleep, and forget awhile that thou wast born,
And on the morrow will I come to thee
To show thee what thy life with us must be."

And with that word he went, and though at first
The other thought that he should never sleep
For wondering what had made that house accursed,
And sunk that seeming bliss in woe so deep,
Yet o'er his soul forgetfulness did creep,
And in a dreamless slumber long he lay,
Not knowing when the sun brought back the day.

But in broad daylight of the following morn
He woke, and o'er him saw his fellow stand,
Who seemed, if it could be, yet more forlorn
Than when he last reached out to him his hand.
But now he said, "Come thou and see the band
Of folk that thou shalt dwell with, and the home
Whereto, fate leading thee, thou now hast come."

He rose without a word, and went with him
Who led the way through pillared passages,
Dainty with marble walls, made cool and dim
By the o'erhanging boughs of thick-leaved trees
That brushed against their windows in the breeze,
And still the work of one all seemed to be
Who had a mind to mock eternity.

Too lovely seemed that place for any one
But youths and damsels, who, not growing old,
Should dwell there, knowing not the scorching sun,
Without a name for misery or cold,
Without a use for glittering steel or gold
Except adornment, and content withal,
Though change or passion there should ne'er befall.

And still despite his fellow's woeful face,
And that sad cry that smote him yesternight,
The strange luxurious perfume of that place,
Where everything seemed wrought for mere delight,
Still made his heart beat, and his eyes wax bright
With delicate desires new-born again,
In that sweet rest from poverty and pain.

And, looking through the windows there askance,
He yet had something like a hope to see
The garden blossom into feast and dance,
Or, turning round a corner suddenly,

Mid voices sweet, and perfumed gowns to be,
Bewildered by white limbs and glittering eyes,
Striving to learn love's inmost mysteries.

But as they went, unto a door they came
That Firuz opened, showing a great hall
Whose walls with wealth of strange-wrought gold did flame
Through a cool twilight, for the light did fall
From windows in the dome high up and small,
And Bharam's lustful hope was quenched in fear,
As he, low moaning and faint sobs could hear.

He stopped and shut his eyes, oppressed with awe,
Thinking the rites of some sad god to see—
The secrets of some blood-stained hidden law—
But Firuz grasped his arm impatiently,
And drew him in. "O friend, look up!" said he,
"Nought dwelleth here but man's accursed race,
And thou art far the mightiest in this place."

Then he, though trembling still, looked up, and there
Beheld six men clad even as his guide,
Who sat upon a bench of marble fair
Against the wall, and some their eyes must hide
When they met his, and some rose up and cried
Words inarticulate, then sank again
Into their places, as out-worn with pain.

But one against the wall, with head back thrown,
Was leaning, and his eyes wide open stared,
And by his side his nerveless hands hung down,
Nor showed his face a glimmer of surprise,
Deaf was he to the wisest of the wise,
Speechless though open-mouthed; for there sat he,
Dead midst the living slaves of misery.

Bharam stared at him, wondering, still in dread;
But no heed took his fellows of his case,
Till Firuz, with a side-glance at him, said,
"Why mourn ye more that yet another face
Must see our shame and sorrow in this place?
Do ye not know this worldly man is come
To lay the last one of us in his home?

"And now in turn another soul is gone,
Get ready then to bear him forth straightway.
Be patient, for the heavy days crawl on!
But thou, O friend, I pray thee from this day
Help thou us helpless men, who cannot pray
Even to die; no long time will it be
Ere we shall leave this countless wealth to thee.

"Behold, a master, not a slave, we need,
For we, I say, have neither will to die
Nor yet to live, yet will we pay good heed
To thy commands, still doing patiently
Our daily tasks, as the dull time goes by;
Drive us like beasts, yea, slay us if thou wilt,
Nor will our souls impute to thee the guilt.

"Yet ask us not to tell thee of our tale,
Why we are brought unto this sad estate,
Nor for the rest will any words avail
To make us flee from this lone house, where fate
With all its cruel sport will we await;
Lo, now thy task, O fellow, in return
A mighty kingdom's wealth thou soon shalt earn."

Now as he spoke, a hard forgetfulness
Of his own lot, the rich man's cruel pride,
Smote Bharam's heart, he thought, "What dire distress
Could make me cast all hope of life aside?
Could aught but death my life and will divide:
Surely this mood of theirs will pass away
And these walls yet may see a merry day."

So thought he, yet, beholding them again,
And seeing them so swallowed up with woe
That they scarce heeded him, a pang of pain
Like pleasure's death throughout his heart did go;
And therewithal a strong desire to know
The utmost of their tale possessed his mind
And made him scorn an easy life and blind.

So midst his silence neither spoke they aught,
Firuz himself, as one, who having laid
His charge upon another, may take thought
Of l is own miseries, sat with head downweighed,
With tears that would not flow; then Bharam said,
"Masters, I bid you rise and do your best
To give your fellow's body its due rest!"

They rose up at his words and straight began,
As men who oft had had such things to do,
To dress the body of the just-dead man
For his last resting-place, then two and two
They bore it forth, passing the chambers through,
Where Bharam on that morn had hoped to see
Fair folk that had no name for misery.

Then through the sunny pleasance slow they passed,
That sweet with flowers behind the palace lay,

Until they reached a thick, black wood at last,
Bounding the garden as the night bounds day,
And through a narrow path they took their way,
Less like to men than shadows in a dream,
Till the wood ended at a swift broad stream,

Beneath the boughs dark green it ran, and deep,
Well-nigh awash with the wood's tangled grass,
But on the other side wall-like and steep,
Straight from the gurgling eddies, rose a mass
Of dark grey cliff; no man unhelped could pass;
But a low door e'en in the very base
Was set, above the water's hurrying race.

Of iron seemed that door to Bharam's eyes,
Heavily wrought, and closely locked it seemed;
But as he stared thereon strange thoughts would rise
Within his heart, until he well-nigh deemed
That he in morning sleep of such things dreamed,
And dreamed that he had seen all this before,
Wood and deep river, cliff, and close-shut door.

But in the stream, and close unto his feet,
A boat there lay, as though for wafting o'er
Whoso had will such doubtful things to meet
As that strange door might hide; and on the shore,
About the path, a rod of ground or more
Was cleared of wood, in which space here and there
Low changing mounds told of dead men anear.

So there that doleful company made stay,
And 'twixt the trees and swift stream hurrying by,
Their brother's body in the earth did lay.
Nor ever to the cliff would raise an eye,
But trembling, as with added agony,
Did their dull task as swiftly as they could,
Then went their way again amidst the wood.

Now with these dreary folk must Bharam live
Henceforward, doing even as he would;
And many a joy the palace had to give
To such a man as e'en could find life good
So prisoned, and with nought to stir the blood,
And seeing still from weary day to day
These wretched mourners cast their lives away.

Yet came deliverance; one by one they died,
E'en as new-come he saw that man die first,
And so were buried by the river-side.
And ever as he saw these men accurst
Vanish from life, he grew the more athirst

To know what evil deed had been their bane,
But still were all his prayers therefor in vain.

His utmost will in all things else they did,
Serving as slaves if he demanded aught,
But in grim silence still their story hid;
Nor did he fare the better when he sought
In the fair parchments that scribes' hands had wrought
Within that house. Of many a tale they told;
But none the tale of that sad life did hold.

Therefore in silence he consumed his days
Until a weary year had clean gone by
Since first upon that palace he did gaze,
And all that doleful band had he seen die,
Except Firuz; and ever eagerly
Did Bharam watch him, lest he too should go,
And make an end of all he longed to know.

At last a day came when the mourner said,
"Beneath the ground my woe thou soon shalt lay,
And all our foolish sorrow shall be dead;
Come then, I fain would show thee the straight way
Through which we came the night of that passed day
When first I brought thee here. This knowledge thine,
Guard thou this house, and use it as a mine;

"While safe thou dwellest in some city fair,—
Hasten, for little strength is in me now!"
But Bharam thought, "Yet will he not lay bare
His story to me utterly, and show
What-thing it was that brought these men so low."
Yet said he nought, but from the house they went,
While painfully the mourner on him leant.

So, the wood gained, by many glades they passed
That Firuz heeded not, though they were wide,
Until they reached a certain one at last,
Whereon he said, "Here did we come that tide;
I counsel thee no longer to abide
When I am dead, but mount my mule and go,
Nor doubt the beast the doubtful way shall know.

"She too shall serve thee when thou com'st again,
With many men, and sumpter mules enow
To gather up the wealth we held in vain,—
Turn me, I would depart! fainter I grow!
And thou the road to happy life dost know.
Alas, my feet are heavy! nor can I
Go any further. Lay me down to die!"

Then 'gainst a tree-root Bharam laid his head,
Saying, "Fear not, thou hast been good to me,
And by the river-side, when thou art dead,
I will not fail to lay thee certainly!"
"Nay, nay," he said, "what matter—let it be!
I bring the dismal rite unto an end.
Hide my bones here, and toward thy city wend!

"Better perchance that thou beholdest not
That place once more, our misery and bane!"
Then at that word did Bharam's heart wax hot;
He seemed at point his whole desire to gain.
He cried aloud, "Nay, surely all in vain
Thy secret hast thou hidden till this day,
Since to the mystic road thou showest the way!"

"My will is weak," his friend said, "thine is strong;
Draw near, and I will tell thee all the tale,
If this my feeble voice will last so long.
Perchance my dying words may yet avail
To make thee wise. This pouch of golden scale,
Open thou it. The gold key hid therein
Opens the story of our foolish sin.

"How thy face flushes, holding it! Just so,
As by that door I stood, did my face burn
That summer morning past so long ago.
Draw nigher still if thou the tale wouldst learn.
I scarce can speak now, and withal I yearn
To die at last, and leave the thing unsaid.
Raise thou me up, or I shall soon be dead!"

His fellow raised him trembling, nor durst speak
Lest he should scare his feeble life away,
Then from his mouth came wailing words, and weak:
"Where art thou then, O loveliest one, to-day?
Beneath the odorous boughs that gladden May,
Laid in the thymy hollow of some hill,
Dost thou remember me a little still?

"Can kindness such as thine was, vanish quite
And be forgotten? Ah, if I forget,
Canst thou forget the love and fresh delight
That held thee then—my love that even yet
Midst other love must make thy sweet eyes wet,
At least sometimes, at least when heaven and earth
In some fair eve are grown too fair for mirth?

"O joy departed, know'st thou how at first
I prayed in vain, and strove with hope to dull
My ravening hunger, mock my quenchless thirst?

And know'st thou not how when my life was full
Of nought but pain, I strove asleep to lull
My longing for the eyeless, hopeless rest,
Lest even yet strange chance should bring the best?

"Farewell, farewell, beloved! I depart,
But hope, once dead, now liveth though I die,
Whispering of marvels to my fainting heart—
Perchance the memory of some written lie,
Perchance the music of the rest anigh;
I know not—but farewell, be no more sad!
For life and love that has been, I am glad."

He ceased, and his friend, trembling, faintly said—
"Wilt thou not speak to me, what hast thou done?'
But even as he spoke, the mourner's head
Fell backward, and his troubled soul was gone;
And Bharam, in the forest left alone,
Durst scarcely move at first for very fear,
And longing for the tale he was to hear.

But in a while the body down he laid,
And swiftly gat him o'er the hot dry plain,
And through the garden, as a man afraid,
Went softly, and the golden porch did gain,
And from the wealth those men had held in vain,
Most precious things he did not spare to take
For his new life and joyous freedom's sake.

So doing he came round unto the door
That led out to the passage through the wood,
Wherethrough the mourners erst their dead ones bore
Down to the river; but as there he stood
He felt a new fire kindling in his blood;
His sack he laid aside, and touched the key
That could unlock that dreadful history;

And his friend's words, that loving tender voice
He sent forth ere he died, smote on his heart:
How could he leave those dead men and rejoice
With folk who in their story had no part?
Yea, as he lingered did the hot tears start
Into his eyes, he wept, and knew not why;
Some pleasure seemed within his grasp to lie,

He could not grasp or name, and none the less
He muttered to himself, "I must be gone
Or I shall die in this fair wilderness,
That every minute seems to grow more lone;
Why do I stand here like a man of stone?"
And with that very word he moved indeed,

But took the path that toward the stream did lead.

Quickly he walked with pale face downward bent,
As 'twixt the trembling tulip-beds he passed,
Until a horror seized him as he went,
And, turning toward the house, he ran full fast,
Nor, till he reached it, one look backward cast;
And by the gathered treasure, left behind
Awhile ago, he stood confused, half blind.

Then slowly did he lift the precious weight,
Yet lingered still. "Ah, must I go?" he said,
"Have I no heart to meet that unknown fate?
And must I lead the life that once I led,
Midst folk who will rejoice when I am dead;
Even as if they had not shared with me
The fear and longing of felicity?"

"And yet indeed if I must live alone,
If fellowship is but an empty dream,
Is there not left a world that is mine own?
Am I not real, if all else doth but seem?
Yea, rather, with what wealth the world doth teem,
When we are once content from us to cast
The dreadful future and remorseful past."

A little while he lingered yet, and then
As fearful what he might be tempted to,
He hurried on until he reached again
The outer door, and, sighing, passed therethrough,
But still made haste to do what he must do,
And found the mule and cast on her the sack,
And took his way to that lone forest-track.

Mattock and spade with him too did he bear,
And dug a grave beneath the spreading tree
Whereby Firuz had died, and laid him there,
Thinking the while of all his misery,
And muttering still, "How could it hap to me?
Unless I died within a day or two
Surely some deed I soon should find to do."

But when the earth on him he 'gan to throw,
He said, "And shall I cast the key herein?
What need have I this woeful tale to know,
To vex me midst the fair life I shall win;
Why do I seek to probe my fellow's sin,
Who, living, saved my life from misery,
And dying, gave this fresh life unto me?"

He kept the key, his words he answered not,

But smoothed the earth above the mourner's head,
Then mounting, turned away from that sad spot,
Feverish with hope and change, bewildered,
And ever more oppressed with growing dread,
As through the dark and silent wood he rode,
And drew the nigher unto man's abode.

But when at last he met the broad sweet light
Upon the hill's brow where that wood had end,
And saw the open upland fresh and bright,
A thrill of joy that sight through him must send,
And with good heart he 'twixt the fields did wend,
And not so much of that sad house he thought
As of the wealthy life he thence had brought;

So amidst thoughts of pleasant life and ease,
Seemed all things fair that eve; the peasant's door,
The mother with the child upon her knees
Sitting within upon the shaded floor;
While 'neath the trellised gourd some maid sung o'er
Her lover to the rude lute's trembling strings,
Her brown breast heaving 'neath the silver rings;

The slender damsel coming from the well,
Smiling beneath the flashing brazen jar,
Her fellows left behind thereat, to tell
How weary of her smiles her lovers are;
While the small children round wage watery war
Till the thin linen more transparent grows,
And ruddy brown the flesh beneath it glows;

The trooper drinking at the homestead gate,
Telling wild lies about the sword and spear,
Unto the farmer striving to abate
The pedler's price; the village drawing near,
The smoke, that scenting the fresh eve, and clear,
Tells of the feast; the stithy's dying spark,
The barn's wealth dimly showing through the dark.

How sweet was all! how easy it should be
Amid such life one's self-made woes to bear!
He felt as one who, waked up suddenly
To life's delight, knows not of grief or care.
How kind, how lovesome, all the people were!
Why should he think of aught but love and bliss
With many years of such-like life as this?

Night came at last, and darker and more still
The world was, and the stars hung in the sky,
And as the road o'ertopped a sunburnt hill
He saw before him the great city lie,

The glimmering lights about grey towers and high,
Rising from gardens dark; the guarded wall,
The gleaming dykes, the great sea, bounding all.

As one who at the trumpet's sound casts by
The tender thought of rest, of wife and child,
And fear of death for hope of victory,
So at that sight those sweet vague hopes and wild
Did he cast by, and in the darkness smiled
For pleasure of the beauty of the earth,
For foretaste of the coming days of mirth.

Surely if any man was blithe and glad
Within that city, when the morrow's sun
Beheld it, he at least the first place had,
And midst of glad folk was the happiest one—
So much to do, that was not e'en begun,
So much to hope for, that he could not see,
So much to win, so many things to be!

Yea, so much, he could turn himself to nought
For many days, but wandering aimlessly
Wherever men together might be brought,
That he once more their daily life might see,
That to his new-born life new seemed to be,
And staving thought off, he awhile must shrink
From touching that sweet cup he had to drink.

Yet when this mood was past by, what was this,
That in the draught he was about to drain,
That new victorious life, all seemed amiss?
If, thinking of the pleasure and the pain,
Men find in struggling life, he turned to gain
The godlike joy he hoped to find therein,
All turned to cloud, and nought seemed left to win.

Love moved him not, yea, something in his heart
There was that made him shudder at its name;
He could not rouse himself to take his part
In ruling worlds and winning praise and blame;
And if vague hope of glory o'er him came,
Why should he cast himself against the spears
To make vain stories for the unpitying years?

The thing that men call knowledge moved him not,
And if he thought of the world's varying face,
And changing manners, then his heart waxed hot
For thinking of his journey to that place,
And how 'twixt him and it was little space,
Then back to listlessness once more he turned,
Quenching the flame that in his sick heart burned.

What thing was left him now, but only this,
A life of aimless ease and luxury,
That he must strive to think the promised bliss,
Where hoping not for aught that was not nigh,
Midst vain pretence he should but have to die,
But every minute longing to confess
That this was nought but utter weariness.

So to the foolish image of delight
That rich men worship, now he needs must cling
Despite himself, and pass by day and night
As friendless and unloved as any king;
Till he began to doubt of everything
Amidst that world of lies; till he began
To think of pain as very friend of man.

So passed the time, and though he felt the chain
That round about his wasting life, was cast,
He still must think the labour all in vain
To strive to free himself while life should last,
And so, midst all, two weary years went past,
Nought done, save death a little brought anear,
The hard deliverance that he needs must fear.

At last one dawn, when all the place was still,
He took that key, and e'en as one might gaze
Upon the record of some little ill
That happed in past days, now grown happy days,
He eyed it, sighing, 'neath the young sun's rays;
And silently he passed his palace through,
Nor told himself what deed he had to do.

He reached the stable where his steeds were kept,
And 'midst the delicate-limbed beasts he found
The mule that o'er the forest grass had stepped,
Then, having on her back the saddle bound,
Entered the house again, and, looking round
The darkened banquet-chamber, caught away
What simple food the nighest to him lay.

Then, with the hand that rich men fawned upon,
The wicket he unlocked, and forth he led
His beast, and mounted when the street was won,
Wherein already folk for daily bread
Began to labour, who now turned the head
To whisper as the rich man passed them by
Betwixt the frails of fresh-plucked greenery.

He passed the wall where Firuz first he saw,
The hostel where the dead man gave him food;

He passed the gate and 'gan at last to draw
Unto the country bordering on the wood,
And still he took no thought of bad or good,
Or named his journey, nay, if he had met
A face he knew, he might have turned back yet.

But all the folk he saw were strange to him,
And, for all heed that unto them he gave,
Might have been nought; the reaper's bare brown limb,
The rich man's train with litter and armed slave,
The girl bare-footed in the stream's white wave—
Like empty shadows by his eyes they passed,
The world was narrowed to his heart at last.

He reached the hill, which e'en in that strange mood
Seemed grown familiar to him, with no pain
He found the path that pierced the tangled wood,
And midst its dusk he gave his mule the reins
And in no long time reached the little plain,
And then indeed the world seemed left behind,
And no more now he felt confused and blind.

He cried aloud to see the white house rise
O'er the green garden and the long white wall,
Which erst the pale moon showed his wondering eyes,
But on the stillness strange his voice did fall,
For in the noon now woodland creatures all
Were resting 'neath the shadow of the trees,
Patient, unvexed by any memories.

How should he rest, who might have come too late?
O'er the burnt plain he hurried, and laid hand
Upon the rusted handle of the gate,
Not touched since he himself thereby did stand,
The warm and scented air his visage fanned,
And on his head down rained the blossoms' dust,
As back the heavy grass-choked door he thrust.

But ere upon the path grown green with weed
'He set his foot, he paused a little while,
And of her gear his patient beast he freed,
And muttered, as he smiled a doubtful smile,
"Behold now if my troubles make me vile,
And I once more have will to herd with man,
Let me get back, then, even as I can."

There 'neath the tangled boughs he went apace,
Remembering him awhile of that sad cry,
That erst had been his welcome to that place,
That showed him first it might be good to die,
When he but thought of new delights anigh;

Thereat he shuddered now, bethinking him
In what a sea he cast himself to swim.

But his fate lay before him, on he went,
And through the gilded doors, now open wide,
He passed, and found the flowery hangings rent,
And past his feet did hissing serpents glide,
While from the hall wherein the mourners died
A grey wolf glared, and o'er his head the bat
Hung, and the paddock on the hearth-stone sat.

He loitered not amid those loathsome things,
That in the place which erst had been so fair,
Brought second death to fond imaginings
Of that sweet life, he once had hoped for there;
So with a troubled heart and full of care,
Though still with wild hopes stirring his hot blood,
He turned his face unto the dreary wood.

No less the pleasance felt its evil day;
The trellis, that had shut the forest trees
From the fair flowers, all torn and broken lay,
Though still the lily's scent was on the breeze,
And the rose clasped the broken images
Of kings and priests, and those they once had loved,
And in the scented bush the brown bird moved.

But with the choking weeds the tulip fought,
Paler and smaller than he had been erst
The wind-flowers round the well, fair feet once sought,
Were trodden down by feet of beasts athirst;
The well-trained apricot its bonds had burst;
The wild-cat in the cherry-tree anear
Eyed the brown lynx that waited for the deer.

A little while upon the black wood's edge
Did Bharam eye the ruin mournfully,
Then turned and said, "I take it as a pledge
That I shall not come back again to die;
The mocking image of felicity
Awaited those poor souls that failed herein,
But I most surely death or life shall win."

Thus saying, through the wood he 'gan to go,
And kindlier its black loneliness did seem
Than all the fairness ruin brought so low;
So with good heart he reached the swift full stream,
And there, as in an old unfinished dream,
He stood among the mourners' graves and saw
Past the small boat the eddies seaward draw.

Slowly, as one who thinks not of his deed,
He gat into the boat, and loosed from shore,
And 'gan to row the ready shallop freed
Unto the landing cut beneath the door,
And in a little minute stood before
Its rusty leaves with beating heart, and hand
His wavering troubled will could scarce command.

But almost ere he willed it, was the key
Within the lock, and the great bolt sprang back,
The iron door swung open heavily,
And cold the wind rushed from a cavern black:
Then with one look upon the woodland track,
He stepped from out the fair light of the day,
Casting all hope of common life away.

For at his back the heavy door swung to,
Before him was thick darkness palpable;
And as he struggled further on to go,
With dizzied head upon the ground he fell,
And if he lived on yet, he scarce could tell,
Amid the phantoms new born in that place
That past his eyes 'gan flit in endless race.

Fair women changing into shapeless things,
His own sad face mirrored, he knew not how,
And heavy wingless birds, and beasts with wings,
Strange stars, huge swirling seas, whose ebb and flow
Now seemed too swift for thought, now dull and slow:
Such things emmeshed his dying troubled thought,
Until his soul to sightless sleep was brought.

But when he woke to languid consciousness
Too well content he was therewith at first,
To ope his eyes, or seek what things might bless
His soul with rest from thought of good and worst,
And still his faint incurious ease he nursed,
Till nigh him rang a bird's note sweet and clear,
And stirred in him the seeds of hope and fear.

Withal the murmur of a quiet sea
He heard, and mingled sounds far off and sweet,
And o'er his head some rustling summer tree;
Slowly thereon he gat unto his feet,
And therewithal his sleep-dazed eyes did meet
The westering golden splendour of the sun,
For on that fair shore day was well-nigh done.

Then from the flashing sea and gleaming sky
Unto the green earth did he turn him round,
And saw a fair land sloping lazily

Up to a ridge of green with grey rocks crowned,
And on those slopes did fruitful trees abound,
And, cleaving them, came downward from the hill
In many a tinkling fall a little rill.

Now with his wakening senses, hunger too
Must needs awake, parched did his dry throat feel,
And hurrying, toward the little stream he drew,
And by a clear and sandy pool did kneel
And quenched his thirst, the while his hand did steal
Unto his wallet, where he thought to find
The bread he snatched from vain wealth left behind.

But when within his hand he held that bread,
Mouldy and perished as with many days,
He wondered much that he had not been dead,
And fell to think with measureless amaze
By what unheard-of, unimagined ways
Unto that lonely land he had been brought;
Until, bewildered in the maze of thought

That needs could lead nowhither, he arose
And from the fairest of those fruit-hung trees
The ripest and most luscious seeds he chose,
And staved his hunger off awhile with these;
Then 'twixt their trunks got back to where the breeze
Blew cool from off the calm sea, thinking still
That thence his fate must come for good or ill.

Thus, looking unto right and left, he passed
Over the green-sward, till he reached the strand,
And nought was 'twixt the sea and him at last,
Except a lessening belt of yellow sand.
There, looking seaward, he awhile did stand,
Until at last the great sun's nether rim,
Red with the sea-mist, in the sea 'gan swim.

But 'gainst it now a spot did he behold,
Nor knew if he were dazzled with the light,
Till as the orb sank and the sea grew cold,
Greater that grew beneath the gathering night,
And when all red was gone, and clear and bright
The high moon was, beneath its light he saw
A ship unto him o'er the waters draw.

Quickly his heart 'gan beat at sight of it,
But what that he could do could change his fate?
So calmly on the turf's edge did he sit
The coming of that unknown keel to wait,
That o'er the moonlit sea kept growing great,
Until at last the dashing oars he heard,

The creaking yard, the master's shouted word.

Then as the black hull 'neath the moonlight lay,
In the long swell, bright against side and oar,
A little shallop therefrom took its way
Unto the low line of the breakers hoar,
And when its keel was firm upon the shore
Two women stepped out thence, and 'gan to go
To Bharam's place with gentle steps and slow.

Then he arose, and wondering what should be
The end hereof, stood gazing at them there,
And even in that doubtful light could see
That they were lovesome damsels young and fair;
And as he watched their garlanded loose hair
And dainty flutter of their rich array,
Full many a hope about his heart 'gan play.

Now they drew nigh, and one of them began
In a sweet voice these hopeful words to say,
"Fear not, but come with us, O happy man,
Nor with thy doubts or questions make delay;
For this soft night gets ready such a day,
As shall thy heart for feeble pining blame,
And call thy hot desire a languid shame."

Therewith she turned again unto the sea,
As though she doubted not what he would do,
And Bharam followed after silently,
And went aboard the shallop with the two,
As one who dreams; and as the prow cleft through
The grey waves, sat beside them, pondering o'er
The days grown dim that led to that strange shore.

None spake to him, the mariners toiled on,
Silent the damsels sat, hand joined to hand,
Until the black sides of the ship were won;
Then folk hauled up the boat, his feet did stand
On the wide deck, the master gave command,
Back went the oars, and o'er the waters wan,
Unto the west 'neath sail and oar she ran.

All night they sailed, and when the dawn was nigh
And far astern the eastern sky grew bright,
A dark line seemed to cross the western sky
Afar and faint, and with the growing light
Another land began to heave in sight,
And when the lingering twilight was all done,
Grey cliffs they saw, made ruddy with the sun.

But when the shadow of their well-shaved mast

Had shortened that it no more touched the sea,
And well-nigh all the windy waste was past
That kept them from the land where they would be,
They turned about a ness, and 'neath their lee
A sandy-beached and green-banked haven lay,
For there a river cleft the mountains grey.

Thither they steered with no delay, and then
Upon the green slopes Bharam could behold
The white tents and the spears of many men,
And on the o'erhanging height a castle old,
And up the bay a ship o'erlaid with gold,
With golden sails and fluttering banners bright,
And silken awnings 'gainst the hot sun dight.

But underneath the tents, anigh that ship,
A space there was amidst of shadowing trees,
Well clad with turf down to the haven's lip;
And there, amongst the pasture of the bees,
Fanned by the long-drawn sweet-breathed ocean-breeze,
Well canopied, was set a wondrous throne,
Amidst whose cushions sat a maid alone.

Crowned as a queen was she, and round her seat
Were damsels gathered, clad just in such guise
As those who on the sands did Bharam meet,
And stood beside him now, with lovesome eyes.
All this saw Bharam in no other wise
Than one might see a dream becoming true,
Nor had he thought of what he next should do.

Only those longings, vague and aimless erst,
Now quickened tenfold, found a cause and aim,
And on his soul a flood of light outburst,
That swallowed up in brightness of its flame
Strange thoughts of death, and hopes without a name,
For now he knew that love had led him on,
Until—until, perchance, the end was won.

Unto that presence straight the shipmen steered,
And as the white foam from the oars did fly,
And the black prow the daisied green-sward neared,
Uprose a song from that fair company,
Which those two damsels echoed murmuringly,
Bearing love-laden words unto his ears
On tender music, mother of sweet tears.

SONG.

O thou who drawest nigh across the sea,
O heart that seekest Love perpetually,

Nor know'st his name, come now at last to me!

Come, thirst of love thy lips too long have borne,
Hunger of love thy heart hath long outworn,
Speech hadst thou but to call thyself forlorn.

The seeker finds now, the parched lips are led
To sweet full streams, the hungry heart is fed,
And song springs up from moans of sorrow dead.

Draw nigh, draw nigh, and tell me all thy tale;
In words grown sweet since all the woe doth fail,
Show me wherewith thou didst thy woe bewail.

Draw nigh, draw nigh, beloved! think of these
That stand around as well-wrought images,
Earless and eyeless as these trembling trees.

I think the sky calls living none but three:
The God that looketh thence and thee and me;
And He made us, but we made Love to be.

Think not of time, then, for thou shalt not die,
How soon soever shall the world go by,
And nought be left but God and thou and I.

And yet, O love, why makest! thou delay,
Life comes not till thou comes, and the day
That knows no end may yet be cast away?

Such words the summer air swept past his ears,
Such words the lovesome maidens murmured,
With unabashed soft eyes made wet with tears,
As though for them the world were really dead,
As though indeed those tender words they said
Each to her love, and each her fingers moved,
As though she thought to meet the hands she loved.

But Bharam heeded not their lonesomeness,
As through his heart there shot one bitter thought
Of those dead mourners and their dead distress
That his own feet to such a land had brought,
But even ere the fear had come to nought,
The thought that made it, yea, all memory
Of what had been, had utterly passed by.

But when the song was done, and on the strand
The bark's prow grated, and the maidens twain
In low words bade him follow them aland,
Still, mid the certain hope of boundless gain,
About him clung the seeming-causeless pain

Of that past thought, that love had driven away,
The dreary teaching of a hopeless day.

And as unto the throne he drew anigh
He tried to say unto himself; "Alas!
Why am I full of such felicity?
How know I that for me the music was?
How know I yet what thing will come to pass?
How know I that my heart can bear the best,
Vain foolish heart that knew but little rest?"

A moment more and toward that golden ship
His face was turned, a hand was holding his;
His eyes with happy tears were wet, his lip
Still thrilled with memory of a loving kiss,
His eager ears drank in melodious bliss
Past words to tell of; joy was born at last,
Surely the bitterness of death was past.

How can I give her image unto you,
Clad in that raiment wonderful and fair?
What need? Be sure that love's eye pierceth through
What web soever hides the beauty there—
To tell her fairness? Measure forth the air,
And weigh the wind, and portion out the sun!
This still is left, less easy to be done.

Into the golden ship now passed the twain,
he maidens followed, and the soldiers moved
Their ordered ranks, the shoreward road to gain;
The minstrels played what tunes the best behoved,
While in the stern the lover and beloved
Had nought to do but each on each to gaze,
Without a thought of past or coming days.

Up stream the gold prow pointed, the long oars
Broke into curves of white the swirling green,
On each side opened out the changing shores;
So lovely there were all things to be seen,
That in the golden age they might have been;
But rather had he gaze upon those eyes
Than see the whole world freed from miseries.

Sometimes she said, "And this, O love, is thine
As thou art mine. Look forth thy land to see!"
But he looked not, but rather would entwine
His fingers in her fingers amorously,
And answer, "Yea, and that one day shall be
When thou shalt go upon the blossoms sweet,
And I must look thereon to see thy feet!"

Now the stream narrowed, and the country girls
Thronged on the banks to see the Queen go by,
And cast fresh flowers upon the weedy swirls.
"Look forth! they sing to our felicity!"
The Queen said, "And the city draweth nigh."
"Nay, nay," said Bharam, "I will look on them
When they shall kneel to kiss thy garment's hem."

Now far ahead, above dark banks of trees
Could they behold the city's high white wall,
And, as they neared it, on the summer breeze
Was borne the tumult of the festival;
And when that sound on Bharam's ears did fall,
He cried, "Ah, will they lengthen out the day,
E'en when kind night has drawn the sun away?"

She sighed and said, "Nay now, be glad, O king,
That thou art coming to thy very own;
Nor one day shalt thou think it a small thing
That thou therein mayst wear the royal crown
When somewhat weary thou at last art grown,
Through lapse of days, of this and this and this—
That something more is left thee than a kiss."

He stared at her wide eyes as one who heard
Yet knew not what the words might signify,
Then said, "And think'st thou I shall be afeard
To slay myself before our love goes by,
That changed by death, if we indeed can die,
Unwearied by this anxious, earthy frame,
I still may think of thee, and know no shame?"

She gazed upon his flushed face tenderly,
Reddening herself for love, but said not aught,
Only her bosom heaved with one soft sigh,
And some unravelled maze of troublous thought
Unbidden tears unto her sweet eyes brought;
And he forgot that shade of bitterness
When such a look his yearning heart did bless.

Thereat the silver trumpet's tuneful blare
Made music strange unto his lovesome dream,
For now before them lay the city fair,
With high white bridges spanning the swift stream,
And bridge and shore with wealth of gold did gleam.
From a great multitude shout followed shout,
And high in air the sound of bells leapt out.

And then the shipmen furled the golden sail—
Slowly the red oars o'er the stream did skim,
As 'twixt the houses the light wind 'gan fail,

Till by a palace on the river's brim,
Whose towering height made half the bells grow dim,
The golden ship was stayed, for they had come
Unto the happy seeker's wondrous home.

"Look up and wonder, well-beloved," she said,
As now they rose to go unto the shore,
"At what the men did for us who are dead,
And praise them for the depth of their past lore,
And thank them though their life is long past o'er.
If they had known that all these things should be
How better had they wrought for thee and me?"

Gravely she looked into his eager eyes,
That turned unto the house a little while,
But took small heed of all the phantasies
Wherewith those men their trouble did beguile,
Though calmly did the vast front seem to smile,
From all its breadth of beauty looking down
Upon the tumult of the joyous town.

Again she sighed, but passed on silently,
And o'er the golden gangway went the twain
Unto the gold shade of the doorway high,
Treading on golden cloths, betwixt a lane
Of girls who each had been a kingdom's bane
In toiling, troubled lands, where loveliness
In scanty measure longing men doth bless.

One moment, and the threshold Bharam passed,
And that desire his heart was set upon
Yet would not name, his heart hath won at last.
Ah, if the end of all thereby were won!
For though, indeed, the noon-tide sun hath shone,
And all the clouds are scattered, who can say
What clouds shall curse the latter end of day?

The days passed—growing sweeter as the year
Declined through autumn into winter-tide;
Perchance, for though no day could be so dear
As that whereon he first had seen his bride,
Yet still no less did love with him abide,
Tempered with quiet days and restfulness;
Desire fulfilled, renewed, his life did bless.

And thereto now were added other joys,
Her gifts indeed, unmeet for him to scorn:
The judgment-seat, the tourney's glorious noise,
The council wherein were the wise laws born;
Sweet tales of lovers vanquished and forlorn,
To make bliss greater when these lovers met,

Silent, alone, all troubles to forget—

All troubles to forget—the winter went,
Spring came, and love seemed worthier therewith weighed,
The summer came, and brought no discontent,
Nor yet with autumn's fading did love fade,
And the cold winter love the warmer made.
So Bharam said, when round his love he clung,
And lonely, still such words were on his tongue.

At last from this and that (it boots not now
To tell the why and wherefore of the thing),
Great war and strife with other lands did grow,
And weeping she around his neck must cling,
Bidding him look for such a welcoming
When he came back again, as should outdo
The day that made one heart and life of two.

Nor did this fail: tried at all points was he,
He met the foe, and, beaten back with shame,
Snatched from victorious hands the victory,
And, winner of a great and godlike name,
Sighing with love, back to his love he came,
Worthy of love and changed by love indeed,
And with most glorious love to be his meed.

Ah, changed by love—the fickle careless earth,
The deeds of men, the troubles that they had,
That in first love he held of little worth,
Now like a well-told tale would make him glad,
And nought therein to him seemed lost or bad;
"And love," he said, "my joyous life doth bound,
E'en as the sea some fair isle flows around."

"Love flows around"—alas, as time went on
Some strong career of striving would he stay,
And falter e'en at point of victory won,
And well-nigh cast the longed-for thing away:
"Nay, let me think of love," then would he say,
"Ah, I have swerved from singleness of heart,
Let me return, nor in these things have part."

"Let me return"—but, ah, what thing was this?
That in his love's arms he would feel the sting
Of vain desire, and ne'er-accomplished bliss.
At whiles, indeed—for he had strength to fling
All thought away, and to his love to cling.
At least as yet, and still he seemed to be
O' Dowered with the depth of all felicity.

So passed the time, till he two years had been

Living that joyous life in that fair land,
When on a day there came to him the Queen,
And said: "Fair love, all folk bow 'neath the hand
Of this or that, and I, at the command
Of one whose will I dare not disobey,
Must leave thee lonely till the hundredth day.

"Nay, now, forbear to ask me why I go!
Thou know'st all things are thine that I have got,
Nathless this one thing never shalt thou know,
Unless the love grow cold that once was hot,
And thou art grown aweary of thy lot.
Ah, love, forgive me! for thy kiss is sweet,
As cool fresh streams to bruised and weary feet.

"Yet one more word; the room where thou and
Were left alone that day of all sweet days;
Enter it not, till that time is passed by
I told thee of, and many weary ways
My feet have worn, to meet thy loving gaze;
For surely as thy foot therein shall tread,
Thou unto me, as I to thee, art dead.

"And yet, for fear of base and prying folk,
Needs must thou bear about that chamber's key.
Ah, love, farewell! no hard or troublous yoke
Thou hast to bear, nor have I doubt of thee.
For all the stream of tears that thou dost see,
They are love's offspring only, for my heart
Yet more than heretofore in thine has part."

Thus did she go, and he so left behind,
Mourned for her and desired her very sore,
Yet, with a pang, he felt that he was blind,
Despite of words, that yet there was a store
Of some undreamed-of and victorious lore
He might not touch—frowning he turned away,
And seemed a troubled, gloomy man that day.

Yet loyally for many days he dwelt
Within that house, or from his golden throne
Good justice to the thronging people dealt;
But when night came, and he was left alone,
Then all that splendour scarcely seemed his own;
And when he fell to thinking of his love,
He 'gan to wish that he his heart might prove.

In agony he strove to cast from him
Fresh doubts of what she was, and all his tale
Rose up once more, now vague indeed and dim,
Yet worse therefore perchance—if he should fail,

And in some half-remembered hell go wail
His happy lot, the days that might have been!
Was she his bane?—his life, his love, his queen.

Then would he image forth her body fair,
And limb by limb would set before his eyes
Her loveliness as he had seen it there;
Then cry, "Why think of these vain mysteries
When still ahead such happy life there lies?
And yet and yet, this that doth so outshine
All other beauty, is it wholly mine?

"How can it change, that throne of loveliness?
How can it change—but I grow old and die.
Perchance some other heart those eyes shall bless,
Some other head upon that bosom lie,
When all that once I was is long gone by:
And now what memory through my mind has passed
Of men from some strange heaven of love outcast?

"Who knows but in that chamber I may find
The clue unto this tangled, weary maze,
And vision clear, whereas I now am blind,
And endless love instead of anxious days—
A glorious end to all these dark strange ways?
Perchance those words she did but say to me,
To try my heart—did she not give the key?"

So passed the days, and sometimes would he strive
To think of nothing but her dear return,
And midst of kingly deeds would think to live,
But then again full oft his heart would burn
The uttermost of all the thing to learn;
Love failed him not, but baneful jealousy
Had scaled his golden throne and sat thereby.

Now he began to wander nigh the door,
And draw from out its place the golden key,
And curse the gift, and wish the days passed o'er,
Till in his arms his love once more should be;
Yet still he dreaded what his eyes should see
In those familiar and beloved eyes,
Changed now perchance in some unlooked-for wise.

At last a day came, on the morn of it
Did he arise from haggard dreamful sleep,
And on the throne of justice did he sit,
In troublous outward things his soul to steep;
Then, armed, upon his war-horse did he leap,
And in the lists right eagerly did play,
As one who every care hath cast away.

Then came the evening banquet, and he sat
To watch the dancers' gold-adorned feet,
And with his great men talked of this and that,
Then rose, with gold a minstrel-man to greet,
Then listened to his pensive song and sweet
With serious eyes, and still in everything
He seemed an unrebuked and glorious king.

But at the dead of night was he alone
Once more, once more within his wavering heart
Strange thought against confused thought was thrown,
Nor knew he how real life from dreams to part,
All seemed to him a picture made by art,
Except the overwhelming strong desire
To know the end, that set his heart afire.

Dawn found him thus; then he arose from bed,
He kissed her picture hanging on the wall,
The linen things that veiled her goodlihead
From all but him, and still, like bitterest gall,
A thought rose up within him therewithal,
And strangely was his heart confused with fears
That checked the rise of tender, loving tears.

He gat the golden key into his hand,
And once more had a glimmering memory
Of how just so he once before did stand,
Ready another golden key to try;
Then murmured he, "Gat I not bliss thereby?
Unless all this is such a gleam of thought,
That to a man's mind sometimes will be brought.

"Of how he lived before, he knows not where."
So saying from the chamber did he pass,
And went a long way down a cloister fair,
And o'er a little pleasance of green grass,
Until anigh the very door he was
That hid that mystery from him; there he stayed,
And in his hand the golden key he weighed.

There stood he, trying hard to think thereof,
The better and the worse, how all would be
If he should do the deed, but thought would move
From this thing unto that confusedly,
And neither past nor future could he see,
Nay scarce could say of what thing then he thought,
Such fever now the fierce desire had wrought.

Not long he lingered, in the lock he set
The golden key, as one constrained thereto,

And thrust the door back, and with scared eyes met
The lovely chamber that so well he knew,
And therein still was all in order due,
No deathlike image seared his wondering eyes,
No strange sound smote his ears with ill surprise.

He sighed, and smiled, as one would say, "Ah, why
Have I feared this, wherein was nought to fear,
Wrapping familiar things in mystery?"
And even therewithal did he draw near
I To well-remembered things his soul held dear,
Gazing at all those matters one by one,
That told of sweet things there in past days done.

There in the grey light were the hangings fair,
No figure in them changed now any whit,
The marble floor half hid with carpets rare
E'en as when first he saw her feet on it,
A grey moth's whirring wings indeed did flit
Across the fair bed's gleaming canopy,
But yet no other change had passed thereby.

And by the bed upon the floor there lay
Soft raiment of his love, as though that she
Had there unclad her, ere she went away.
He stopped and touched the fair things tenderly,
And love swept over him as some grey sea
Sweeps o'er the dry shells of a sandy bank,
And with dry lips his own salt tears he drank.

He rose within a while, and turned about
Unto the door, and said, "Three days it is
Before she comes to take away all doubt
And wrap my soul again in utter bliss;
I will depart, that she may smile at this,
Giving the pity and forgiveness due
Unto a heart whose feebleness she knew.

Therewith he turned to go, but even then,
Upon a little table nigh his hand,
Beheld a cup the work of cunning men
For many a long year vanished from the land,
And up against it did a tablet stand;
Whereon were gleaming letters writ in gold;
Then breathlessly these things did he behold;

For never had his eyes beheld them erst,
And well he deemed the secret lay therein;
Trembling, he said, "This cup may quench my thirst,
Fair rest from this strange tablet may I win,
And if I sin she will forgive my sin;

Nay, rather since her word I disobey
In entering here, no heavier this will weigh."

Withal he took the tablet, and he read;
"O thou who, venturing much, hast gained so much,
Drink of this cup, and be remembered
When all are gone whose feet the green earth touch:
Dull is the labouring world, nor holdeth such
As think and yet are happy; then be bold,
And things unthought of shall thine eyes behold!

"Yea, thou must drink, for if thou drinkest not
Nor soundest all the depths of this hid thing,
Think'st thou that these my words can be forgot,
How close soever thou to love mayst cling,
How much soever thou art still a king:
Drink then, and take what thou hast fairly won,
For make no doubt that thine old life is done."

He took the cup and round about the bowl
Beheld strange figures carved, strange letters writ,
But mid the hurrying tumult of his soul,
He of their meaning then could make no whit,
Though afterwards their smallest lines would flit
Before his eyes, in times that came to him
When many a greater matter had grown dim.

So with closed eyes he drank, and once again,
While on his quivering lip the sweet draught hung,
Did he think dimly of those mourning men
And saw them winding the dark trees among,
And in his ears their doleful wailing rung;
His love and all the glories of his home
E'en in that minute shadows had become.

E'en in that minute, though at first indeed
In one quick flash of pain unbearable,
His love, his queen, made bare of any weed,
Seemed standing there, as though some tale to tell
From opened lips; and then a dark veil fell
O'er all things there, a chill and restless breeze
Seemed moaning through innumerable trees.

Yet still he staggered onwards to the door
With arms outspread, as one who in dark night
Wanders through places he has known before;
Wide open were his eyes that had no sight,
And with a feverish flush his cheeks were bright,
His lips moved, some unspoken words to say,
As, sinking down, across the door he lay.

What strange confused dreams swept through his sleep!
What fights he fought, nor knew with whom or why;
How piteously for nothing he must weep,
For what inane rewards he still must try
To pierce the inner earth or scale the sky!
What faces long forgot rose up to him!
On what a sea of unrest did he swim!

He woke, the wind blew cold upon his face,
The sound of swirling waters smote his ear,
Through the deep quiet of some lonely place;
Shuddering with horror at what might be near,
He closed his dazzled eyes again for fear,
Ere they had seen aught but the light of day
And formless things against it, black and grey.

Trembling awhile he lay, and scarcely knew
Why he was sick with fear, but when at last
His wretched soul unto his body drew,
And somewhat he could think about the past,
As one might wake to hell, around he cast
A haggard glance, and saw before him there
A grey cliff rising high into the air

Across a deep swift river, and the door
Shut fast against him, did he see therein,
Wherethrough with trembling steps he passed before
That happy life above all lives to win,
And round about him the sharp grass and thin,
Covered low mounds that here and there arose,
For to his head his forerunners were close.

Then with changed voice he moaned and to his feet
Slowly he gat, and 'twixt the tree-boles grey
He 'gan to go, and tender words and sweet
Were in his ears, the promise of a day
When he should cast all troublous thoughts away.
He stopped, and turned his face unto the trees
To hearken to the moaning of the breeze;

Because it seemed well-nigh articulate;
He cried aloud, "Come back, come back to me!"
If yet the echo of the fearful gate
Had any sound to help his misery;
He shut his eyes, lest he perchance might be
Caught by some fearful dream within a dream,
That he might wake up to his gold bed's gleam.

Voiceless the wind was, the grey cliff was dumb,
His eyes could show him nought but that same place
Whereto in days of hope his feet had come;

He cast himself adown, and hid his face
Within the grass, and heeding no disgrace,
Howled beastlike, till his voice grew hoarse and dim.
And little life indeed seemed left in him.

Then in a while he rose and tottered on
Adown that path, scarce knowing what had been
Or why his woe was such, until he won
To where had been of old the pleasance green,
Whose beauty, whose decay he erst had seen
That now indeed a tangled waste had grown,
Whose first estate scarce any man had known.

Roofless above it then he saw the house,
Whose vanished loveliness his heart had filled
With fresh luxurious longings amorous,
And thitherward, though thus he scarcely willed,
His feet must stray to see the wild bird build
Her nest within the chambers, once made bright,
To house the delicate givers of delight.

And now the first rage of his grief being o'er,
Madness was past, though pain was greater still,
And he remembered well the days of yore,
And how his great desire made all things ill,
And aye with restlessness his life did fill;
Too hard to bear that he must cast away
Honour and wealth, to reach e'en such a day.

Now in the hall upon that bench of stone,
Where erst the mourners used to sit, he sat,
Striving to think of all that he had done
Before his heart's unnamed desire he gat,
Striving to hope that still in this or that
He might take pleasure yet before he died,
That the hard days a little joy might hide.

He moaned to think that he had cast away
All hope of quiet life then when his hand
Was on the key 'neath that high cliff and grey,
And looking backward he awhile did stand-
Needs must he deem him worse than that sad band
Who therein erst their wretched lives outwore,
However great the burden that they bore.

For they, he said, had somewhat left of rest,
Since in that place indeed they could abide,
But on his heart the weight of woe so pressed
That he his wretched head could never hide,
But needs must wander forth until he died—
Ah God, more full of horror seemed that place,

Than the world's curious eyes upon his face.

For there he seemed to sleep that he might dream
The worst of dreams, he seemed to be awake,
That through them all might pierce no hopeful gleam,
That he the fearful chain might never break;
And shameful images his eyes must make
That shuddering he must call by his love's name,
And on his lips must gather words of shame.

Midst this, I say, what will was left to him,
Still urged him unto men's abodes again,
So that he rose, and though his eyes were dim
With misery, he crossed the sunburnt plain,
And as one walks in sleep, with little pain
He pierced the forest through, and came once more
Unto the hill that looked the uplands o'er.

Fierce was the summer sun of that bright day,
When on the upland road he set his feet,
And man and beast within the shadow lay
And rested, but no rest to him was sweet
That he could gain, and when the hot sun beat
Upon his head as from the wood he passed,
Nought noted he that flame upon him cast.

At end of day he reached the city gate,
And now no more he moaned, his eyes were dry;
Shut in his body's bonds, his soul would wait,
The utmost term of all its misery,
Nor hope for any ease, nor pray to die.
Some poor abode within that city fair
He gat himself and passed the long days there.
But now and then men saw him on the quays,
Gazing on busy scenes he heeded nought,
Or passing through the crowd on festal days,
Or in some net of merry children caught,
And when they saw his dreamy eyes distraught,
His changeless face drawn with that hidden pain,
They said, "THE MAN WHO NE'ER SHALL LAUGH AGAIN."

Ah, these, with life so done with now, might deem
That better is it resting in a dream,
Yea, e'en a dull dream, than with outstretched hand,
And wild eyes, face to face with life to stand,
No more the master now of anything,
Through striving of all things to be the king—
Than waking in a hard taskmaster's grasp
Because we strove the unsullied joy to clasp—
Than just to find our hearts the world, as we
Still thought we were and ever longed to be,

To find nought real except ourselves, and find
All care for all things scattered to the wind,
Scarce in our hearts the very pain alive.
Compelled to breathe indeed, compelled to strive,
Compelled to fear, yet not allowed to hope—
For e'en as men laid on a flowery slope
'Twixt inaccessible cliffs and unsailed sea,
Painless, and waiting for eternity
That will not harm, were these old men now grown.
The seed of unrest, that their hearts had sown,
Sprung up, and garnered, and consumed, had left
Nought that from out their treasure might be reft;
All .was a picture in these latter days,
That had been once, and they might sit and praise
The calm, wise heart that knoweth how to rest,
The man too kind to snatch out at the best,
Since he is part of all, each thing a part,
Beloved alike of his wide-loving heart.

Ah, how the night-wind raved, and wind and sea
Clashed wildly in their useless agony,
But dulled not or made weak the minstrel's song
That through the hall bemocked the lost year's wrong.

NOVEMBER

Are thine eyes weary? is thy heart too sick
To struggle any more with doubt and thought,
Whose formless veil draws darkening now and thick
Across thee, e'en as smoke-tinged mist-wreaths brought
Down a fair dale to make it blind and nought?
Art thou so weary that no world there seems
Beyond these four walls, hung with pain and dreams?

Look out upon the real world, where the moon,
Half-way 'twixt root and crown of these high trees,
Turns the dead midnight into dreamy noon,,
Silent and full of wonders, for the breeze
Died at the sunset, and no images,
No hopes of day, are left in sky or earth—
Is it not fair, and of most wondrous worth?

Yea, I have looked and seen November there;
The changeless seal of change it seemed to be,
Fair death of things that, living once, were fair;
Bright sign of loneliness too great for me,
Strange image of the dread eternity,
In whose void patience how can these have part,
These outstretched feverish hands, this restless heart?

On a clear eve, when the November sky
Grew red with promise of the hoar-frost nigh,
These ancient men turned from the outside cold,
With something like content that they, grown old,
Needed but little now to help the ease
Of those last days before the final peace.
The empty month for them left no regret
For sweet things gained and lost, and longed for yet,
'Twixt spring-tide and this dying of the year.
Few things of small account the whole did bear,
Nor like a long lifetime of misery
Those few days seemed, as oft to such may be
As, seeing the patience of the world, whereby
Midst all its strife it falls not utterly
Into a wild, confused mass of pain,
Yet note it not, and have no will to gain,
Since they are young, a little time of rest,
Midst their vain raging for the hopeless best.

Such thought, perchance, was in his heart, who broke
The silence of the fireside now, and spoke;
"This eve my tale tells of a fair maid born
Within a peaceful land, that peace to scorn,
In turn to scorn the deeds of mighty kings,
The council of the wise, and far-famed things,
And envied lives; so, born for discontent,
She through the eager world of base folk went,
Still gaining nought but heavier weariness.
God grant that somewhere now content may bless
Her yearning heart; that she may look and smile
On the strange earth that wearied her awhile,
And now forgets her! Yet so do not we,
Though some of us have lived full happily!"

THE STORY OF RHODOPE

ARGUMENT

There was in a poor land a certain maid, lowly but exceeding beautiful, who, by a strange hap, was drawn from her low estate, and became a queen and the world's wonder.

A Grecian-speaking folk there dwelt of yore,
Whose name my tale remembers not, between
The snow-topped mountains and the sea-beat shore,
Upon a strip of plain, and upland green,
Where seldom was the worst of summer seen,
And seldom the last bond of winter's cold;
Easy was life 'twixt garden, field, and fold.

My tale says these dealt little with the sea,
But for the mullet's flushed vermilion,
And weight o' the tunny, and what things might be
Behind the snowy tops but moon and sun
They knew not, nor as yet had anyone
Sunk shaft in hill-side there, or dried the stream
To see if 'neath its sand gold specks might gleam.

Yet rich enow they were; deep-uddered kine
Went lowing towards the pails at eventide;
The sheep cropped close unto the well-fenced vine,
Whose clusters hung upon the southering side
Of the fair hill; the brown plain far and wide
Changed year by year through green to hoary gold,
And the unherded, moaning bees untold

Blind-eyed to aught but blossoms, ranged the land,
Working for others; and the clacking loom
Not long within the homestead still did stand;
The spindles twirled within the women's room,
And oft amidst the depth of winter's gloom,
From off the poplar-block white chips would fly
'Neath some deft hand, watched of the standers-by.

Sometimes too would the foreign chapmen come,
And beach their dromond in the sandy bay,
And then the women-folk from many a home,
With heavy-laden beasts would take their way,
And round the black-keeled ship expend the day,
And by the moon would come back, light enow,
With things soon told, for that rough wealth to show.

Therefore of delicate array, full oft
Small lack there was in coffers of that land,
And gold would shine on shoulders smooth and soft,
And sparklike gems glitter from many a hand,
And by the altar would the goodman stand
Upon the solemn days of sacrifice,
Clad in attire of no such wretched price.

But the next morn the yellow headed girls
Would be afield, or 'twixt the vine-rows green,
And on the goodman's forehead would no pearls,
But rather sundrawn beaded drops be seen,
As the bright share carved out the furrow clean,
Or the thick swath fell 'neath the sturdy stroke:
For all must labour midst that simple folk.

Now, in a land where few were poor, if none
Were lordly rich, a certain man abode,

Who poorer was perchance than anyone
That ruled a house; yea, somewhat of a load
Of fears he bare adown life's latter road,
For, touching now upon his sixtieth year,
His wealth still waned, and still his house grew bare.

Why this should be none knew, for he was deft
In all the simple craft of that fair land,
Plough-stilt, and spade, and sickle, and axe-heft,
As much as need be pressed his hardened hand,
And creeping wanhope still did he withstand;
Wedded he was, and his grey helpmate too
Was skilled in all, and ever wrought her due.

Yet did his goods decrease: at end of dry
He cut his hay, to lie long in the rain;
And timorous must he let the time go by
For vintaging; and August came in vain
To his thin wheat; his sheep of wolves were slain;
Lame went his horses, barren were his kine,
His slaughtering-stock before the knife would pine.

All this befell him more than most I say,
And yet he lived on; gifts were plenty there,
The rich man's wealth but seldom hoarded lay;
And at a close-fist would the people stare,
And point the finger as at something rare—
Yet ever giving is a burden still,
And fast our goodman trundled down the hill.

Not always though had fortune served him thus,
In earlier days rich had he been and great,
But had no chick or child to bless his house,
And much did it mislike him of his fate,
And early to the Gods he prayed and late,
To give him that if all they took besides,
As to fate's feet will blind men still be guides.

So on a day when more than twenty years
Of childless wedlock had oppressed his wife,
She spake to him with smiles and happy tears;
And said, "Be glad, for ended is the strife
Betwixt us and the Gods, and our old life
Shall be renewed to us; the blossom clings
Unto the bough long barren, the waste sings."

Joyful he was at those glad words, and went
A changed man through his homestead on that morn,
And on fair things stored up he stared intent,
And hugged himself on things he erst did scorn,
When life seemed quickly ended and forlorn.

And so the days passed, till the time was come
When a new voice should wail on its cold home.

March was it, but a foretaste of the June
The earth had, and the budding linden-grove
About the homestead, with the brown bird's tune
Was happy, and the faint blue sky above
The black-thorn blossoms made meet roof for love,
For though the south wind breathed a thought of rain,
No cloud as yet its golden breadth did stain.

That afternoon within his well-hung hall,
Amidst of many thoughts the goodman lay
Until a gentle sleep on him 'gan fall,
And he began to dream, but the sweet day
The dream forgat not, nor could wipe away
The pictures of his home that seemed so good,
For midst his garden in his dream he stood;

Hand in hand with his wife he seemed to be,
And both their eyes were lovingly intent
Upon a little blossom fair to see
Before their feet, that through the fresh air sent
Sweet odours; but as over it they bent,
The day seemed changed to cloudiness and rain,
And the sweet flower, whereof they were so fain,

Was grown a goodly sapling, and they gazed
Wondering thereat, but loved it nothing less.
But as they looked a bright flame round it blazed,
And hid it for a space, and weariness
The souls of both the good folk did oppress,
And on the earth they lay down side by side,
And unto them it was as they had died.

Yet did they know that o'er them hung the tree
Grown mighty, thick-leaved, on each bough did hang
Crown, sword, or ship, or temple fair to see;
And therewithal a great wind through it sang,
And trumpet blast there was; and armour rang
Amid that leafy world, and now and then
Strange songs were sung in tongues of outland men.

Amid these sounds the goodman heard at last
A song in his own tongue, and sat upright
And blinking at the broad bright sun that cast
A straight beam through the window, making bright
The dusky hangings; till his gathering sight
Showed him outside two damsels, pail on head,
Who went by, singing, to the milking shed.

And meeting them with jingling bit and trace
Came the grey team from field; a merry lad
Sat sideways on the foremost, broad of face,
Freckled and flaxen-haired, whose red lips had
A primrose 'twixt them, yet still blithe and glad,
With muffled whistle, swinging, did he mock
The maidens' song and the brown throstle-cock.

Then rose the goodman, happy, for his dream
Seemed nowise ill to think on; rather he
Some echo of his hopes the thing did deem
If hardly any certain prophecy
Of happy things in time to come to be;
And into the March sun he wandered forth,
With life and wealth all grown of double worth.

From barn to well-stocked field he went that eve,
Smiling on all, and wondering how it was
That any one in such a world might grieve,
At least for long, at what might come to pass;
The soft south-wind, the flowers amid the grass,
The fragrant earth, the sweet sounds everywhere,
Seemed gifts too great almost for man to bear.

Long wandered he, the happiest of all men
Till day was gone, and the white moon and high
Cast a long shadow on the white stones, when
He came once more his homestead door anigh;
And there a girl stood watching, and a cry
Burst from her lips when she beheld him come;
She said, "O welcome to thy twice-blessed home!

"Thy wife hath borne to thee a maiden fair,
Come and behold it, and give thanks withal
Unto the Gods, who thus have heard thy prayer."
Sweetly that voice upon his ears did fall,
'Twixt him and utter bliss no bounding wall
Seemed raised now, nor did end of life-seem nigh;
Once more he had forgot that he must die.

So on the morrow high feast did he hold,
And all the guests with gifts were satisfied,
And gladdened were the Gods of field and fold,
With many a beast that at their altars died.
How should the spring of all that wealth be dried?
Nought did he deal with untried things or strange,
'Twixt year and year how might the seasons change?

Well, by next year, grown had the child and thriven
Unto his heart's desire, and in his hall
Again was high feast held, and good gifts given

To the departing guests; yet did it fall
That somewhat his goods minished therewithal,
But little grief it gave him; "Ah, let be
This year will raise the scale once more," said he.

But as the time passed, with the child's increase
Did ill luck grow apace, till field by field
Fell his lands from him; nought he knew of ease,
Yet little good hap did his trouble yield;
The Gods belike a new bag had unsealed
Of hopeless longing for him, and his day
Mid restless yearning still must pass away.

So things went on, till June of that same year
Whereof I tell, when nineteen May-tides green
The maid had looked on, and was grown so fair
That never yet the like of her had been
Within that land; and her divine soft mien,
Her eyes and her soft speech, now blessed alone
A house wherefrom all fair things else were gone.

Yet whoso gloomed thereat, not she it was
Who with her grave set face and heart unmoved,
Watched, wearied not nor pleased, each new day pass;
Nor thought of change, she said. As well behoved,
By many men ere now was she beloved;
Wild words she oft had heard, and harder grown
At bitter tears about her fair feet strown.

For far apart from these she seemed to be,
Their joys and sorrows moved her not, and they
Looked upon her as some divinity,
And cursed her not, though whiles she seemed to lay
A curse on them unwitting, and the day
Seemed grown unhappy, useless, as she came
With eyes fulfilled of thoughts of life and shame

Across their simple merriment. Meanwhile
She laboured as need was, nor heeded aught
What thing she did, nor yet did aught seem vile
More than another that the long day brought
Unto her hands; and as her father fought
Against his bitter foe, she watched it all
As though in some strange play the thing did fall.

And he, who loved her yet amidst of fear,
Would look upon her, wondering, even as though
He, daring not her soul to draw anear,
Yet of her hopes and fears was fain to know,
Was fain to hope that she one day would show
In what wise he within her heart was borne;

Yea, if that day he found in her but scorn.

It fell then in the June-tide, mid these things,
That on an eve within the bare great hall,
When nigh the window the bat's flickering wings
Were brushing, and the soft dew fast did fall,
And o'er the ferry far away did call
The homeward-hastening traveller? that the three
Sat resting in that soft obscurity.

Some tale belike unto the other two
The goodman had been telling, for he said,
"Well, in the end no more the thieves might do,
For when enough of them were hurt or dead
Needs must they cry for quarter; by Jove's head,
That parley as sweet music did I hear,
Who for three hours had seen grim death anear.

"So then their tall ship did we take in tow,
And beached her in the bay with no small pain.
The painted dragon-head, that ye note now
Grin at Jove's temple-door with gapings vain,
And her steel beaks the merchant-galleys' bane,
We smote away; with every second oar
We roofed that house of refuge nigh the shore.

"Then fell we unto ransacking her hold,
And left them store of meal, but took away
Armour, fair cloths, and silver things and gold,
Rich raiment, wine and honey; then we lay
Upon the beach that latter end of day,
And shared the spoil by drawing short and long—
That was before my fate 'gan do me wrong,

"And good things gat I; two such casks of wine,
And such a jar of honey, as would make
The very Gods smile, had they come to dine
E'en in this bare hall; ah! my heart doth ache,
O daughter Rhodope, for thy sweet sake
When of the gold-sewn purple robe I tell
That certes now had matched thy beauty well.

"What else? a crested helm all golden wrought,
A bow and sheaf of arrows—there they hang
Since they with one thing else came not to nought
Of all the things o'er which the goodwife sang,
When on the threshold first my spear-butt rang,
And o'er the bay the terror of the sea
With clipped wings laboured slow and painfully.

"Take down the bow, goodwife; a thing of price

Though unadorned, therefore it yet bides here;
For trusty is it in the wood, and wise
The long shafts are to find the dappled deer
And mend our four days' fast with better cheer.
But for the other thing—the twilight fails
Amid these half-remembered woeful tales;

"So light the taper for a little while
To see a marvel." Therewith speedily
The goodwife turned and lighted up her smile,
And deep-set eyes turned full on Rhodope
As hoping there some eagerness to see;
But on the brightening stars her wide eyes stared
E'en when the taper through the darkness glared.

Then to the great chest did the goodman go,
And turning o'er the coarser household gear
That lay therein, much stuff aside did throw
Ere from the lowest depths his hand did bear
A silken cloth of red, embroidered fair,
Wrapped about something; this upon the board
He laid, and 'gan unfold the precious hoard.

With languid eyes that hoped for little joy
Did Rhodope, now turning, gaze thereon,
And wait the showing forth of the fair toy,
In days long past from fear and battle won;
But yet a strange light in her bright eyes shone
When now the goodman did the cloth unfold,
And showed the gleam of precious gems and gold.

And there upon the silken cloth now lay
Twin shoes first made for some fair woman's feet,
Wrought like the meadows of an April day,
With gems amidst the sun of gold; most meet
To show in kings' halls, when the music sweet
Is at its softest, and the dance grown slow,
Midst of white folds the feet of maids may show.

Now unto these fair things went Rhodope,
And, blushing faintly, 'gan the latchets touch,
And drew her hand across them daintily,
Then let it fall, smiling, that overmuch
She thought of them, then turned away to such
Rude work as then the season asked of her,
With face firm set that weary life to bear.

Then said the goodman, with a rueful smile
Upon her, "Chick or child I had not then,
But riches, wherewith fortune did beguile
My heart to ask for more; and now again

That thou grow'st fairer than the seed of men,
All goes from me—and let these go withal,
Since I am thrust so rudely to the wall!

"Long have I kept them; first, for this indeed,
That few men of our land have will therefor
To pay me duly; and the coming need
Still did I fear would make the past less sore;
And then withal a man well skilled in lore
Grew dreamy o'er them once, and said that they
Bore with them promise of a changing day.

"Yet bread is life, and while we live we yet
May turn a corner of this barren lane,
And Jove's high-priest hath ever prayed to get
These fair things, and prayed hitherto in vain:
Belike a yoke of oxen might I gain
To turn the home-field deeper, when the corn,
Such as it is, to barn and stack is borne.

"The meal-ark groweth empty too, and thou,
O fairest daughter, worthy to be clad
In weed like this, shalt feel November blow
No blessing to thee; cask-staves must be had
Against the vintage, seeing that men wax glad
Already o'er the bunches, and the year
Folk deem great wealth to all men's sons will bear.

"So, daughter, unto thee this charge I give
To take these things tomorrow morn with thee
Unto Jove's priest, and say, we needs must live;
Therefore these fair shoes do I let him see,
That he may say what he will give to me,
That they may shine upon his daughter's feet,
When she goes forth the sacrifice to meet."

Now as he spake again a light flush came
Into her cheek, and died away again;
Then cried the goodwife; "Ah, thou bearest shame,
That we are fallen 'neath the feet of men,
That thou goest like a slave! what didst thou then
So coldly e'en on this man's son to look,
That he thy scornful eyes no more might brook?"

But still sat Rhodope, as though of stone
Her face was, and the goodman spake and said;
"Nay, mother, nay, she is not such an one
As lightly to our highest to be wed
Before the crown of love has touched her head:
Be patient; hast thou ne'er heard stories tell
What things to such as her of old befell?"

Kindly he smiled at her, as half he meant
The words he said; but now her changeless eye
Cast on him one hard glance, and then she bent
Over her work, and with a half-choked sigh
The goodman rose, and from a corner nigh
Took up some willow-withes, and so began
To shape the handle of a winnowing fan.

But with the new day's sun might you behold
The maiden's feet firm planted on the way
Which led unto the vale, where field and fold
About the temple of the Thunderer lay,
And the priest wrought, a sturdy carle today
Within the hay-field or behind the plough,
Tomorrow dealing with high things enow.

First betwixt sunny meads the highway ran
With homesteads set therein, and vineyards green,
Now merry with the voice of maid and man,
Who shouted greetings the tall rows between,
Whereto she answered softly, as a queen
Who feels herself of other make to be
Than those who worship her divinity.

The dark-eyed shepherd slowly by her passed,
And from his face faded the merry smile,
And down upon the road his eyes he cast,
And strove with other names his heart to wile
From thought of her; so coarse he seemed and vile
Before her smileless face, o'er which there shone
Some glory, as of a bright secret sun,

That was for her alone. The mother stood
Within her door, and as the gown of grey
Fluttered about her, and the coarse white hood
Flashed from the oak-shade o'er the sunlit way,
She muttered after her; "Ah, have thy day,
If thou wert set high up as thou art low,
On many a neck those feet of thine should go!"

But heeding little of the hearts of these
She went upon her way, and walking fast
Soon left the tilled fields and the cottages,
For toward the mountain-slopes the highway passed,
And turned unto the south, and 'gan at last
To mount aloft 'twixt heathery slopes set o'er
With red-trunked pines, and mossy rocks and hoar.

Still fast she went, though high the sun was grown,
For on strange thoughts and wild her heart was set;

Those things held in the bosom of her gown
Seemed teaching hopes she might not soon forget;
She clenched her hands harder and harder yet,
And cried aloud; "So small, so quickly done,
O idle, timorous life beneath the sun!

"And here amid these fields and mountains grey,
Drop after drop slowly it ebbs from me,
And leaves no new thing gained; day like to day,
Face like to face, as waves in some calm sea!
With memory of our sad mortality
Pipes the dull tune of earth, nought comes anigh
To give us some bright dream before we die.

"What say'st thou—'Beautiful thou art and livest,
And men there are, strong, young and fair enow,
To take with thankful heart e'en what thou givest;
Love and be loved then!'—Nay, heart, dost thou know
How through thin flame of love thou still wilt show
The long years set with mocking images,
Ready to trap me if I think of these?

"Ah, love they say, and love! Shall not love fade
And turn a prison, barred with vain regret
And vain remorse that we so lightly weighed,
The woes wherein our stumbling feet were set,
Stifling with thoughts we never may forget;
Because life waneth, while we strive to turn
And seek another thing for which to yearn.

"So deem I of the life that holds me here,
As though I were the shade of one long dead,
Come back a while from Pluto's region drear
To mine own land where unremembered
My fathers are—Lo, now, these words just said,
This heathery slope my feet are passing o'er,
Yon grey-winged dove—has it not been before?

"Would then that I were gone, and lived again
Another life;—if it must still be so,
That life on life passes, forgotten, vain
To still our longings, that no soul can know
By what has been how this and this shall go—
Because methinks I yet have heard men tell
How lives there were wherein great things befell.

"How mid such life had I forgot the past,
Nor thought about the future! but been glad
While round my head a dreamy veil I cast,
And seemed to strive with seeming good or bad;
Till at the last some dream I might have had

That nigh a god I was become to be,
And, dying, yet should keep all memory;

"Know what I was, nor change my hope and fear
All utterly, but learn why I was born,
Nor come to loathe what once to me was dear,
Nor dwell amidst a world of ghosts forlorn,
Nor see kind eyes, and hear kind words, with scorn.
—But ye, O fields, and hills, and steads of men,
Why are ye fair to mock my longings then?"

And therewithal panting she turned, and stood
High up the hillside; a light fitful wind
Sung mournful ditties through the pine-tree wood
That edged the borders of the pass behind,
And made most fitting music to her mind,
But clear and hot the day of June did grow,
And a fair picture spread out down below.

The green hill-slopes, besprinkled o'er with kine,
And a grey neat-herd wandering here and there,
And then the greener squares of well-propped vine,
The changing cornfields, and the homesteads fair,
The white road winding on, that yet did bear
Specks as of men and horses; the grey sea
Meeting the dim horizon dreamily.

A little while she gazed, then, with a sigh,
She turned again, and went on toward the pass,
But slowly now, and somewhat wearily,
And murmuring as she met the coarser grass
Within the shade: "What, something moved I was,
By hope, and pity of myself! Well then,
I shall not have that joy so oft again."

Then with bent head, 'twixt rocky wall and wall,
Slowly she went, and scarce knew what she thought,
So many a picture on her heart did fall,
Nor would she let one wish to her be brought
Of good or better. Going so, distraught,
The long rough road was nothing to her feet,
Nor took she heed of what her eyes might meet.

But so far through the pass at last she came,
That the road fell unto the temple-vale,
And there she stopped and started, for her name
She heard called out. She thought of many a tale
Of gods who brought to mortals joy or bale,
For so, despite herself, her thoughts would run,
That all the joy of life was not yet done.

But from the hillside came a dappled hound
That fawned upon her e'en as one he knew,
And when she raised her eyes, and looked around,
She saw the man indeed he 'longed unto,
A huntsman armed, and clad in gown of blue,
Come clattering down the stones of the pass-side;
So, standing still, his coming did she bide.

She smiled a smile that was not all of bliss,
For this was he of whom her mother spake,
The high-priest's son, who fain had made her his;
And at the sight of him her heart did ache
With hapless thoughts, and scorn and shame 'gan wake
Within her mind, that still she strove to lull,
Calling herself both cursed and beautiful.

So, while she gathered heart of grace to meet
The few words they might speak together there,
He was beside her; slim he was and fleet,
Well knit, with dark-brown eyes and crisp black hair,
Eager of aspect, round-chinned, fresh, and fair,
And well attired as for that simple folk
Who in those days might bear no great man's yoke.

Now his lip trembled, and he blushed blood-red,
Then turned all pale again. "O Rhodope,
Right fair thou go'st afoot this morn," he said;
"Hast thou some errand with my sire or me?"
And therewithal, as if unwittingly,
Unto her hand did he stretch out his hand;
But moveless as an image did she stand,

But that her gown was fluttering in the wind
That came up from the pass. She spake as one
That hath no care at heart: "I thought to find
Thy father, and to give to him alone
A message from my father. Is he gone?"
He seemed to swallow something in his throat:
"These two nights, maiden, hath he been afloat,

"Watching the tunnies; if thou turn'st again
Thou well mayst meet him coming from the sea."
"Nay," said she, "neither wholly shall be vain
My coming so far, since I have with me
Poor offerings meet for the divinity
From poor folk, which my mother bade me bear
To bless this midmost month of the glad year."

"In a good hour," he said, "for I have done
Little against the roes whereof to tell,
So I will fare with thee; and till the sun

Is getting low, in our house shalt thou dwell,
And in the evening, if it like thee well,
With helmet on the head, and well-strung bow,
Beside thee to thine own home will I go."

Nought spake she for a while, and his heart beat
Quicker with hope of some small happiness;
But at the last her eyes his eyes did meet.
She spake: "Few hearts this heart of mine will bless,
And yet for thee will I do nothing less
Than save thee from the anguish of the strife,
Wherewith thou fain wouldst make my life thy life.

"Thou art unhappy now, but we may part,
And to us both is left long lapse of time
To gain new bliss. What wouldst thou? To my heart
Cold now and alien are this folk and clime,
And while I dwell with them no woe or crime,
If so I may, shall stain my garments' hem;
Thou art an image like the rest of them:

"Yea, but an image unto me alone,
For unto thee this world is wide enow,
Full of warm hearts enow—so get thee gone
Upon thy way. I am not fallen so low
As unto thee dreams of false love to show,
Or for my very heart's own weariness
To give thee clinging life-long sharp distress.

"Now fain I would unto the temple-stead;
And, if thou mayst, do thou go otherwhere,
For good it were that all thy hopes were dead,
Since nought but bitter fruit they now can bear."
He gazed at her as one who doth not hear,
Or hears an outland tongue ill understood;
Wild love and hate made wild-fire of his blood.

Yea, she belike was nigher unto death
Than she might know; yet did he turn at last
And, clutching tight his short-sword's gold-wrought sheath,
Slowly along the seaward way he passed,
Nor backward at her any look he cast,
For fate would not that his blind eyes should see
How on the way her tears fell plenteously.

Yet not long there she stayed, but set her face
Unto the downward road, but had not fared
A many yards from that their meeting-place,
Before upon the wind a sound she heard,
As though some poor wretch a great sorrow bared
Unto the eyes of heaven, and then her feet

With quicker steps the stony way did meet.

And soon she said: "O fate, all left behind,
I follow thee adown the bitter road
With weary feet, and heavy eyes and blind,
That leadeth to thy far unknown abode;
No need, then, with thy stings my flesh to goad,
Keep them for those that strive with thee in vain,
And leave me to my constant weary pain."

Now the pass, widening, to her eyes did show
The little vale hemmed in by hills around,
Wherein was Jove's house fair and great enow,
Some three miles thence, but on a rising ground,
And with fair fields as a green girdle bound,
And guarded well by long low houses white,
Orchards for fruit, and gardens for delight.

Far off, like little spots of white, she saw
The long-winged circling pigeons glittering
Above the roofs, the noise of rook and daw
Came sweet upon the wind from the dark ring
Of elms that edged the cornfields; with wide wing
The fork-tailed restless kite sailed over her,
Hushing the twitter of the linnets near.

She stayed now, gazing downward; at her feet
A dark wood clad the hollow of the hill,
And its black shade a little lake did meet,
Whose waters smooth a babbling stream did still,
Then toward the temple-stead stretched on, until
Green meads with oaks beset 'gan hem it in,
And from its nether end the stream did win.

She gazed and saw not, heard and did not hear,
But said: "Once more have I been vehement,
Have spoken out, as if I knew from where
Come good and ill, and whither they are sent,
As though I knew whereon I was intent;
So, knowing that I know not, e'en as these
Who think themselves as gods and goddesses

"To know both good and evil must I do.
Now ne'er again in this wise shall it be
While here I dwell, nor shall false hope shine through
My prison bars, false passion jeer at me
With what might hap if I were changed and free;
The end shall come at last, and find me here,
Desiring nought, and free from hope or fear."

So saying, but with face cleared not at all,

Rather with trembling lips, upon her way
Once more she went; short now did shadows fall,
It grew unto the hottest of the day,
And round the mountain-tops the sky waxed grey
For very heat; June's sceptre o'er the earth,
If rest it gave, kept back some little mirth.

At last upon the bridge the stream that crossed
Just ere it met the lake she set her feet,
And walked on swiftly, e'en as one clean lost
In thought, till at its end her skirt did meet
A bough of briar-rose, whose pale blossoms sweet
Were draggled in the dust; she stooped thereto
And from her hem its hooked green thorns she drew.

Then drawing a deep breath, she cast aside
The broken bough; and from the dusty road
She turned, and o'er the parapet she eyed
The broad blue lake, the basking pike's abode,
And the dark oakwood where the pigeons cooed;
And as she gazed, some little touch of bliss
Came over her amidst her loneliness.

Drowsy she felt, and weary with the way,
And mid such listlessness that brought no pain,
She drew her arms from off the coping grey,
And o'er the bridge went slowly back again,
As though no whit of purpose did remain
Within her mind; but when the other end
She passed, along the stream she 'gan to wend.

She watched its eddies till it widened out
Into the breezy lake, and even there
Began the wood; so then she turned about,
And shading her grave eyes with fingers fair,
Beneath the sun beheld temple glare
O'er the far tree-tops; then down
Within the shade on last year's oak-leaves brown.

There as she lay, at last her fingers stole
Unto the things that on her bosom lay,
She drew them forth and slowly 'gan unroll
The silken cloth, until a wandering ray
Upon the shoes' bright 'broideries 'gan to play
Through the thick leaves; and with a flickering smile
She 'gan her mind with stories to beguile.

Pondering for whom those dainty things were wrought,
And in what land; and in what wondrous wise
She missed the gift of them; and what things brought
The sea-thieves to her land—until her eyes

Fell on her own gear wrought in homely guise,
And with a half smile she let fall the gold
And glistening gems her listless hand did hold.

Then long she lay there, gazing at the sky
Between the thick leaves, growing drowsier,
While slowly the grey rabbit hobbled by,
And the slim squirrel twisted over her
As one to heed not; as if none were near
The woodpecker slipped up the smooth-barked tree,
The water-hen clucked nigh her fearlessly.

But in a little while she woke, and still
Felt as if dreaming, all seemed far away
Save present rest, both hope and fear and ill;
The sun was past the middle of the day,
But bathed in flood of light the world still lay,
And all was quiet, but for faint sounds made
By the wood creatures wild and unafraid.

From out her wallet now coarse food she drew,
And ate with dainty mouth, then o'er the strip
Of dazzling sunlight where the daisies grew
Unto the babbling streamlet's rushy lip
She went, and kneeling down thereby did dip
Her hollow hand into the water grey
And drank, then back again she went her way.

There 'neath the tree-bole lay the glittering shoes,
And over them she stood awhile and gazed,
Then stooped adown as though one might not choose;
And from the grass one by the latchet raised,
And with the eyes of one by slumber dazed
Did off her own foot-gear, and one by one
Set the bright things her shapely feet upon.

Then to the thick wood slowly did she turn,
And through its cool shade wandered till once more
Thinner it grew, and spots of light did burn
Upon her jewelled feet, till lay before
Her upraised eyes a bay with sandy shore;
And 'twixt the waves and birds' abiding place
Was stretched a treeless, sunlit, grassy space.

Friendly the sun, the bright flowers, and the grass
Seemed after the dark wood; with upraised gown
Slowly unto the water did she pass,
And on the grassy edge she sat her down;
And since right swift these latter hours had flown
Less did the sun burn; there awhile she lay
Watching a little breeze sweep up the bay.

Shallow it was, a shore of hard white sand
Met the green herbage, and as clear as glass
The water ran in ripples o'er that strand,
Until it well-nigh touched the flowery grass;
A dainty bath for weary limbs it was,
And so our maiden thought belike, for she
'Gan put her raiment from her languidly.

Until at last from out her poor array,
Pure did she rise e'en as that other One
Rose up from out the ragged billows grey,
For earth's dull days and heavy to atone;
How like another sun her gold hair shone;
In the green place, as down she knelt, and raised
The glittering shoes, and long time on them gazed,

As on strange guides that thus had brought her there,
Then cast them by, so that apart they fell,
And in the sunlight glittering lay and fair,
Like the elves' blossoms, hard and lacking smell;
Then to the sward she stooped, and bud and bell
Of the June's children gat into her hand,
And left the grass for the scarce-covered sand.

She stood to watch the thin waves mount her feet
Before she tried the deep, then toward the wide,
Sun-litten space she turned, and 'gan to meet
The freshness of the water cool, and sighed
For pleasure as the little rippling tide
Lapped her about, and slow she wandered on
Till many a yard from shore she now had won.

There, as she played, she heard a bird's harsh cry,
And looking to the steep hill-side could see
A broad-winged eagle hovering anigh,
And stood to watch his sweeping flight and free
Dark 'gainst the sky, then turned round leisurely
Unto the bank, and saw a bright red ray
Shoot from a great gem on the sea-thieves' prey.

Then slowly through the water did she move,
Down on the changing ripple gazing still,
As loth to leave it, and once more above
Her golden head rang out the erne's note shrill,
Grown nigher now; she turned unto the hill,
And saw him not, and once again her eyes
Fell on the strange shoes' jewelled 'broideries.

And even therewithal a noise of wings
Flapping, and close at hand—again the cry,

And then the glitter of those dainty things
Was gone, as a great mass fell suddenly,
And rose again, ere Rhodope could try
To raise her voice, for now might she behold
Within his claws the gleam of gems and gold.

Awhile she gazed at him as, circling wide,
He soared aloft, and for a space could see
The gold shoe glitter, till the rock-crowned side
Of the great mountain hid him presently,
And she 'gan laugh that such a thing should be
So wrought of fate, for little did she fear
The lack of their poor wealth, or pinching cheer.

But when she was aland again and clad,
And turned back through the wood, a sudden thought
Shot through her heart, and made her somewhat glad;
"Small things," she said, "her feet had thither brought:
Perchance this strange hap should not be for nought."
And therewithal stories she 'gan to tell
Unto her heart how such things once befell,

How as it had been it might be again.
Then from her odorous breast she took the shoe
Yet left, and turned it o'er and o'er in vain,
If yet she might therein find aught of new
To tell her what all meant; and thus she drew
Unto the wood's edge, and once more sat down
Upon the fresh grass and the oak-leaves brown.

And there beneath the quickly sinking sun
She took again her foot-gear cast aside,
And, scarce beholding them now, did them on;
And while the pie from out the oak-boughs cried
Over her head, arose and slowly hied
Unto the road again, and backward turned
Up through the pass. Blood-red behind her burned

The sunless sky, and scarce awake she seemed,
As 'gainst the hill she toiled, and when at last
Beneath the moon far off the grey sea gleamed,
And all the rugged mountain road was passed,
Back from her eyes the wandering locks she cast,
And o'er her cheeks warm ran the tears, as she
Told herself tales of what she yet might be.

But cold awakening had she when she came
Unto the half-deserted homestead gate,
And she must think hoed she would take the blame
That from her mother did her deed await,
Without a slave-like frightened frown at fate;

Must harden yet her heart once more to face
Her father's wondering sigh at his hard case.

So when within the dimly-lighted hall
Her mother's wrath brake out, as she did hear
Her cold words, and her father's knife did fall
Clattering adown; then seemed all life so drear,
Hapless and loveless, and so hard to bear,
So little worth the bearing, that a pang
Of very hate from out her heart up-sprang.

With cold eyes, but a smile on her red lips,
She watched them; how her father stooped again
And took his knife, and how once more the chips
Flew from the bowl half finished, but in vain,
Because he saw it not; she watched the rain
Of tears wherewith her mother did bewail
That all her joy in her one child should fail.

But when her mother's tears to sobs were turned
The goodman rose and took her hand in his,
And then, with sunken eyes for love that yearned,
Gazed hard at her, and said, "Nay, child, some bliss
Awaits thee surely yet; enough it is;
Trouble and hunger shall not chase me long,
The walls of one abiding-place are strong;

"And thither now I go apace, my child."
Askance she looked at him with steady eyes,
But when she saw that midst his words he smiled
With trembling lips, then in her heart 'gan rise
Strange thoughts that troubled her like memories
And changed her face; she drew her hands from him,
And yet before her eyes his face waxed dim.

Then down the old man sat, and now began
To talk of how their life went, and their needs,
In cheerful strain; and, even as a man,
Unbeaten yet by fortune's spiteful deeds,
Spoke of the troublous twisted way that leads
To peace and happiness, till to a smile
The goodwife's tearful face he did beguile.

So slipped the night away, and the June sun
Rose the next morn as though no woe there were
Upon the earth, and never anyone
Was blind with love or bent by hopeless care;
But small content was in the homestead there,
Despite the bright-eyed June, for unto two
That dwelt there life still held too much to do.

While to the third, empty of deeds it seemed,
A dragging dulness changed by here a pain
And there a hope, waking or sleeping dreamed,
But, waking still or sleeping, dreamed in vain;
For how could anything be loss or gain
When still the order of the world went round,
And still the wall of death all hopes did bound?

So said she oft, and fell to hating men;
Nevertheless with hope still beat her heart,
And changing thoughts that rose and fell again
Would stir within her as she sat apart,
And to her brow the unbidden blood would start,
And she would rise, nor know whereon she trod,
And forth she walked as one who walks with God.

Oftener indeed that dull and heavy mood
Oppressed her, and when any were anigh,
Little she spake, either of bad or good,
Nor would she heed the folk that were thereby
So much as thereon to look scornfully;
Unless perchance her father stood anear,
And then her set hard face she strove to clear.

And if he, fearful, answered with no smile
Unto the softening eyes, yet when he went
About his labour, would he so beguile
His heart with thought of her, that right content
He 'gan to feel with what the Gods had sent;
The little flame of love that in him burned,
Hard things and ill to part of pleasure turned.

Withal his worldly things went not so ill
As for a luckless man; the bounteous year
More than before his barn and vats did fill
With the earth's fruit, and bettered was his cheer,
So that he watched the winter draw anear
Calmly this tide, and deemed he yet might live,
Some joy unto his daughter's heart to give.

But for the one shoe that the erne had left,
The goodwife's word was, "Take the cursed thing,
And when the gems from out it are all reft,
Into the fire the weaver's rag go fling;
Would in like wise the fond desires, that cling
To Rhodope's proud heart, we thus might burn,
That she to some good life at last might turn!

"I think some poison with a double curse
Hath smitten her, and double wilfulness,
For surely now she groweth worse and worse,

Since the bright rag her wayworn foot did press—
Well then—and surely thou wilt do no less
Than as I bid—a many things we need,
More than this waif of cast-off-royal weed."

With querulous voice she spake, because she saw
Her husband look at Rhodope, as she
Still through her fingers did the grey thread draw
From out the rock, and sitting quietly
Seemed not to heed what all the talk might be;
But for the goodman's self he answered not
Until at last the goodwife waxed o'er hot;

And laid hard word on word, till she began
To say, "Alas, and wherefore was I wed
To such an one as is a foredoomed man?
Lo, all this grief hast thou brought on my head,
So wander forth, and dream as do the dead
When to the shadowy land they first are brought!
Surely thou knowest that we lack for nought!"

Then blind with rage from out the place she went,
But still the goodman stood awhile, and gazed
At Rhodope, who sat as if intent
Upon her work, nor aught her fair head raised.
At last he spake: "Well, never was I praised
For wisdom overmuch before this day,
And can I now be certain of the way?

"True is it that our needs are many and sore,
And that those gems would help us plenteously,
Yet do I grudge now more than heretofore
The very last of that strange gift to see.
What sayest thou, how dost thou counsel me,
O daughter? didst thou ever hear folk tell
Of the strange dream that at thy birth befell?"

Blood-red her face grew as she looked on him,
And with her foot the twirling spindle stayed.
"Yea," said she, "something have I heard, but dim
My memory is, and little have I weighed
The worth thereof." The goodman smiled and said,
"Nay, child, as little wise as I may be,
Yet know I that thou liest certainly.

"And so no need there is to tell the tale,
Or ask thee more what thou wouldst have me do;
Have thou thy will, for fate will still prevail,
Though oft we deem we lead her thereunto
Where lies our good—Daughter, keep thou the shoe,
And let the wise men with their wisdom play,

While we go dream about a happier day."

While he was speaking had she laid adown
The rock, and risen unto her feet, and now
Upon her bosom lay his visage brown,
As round him both her fair arms did she throw;
Softly she said, "Somewhat thy need I know,
Remember this whatever happeneth,
Let it make sweet the space 'twixt this and death!

"Hard is the world; I, loved ere I was born,
This once alone perchance thy heart shall feel,
And thou shalt go about, of love forlorn,
And little move my heart of stone and steel:
Ah, if another life our life might heal,
And love become no more the sport of time,
Chained upon either hand to pain and crime!"

A little time she hung about him thus,
And then her arms from round his neck unwound,
And went her ways; his mouth grew piteous
When he had lost her fluttering gown's light sound,
And fast his tears 'gan fall upon the ground.
At last he turned: "So is it now," he said,
"With me as with a man soon to be dead.

"Wise is he all at once, and knows not why,
And brave who erst was timorous; fair of speech,
Whose tongue once stammered with uncertainty,
Because his soul to the dark land doth reach.
And is it so that love to me doth teach
New things, because he needs must get him gone,
And leave me with his memories all alone?"

So the year passed, as has been writ afore,
With better hopes; the pinching winter-tide
Went by, and spring his tender longings bore
Into all hearts, and scattered troubles wide,
Nor yet to see the fruit of them would bide,
But left the burning summer next to deal
With hearts of men, and hope from them to steal.

Now came the time round even to the day
When Rhodope had made her journey vain
Unto the valley where the temple lay,
And now, too, when the morn was on the wane,
Before the homestead door she stood again,
For to the town she needs must go to bring,
For their poor household work, some needful thing.

So with slow feet she crossed the threshold o'er

With brow a little knitted, as if she
Dealt with some troublous thought, that oft before
Had mazed her mind: then no less, steadily
Through the fair day she went on toward the sea,
For by the port, and lying low adown,
Stretched out their unwalled simple market-town.

Some mile of highway had she got to pace,
Ere she might reach the first house of the street
That led unto the lowly market-place;
So on she went, and still her eyes did meet
The elm-tree shade that flickered o'er her feet.
Though thronged beyond its wont the white way was,
With folk well clad, who toward the town did pass,

Swiftly she went, till come half-way belike,
Then stayed her feet and looked up suddenly;
There by the way-side the hot sun did strike
Upon a patch of grass, whereon did lie
A grey old hound, and 'gainst an elm thereby
His master leaned, a shepherd older yet,
Whose deep-sunk eyes her eyes unwitting met.

Therewith a knot of folk she had just passed
Passed her in turn, maidens and youths they were,
Blithe with their life and youth; on her they cast
Such looks as if they had a mind to jeer,
Yet held back, some by wonder, some by fear,
Went on a space until they deemed them free,
Then through the summer day outburst their glee.

Her deep eyes followed them, and yet, indeed,
As images she saw them; there a space
Musing she stood, then turned, and at slow speed
Went back again to her abiding-place,
Just as the old man moved his puckered face
To speak some word to her; and so at last,
O'er her own threshold inward her feet passed.

Then to her sleeping-room she went, and knelt
Beside a chest, and raised the lid, and drew
From out the dark where year-long it had dwelt,
Remembered yet the while, the precious shoe,
And dreamy over it awhile she grew,
Then set it in her bosom, and went forth,
Pondering o'er what her fond desires were worth.

Still folk thronged on the highway; as she went
Some fragment of their talk would reach her ear
Howso upon her dreams she was intent;
Of new-come men they spake, their ways and gear,

How glorious of array, how great they were,
How huge and fair their galley, that last eve
The little black-quayed haven did receive.

That talk of strange and great things raised at last
New and wild hopes in her, but none the less
Straightway unto her journey's end she passed,
And did what she must do, nor cared to guess
Why in the market-place all folk did press
Around a glitter as of steel and gold
That in the midst thereof she did behold.

Yet, her work done, she gat her back again
Unto the market-place, and curiously
'Gan eye the concourse, yea, at last, was fain
Unto the heart thereof to come anigh;
Her heart beat; strange she felt and knew not why,
As on she went, and still the wondering folk
To right and left before her beauty broke.

A temple midmost of the market-place,
Raised to the Mother of the Gods there stood,
An ancient house in guise of other days,
And e'en amid that simple folk deemed rude;
Such as it was the country-folk thought good
To meet and talk there, o'er such things as they
Found hard to deal with as day passed by day.

So when she drew anigh its steps, thereon
She saw indeed a goodly company,
For there sat strange men, young and old, who shone
In such attire as scarce she thought could be,
And by these glittering folk from over sea
Were the land's fathers, and the chief-priest dight
To do a solemn sacrifice aright.

E'en as she came into the foremost rank,
Bright gleamed the slayer's falchion in the sun,
And silently the rose-crowned heifer sank
Upon the time-worn pavement; yet not one
Of all the sea-farers might gaze upon
Victim or priest, for forth stood Rhodope
Lone on the steps, a glorious thing to see.

For on a tripod by the altar's side,
Gleaming, as that day year agone it gleamed,
The shoe her foot had pressed she now espied,
And o'er her soul a sudden light there streamed,
While from her eager eyes such glory beamed,
That all folk stared astonished, all must wait
For her first word as for the stroke of fate.

Yea, there she stood, that all fair things did lack,
Clad in a gown of dark grey woollen stuff,
The wares she had just dealt for at her back,
And all about her homely, coarse, and rough,
Yet, since her beauty blessed them, good enough:
For, as a goddess wandering on the earth,
How might she deem earth's richest gauds of worth?

Gently, yet with no flush on her smooth cheek,
She mounted up the steps, and spake out clear:
"Perchance a match for yon fair thing ye seek
Ye seem to prize so much; it lieth here,
And both of them on this day was-a-year
Were on my feet. My father will be glad
Because great joy in them the old man had."

Then rose a great shout up into the sky,
And in despite herself the blood would rise
Unto her cheek and brow, as quietly
From her white fragrant bosom, a world's prize,
She drew the mass of blazing 'broideries,
And laid it by its fellow, and her hand
Trembled, as there sun-litten she did stand.

Then cried a grey-beard, clad in gems and gold:
"Praise to the Gods who do all things aright,
And thus have given my weak eyes to behold
Now, at the end of life, so fair a sight,
Have given withal unto the worth and might
Of the great king so fair a mate as thee—
How good, how good it is thine eyes to see!"

She was pale now, though never a word she spake,
And held her head, as though a crown it wore
And 'gan 'neath gold, and golden hair to ache
With new-born longings, fears unknown before,
And calmly her deep eyes the men passed o'er
Who sat there marvelling; till the old man said:
"Wonder not overmuch, O glorious maid,

"At all these things! The Gods who wrought thee thus,
And kept thee here apart from ill men's eyes
To show thee forth so much more marvellous,
Have led our hearts unto thee in this wise;
For the great king did solemn sacrifice
Unto the Gods well-nigh a year agone,
And in the bright sun bright the altar shone.

"But e'en as to its highest shot the flame,
And to the awful Gods our hearts did turn,

A cry from out the far blue sky there came,
And a bright thing 'twixt flame and sun did burn,
And some there were who said they could discern
An eagle, like a faint speck, far above
The altar, whereon lay this gift of love.

"How this may be I know not, but the king
Trembled, and toward the altar stretched his hand,
And drew to him the strange-sent, fair-wrought thing,
And, thereon staring, a long while did stand,
And left the place, not giving such command
As he was wont, and still from that day forth
Took little heed of things once held of worth.

"Silent and pale, and strange-eyed still he grew,
And yet said nought hereon for many days,
Until at last he bade us take this shoe
And diligently search in every place
That we might come to, till we saw the face
Of her whose foot had touched it. 'Certainly,
Whereso she is, she hath been wrought for me.

"'Whereso she is, and by what name men name
Her loveliness and love unknown: to now,
Young am I, and have heretofore had shame
To bend to love, e'en as my folk bend low
Before my throne, but now my pride doth grow
As a quenched candle in a golden house,
And through the dark I wander timorous.'

"We marvelled at his word, but deemed some God
Possessed his heart; but thenceforth constantly
Have we gone over the wide world, and trod
Rough ways enow, been tossed o'er many a sea,
And dealt with many a lie, until to thee
The Gods have brought us, O thou wondrous one!
That we might see thee ere our days are done."

"Ah me!" she said, "what thing do ye demand?
Is it a little thing that I should go,
Leaving my people and my father's land, .
To wed some proud great man I do not know?
I look for no glad life; yea, it is so
That if a grain of love were left in me
In vain your keel had cleft our girdling sea.

"No need to speak; I know what ye would say—
That where I go, still I and love shall rule,
That where I go I bear about the day
Made golden by my beauty—base and dull,
Mid hollow shows to strive with knave and fool,

With death, and nothing done, to end it all!
Yet fear ye not! for surely I shall fall

"Where the Gods cast me, nor turn round about
To gaze on bygone time—so it shall be
E'en as ye will." They stared at her, in doubt
If her sweet lips had spoken; yea, and she
Flushed 'neath their eyes fixed on her wonderingly,
Wondering herself at the new fear, new scorn
That with beginning of new days was born.

But they, abased before the rough-clad maid,
Now led her to an empty ivory chair,
And each man knee unto the pavement laid,
And, unashamed, did reverence to her there;
And ever did she seem to grow more fair
Before their eyes, till fear arose in them
As they bent down to her rude garment's hem.

And then the rites unto the Gods went on,
While she sat musing on the wondrous tale;
And when all these at last were duly done,
They prayed her give command when they should sail;
She raised her face, grown quiet now and pale,
And said in a low voice: "Today were best,
For here at least may I have nought of rest.

"The old is gone, the new is not yet come,
Familiar things with strange eyes I behold,
And nowhere now I seem to have a home.
But when I go from homespun unto gold,
My father and mother, poor folk bent and old,
Beaten by fortune, needs must go with me,
And share my new proud life beyond the sea.

"And since the old man loveth me too well,
And hitherto small joy from me hath gained,
Meet is it that my lips alone should tell
How all is changed, and weal that long hath waned
Is waxen now, and the cold rain that rained
Upon his life's grey day hath met the sun,
And blossoms spring from the dull earth and dun.

"And, O ye folk, midst whom my feet have dwelt,
And whom I leave now, if so be, that I
Hard anger in my heart at whiles have felt
'Gainst things that pressed upon me wearily,
Yet now the kindness of time past draws nigh,
And ye will be my folk still, when I go
Unto a land where e'en your name none know."

Then, midst their marvelling silence, she arose,
And took her cast-down fardel up again,
And went her ways; and they, by whom all close
Her body passed, must tremble, and be fain
To think of common things to dull the pain
Of longing, as her lovely majesty,
Too sweet and strange for earth, brushed swiftly by.

And yet of earth she was, and as she went
Through the shrunk shadow to her old abode,
Fresh hope a new joy through her body sent,
The clear cold vision of her soul to cloud;
And less the striving world seemed like a load
To weary her, than a strange curious toy,
To solace life with foolish grief and joy.

Still grew that hope in her, and when she carne
Unto the homestead, and her father met
Anigh the byre, then doubt, and fear, and shame,
Amid the joy of change did she forget,
As firm feet mid the loitering kine she set,
And cried aloud, "O father, turn and gaze
On Fortune's friend, the Queen of glorious days!"

He turned and stared upon her glittering eyes
And godlike mien, and 'gan to speak, but she
Cried out, "The very Gods may call us wise,
For great days have they given to thee and me,
Things stranger than these meadows shall we see,
And thou shalt wonder that thou ere didst keep
These kine, as Phœbus erst Admetus' sheep!"

Then did she pour the whole tale out on him
Eager at first, but faltered to behold
How he fell trembling in his every limb;
Through the new fever that her heart did fold,
Again shame thrust its steely point and cold:
"Alas," she thought, "when all the tale is done,
Why go we thus alone beneath the sun?"

He tried to speak, and the words came at last;
"If thou art glad, then surely I am glad—
And yet, we thought our evil time had passed;
Surely the days grew not so wholly bad!
Ah me, a growing hope of late I had
Of quiet days and sweet—yet shame of me,
That I should dull the joy that gladdeth thee!

"Daughter, thy bidding I will surely do,
And go with thee; nathless bethink thee yet,
How yesterday shall seem full long ago,

When with to-morrow's dew the grass is wet.
Child, I will pray thee never to forget
This face of mine, this heart that loves thee well;
Let distance though, and time that sweet tale tell!"

She cried: "Ah, wilt thou have me lonelier
Than the Gods made me? As day passes day
The life of fear and hope that happened here,
Most oft no doubt shall seem full far away;
Yet be thou nigh, to be a scarce-felt stay
To my mazed steps, a green close fresh and sweet,
On life's hard way, to cool my weary feet.

"I will not take my bidding back; go thou,
And get thee ready swiftly to be gone.
The sails are flapping in the haven now,
And we depart before the clay is done.
O be thou glad, thou shalt not be alone!
Canst thou not see e'en now how this my face
I softened to thee by the happy days?"

He said no more, but eyed her lovingly,
Upon his worn old face a trembling smile;
Then turned him toward the house with one great sigh,
And she was left alone a little while,
Her restlessness with strange dreams to beguile,
And though bright things those dreams did nowise lack,
Yet oft oft-conquered cold fear would come back.

But midst her thoughts from out the house there came
Her father and her mother, and she gazed
Upon the twain with something more than shame,
As she beheld what timid eyes and mazed
The goodwife to her queenly beauty raised,
And how with patient mien her father went,
On all her motions lovingly intent.

Then to the market-place passed on the three,
And though her grey gown only covered her,
Her mother bore some shreds of bravery
And clad her father was in scarlet gear,
Worn now and wretched, that he once did bear
When long ago at his rich board he sat,
And all that land's best cheer the glad guests gat.

And as they stood there now, the simple folk,
Grown used unto the wonder of the tale,
Warmed with new joy, and into shouts outbroke;
The goodwife flushed, but the old man turned pale,
And gazed round helpless, his limbs seemed to fail
As though age pressed him sore; while Rhodope

Grew softer-eyed and spake majestically;

"Fain am I, lords, that we depart straightway;
For if a dream this is, I long full sore
E'en in my dream to feel the wind-blown spray,
And hear the well-timed rolling of the oar,
And ere dark night behold the lessening shore
From your dreamed dromond's deck—so pass we on,
If e'en so far as this my dream hath won."

Then said they: "All is ready in due wise,
E'en as thou bad'st, the ship has been warped round
And rideth toward the sea, and sacrifice
Has there been done, and goodly gifts been found
For this land's folk: but wilt thou not be crowned
And clad in fair array of gold, that we
May show thy beauty meetly to the sea?"

"Nay," said she, "in this lowly guise of mine
Let the king first behold me standing there
The Gods' gift, that his heart may more incline
Towards mine, if thus he note me strange and fair,
Grown up a queen, yet with no wondrous care
For what I should be. Make no more delay,
Low looks the sun upon the watery way."

So seaward now with these all people moved
Rejoicing, though belike they scarce knew why,
And Rhodope 'gan feel herself beloved;
And as the south wind breathed deliciously
O'er flowers and sweet things, and the sun did die
Amid soft golden haze, her loveliness
She 'gan to feel, and all the world to bless.

In her slim hand her father's hand she took,
Her red lips trembled, and her eyes were wet
With tears that fell not; but the old man shook
As one who sees death; then a hand she set
Upon his shoulder, and said, "Long years yet,
With loving eyes these eyes shalt thou behold
Among the glimmer of fair things and gold."

But nought he answered, and they came full soon
To where the gangway ran from out the ship
On to the black pier; white yet was the moon,
And the sun's rim nigh in the sea did dip,
And from the place where sky met ocean's lip,
Ran a great road of gold across the sea,
Where played the unquiet waves impatiently.

Now was her foot upon the gangway plank;

Now over the green depths and oars blood-red
Fluttered her gown, and from the low green bank
Above the sea a cry came, as her head
Gleamed golden in the way that westward led,
And on the deck her feet were, but no more
She looked back then unto the peopled shore.

But with one hand held back as if to take
Her father's hand, she went on toward the prow;
And there she stood, and watched the billows break,
Nor noted when men back the ropes did throw,
And scarce knew when the sea fell from the bow
And the ship moved, nor turned, till, cold and grey,
And darkling fast, the waste before her lay.

But at the last she turned on well-poised feet,
And gazed adown the twilight decks, and heard
The freshening wind about the cordage beat,
The master's and rough helmsman's answering word,
And all alone she felt now, and afeard,
In spite of all the folk who stood around,
Unto her lightest service straightly bound.

A terror seized her; down the deck she passed,
Her gown driven close against her, and her hair
Loosed by the driving wind; till at the mast
She stayed, and muttered: "Ah, he is not there!
And I, where am I? the dream seemed so fair
When it began; but now am I alone,
Waiting, I know not what, till life be done."

Trembling she drew her hand across her brow
As one who wakes; and then, grown calm once more,
She went with steady feet unto the prow,
And ran the line of reverent faces o'er
With anxious eyes, and stayed at last before
The ancient grey-haired man, the chief of these,
And spoke amid the washing of the seas:

"Where is my father? I am fain to speak
Of many things with him, we two alone;
For mid these winds and waves my heart grows weak
With memory of the days for ever gone."
The moon was bright, the swaying lanterns shone
On her pale face, and fluttering garment's hem—
Each stared on each, and silence was on them.

And midst that silence a new lonely pain,
Like sundering death, smote on her, till he spoke:
"O queen, what sayst thou? the old man was fain,
He told us, still to dwell among his folk;

He said, thou knew'st he might not bear the yoke
Of strange eyes watching him—what say I more,
Surely thou know'st he never left the shore?

"I deemed him wise and true: but give command
If so thou willest; certes no great thing
It is, in two hours space to make the land,
Though much the land-wind now is freshening."
One slender hand to the rough shroud did cling,
As her limbs failed; she raised the other one,
And moved her lips to bid the thing be done:

Yet no words came, she stood upright again,
And dropped her hand and said, "I strive with change,
I strive with death the Gods' toy, but in vain:
No otherwise than thus might all be strange."
Therewith she turned, her unseeing eyes did range
Wide o'er the tumbling waste of waters grey,
As swift the black ship went upon her way.

Dark night upon the cold still eve did fall
Amidst the tale, and now the fair guest-hall
Was lit with nought but firelight, as they sat,
Silent, soft-hearted, and compassionate
Midst their own flickering shadows; yet too old
They were, to talk about the story told,
Too old, and knew too well what each man thought,
And feared in any pleasure to be caught,
That hid a snare of sadness at its end.
So slowly did the tale's sweet sorrow blend
With their own quenched desires, and past regret,
And dear-loved follies they might scarce forget;
That in these latter days indeed, were grown
Nought but a tale, for others to bemoan,
Who had not learned with sorrow's self to deal;
Who had no need an hour of bliss to steal,
With trembling hands, from the dark treasury
Of time long unregarded, long gone by,
Where cobwebbed o'er amid the dust it lay.
But these stole not, nor strove, from day to day
Enough of pleasure to their lot did fall
To stay them, that on death they should not call
With change or rest to end the weary tide;
Though careless now, his coming did they bide.

Scarce aught was left of autumn-tide to die
When next they met; the north-east wind rushed by
The house anigh the woods, wherein they were,
And in the oaks and hollies might they hear
Its roar grow greater with the dying morn:
A hard grey day it was, yet scarce forlorn,

Since scarcely aught of tender or of sweet
Was left the year, its ruggedness to meet.
Bare was the country-side of work and folk:
There from the hill-side stead straight out the smoke,
Over the climbing row of corn-ricks, sailed;
And few folk stirred; a blue-clad horseman hailed
A shepherd from the white way, little heard
'Twixt ridge and hollow by November seared;
The ferryman stared long adown the road
That led unto his tottering thatched abode,
Ere the dark speck into a goodwife turned;
The smouldering weed-heap by the garden burned;
Side-long the plough beside the field-gate lay,
With no one nigh to. scare the birds away,
That twittered mid the scanty wisps of straw.
So round the fire the ancient folk did draw,
And, mid the day-dreams, that hung round about,
Rather beheld the wild-wood dim with doubt,
And twilight of the cloudy leafless tide,
Than the scant-peopled fallow country-side,
Whose fields the woods hemmed in: the world grew old
Unto their eyes, and lacked house, field, and fold.

Then spake a wanderer; "Long the tale I tell
Though in few years the deeds thereof befell,
In a strange land and barren, far removed
From southlands and their bliss; yet folk beloved,
Yearning for love, striving 'gainst change and hate,
Strong, uncomplaining, yet compassionate,
Have dwelt therein—a strange and awful land
Where folk, as in the hollow of God's hand,
Beset with fearful things yet fearing nought,
Have lived their lives and wondrous deeds have wrought—
Wild deeds, as other men. Yet these at least,
If death from but a rough and homely feast
Drew them away, lived not so full of care, .
They and their sons, but that their lives did bear
The fruit of deeds recorded. Bear with me
If I shall seem to hold this history
Of a few freemen of the farthest north,
A handful, as a thing of too much worth;
Because this Iceland was my fathers' home,
Nay, somewhat of the selfsame stock they come
As these I tell of: know withal that we
Have ever deemed this tale as true to be,
As though those very Dwellers in Laxdale, p. 336
Risen from the dead had told us their own tale;
Who for the rest while yet they dwelt on earth
Wearied no God with prayers for more of mirth
Than dying men have; nor were ill-content
Because no God beside their sorrow went

Turning to flowery sward the rock-strewn way,
Weakness to strength, or darkness into day.
Therefore, no marvels hath my tale to tell,
But deals with such things as men know too well;
All that I have herein your hearts to move,
Is but the seed and fruit of bitter love."

ARGUMENT

This story shows how two friends loved a fair woman, and how he who loved her best had her to wife, though she loved him little or not at all; and how one of these two friends gave shame to and received death of the other, who in his turn came to his end by reason of that deed.

Of Herdholt and Bathstead

Herdholt my tale names for the stead, where erst
Olaf the Peacock dwelt; nowise the worst
Among the great men of a noble day:
Upon a knoll amidst a vale it lay,
Nigh where Laxriver meets the western sea,
And in that day it nourished plenteously
Great wealth of sheep and cattle.

Ye shall know
That Olaf to a mighty house did go
To take to him a wife: Thorgerd he gat,
The daughter of the man, at Burg who sat,
After a great life, with eyes waxing dim,
Egil, the mighty son of Skallagrim.
Now of the sons the twain had, first we name
Kiartan alone, for eld's sake and for fame,
Then Steinthor, Haldor, Helgi, and Hauskuld,
All of good promise, strong and lithe and bold,
Yet little against Kiartan's glory weighed;
Besides these props the Peacock's house that stayed,
Two maidens, Thurid, Thorbiorg there were;
And furthermore a youth was fostered there,
Whom Thorleik, Olaf's brother, called his son:
Bodli his name was. Thus the tale is done
Of those who dwelt at Herdholt in those days.

Midst the grey slopes, Bathstead its roof did raise
Seven miles from Herdholt; Oswif, wise of men,
Who Thordis had to wife, abode there then
With his five sons, of whom let names go past
That are but names; but these were first and last,
Ospak and Thorolf: never, says my tale,

That Oswif's wisdom was of much avail
In making these, though they were stout enow;
But in his house a daughter did there grow
To perfect womanhood, Gudrun by name,
Whose birth the wondering world no more might blame
Than her's who erst called Tyndarus her sire,
What hearts soe'er, what roof-trees she might fire,
What hearts soe'er, what hearths she might leave cold,
Before the ending of the tale be told.
But where we take the story up, fifteen
The maiden's years were; Kiartan now had seen
His eighteenth spring, and younger by a year
Was Bodli, son of Thorleik.

Now most fair
Seemed Olaf's lot in life, and scarcely worse
Was Oswif's, and what shadow of a curse
Might hang o'er either house, was thought of now
As men think of a cloud the mountain's brow
Hides from their eyes an hour before the rain;
For so much love there was betwixt the twain,
Herdholt and Bathstead, that it well might last
Until the folk aforenamed were all passed
From out the world; but herein shall be shown
How the sky blackened, and the storm swept down.

The Prophecy of Guest the Wise

Upon a day, amid the maids that spun
Within the bower at Bathstead, sat Gudrun,
Her father in the firth a-fishing was,
The while her mother through the meads did pass
About some homely work. So there she sat,
Nor set her hand to this work or to that,
And a half-frown was on her pensive face,
Nor did she heed the chatter of the place
As girl spake unto girl. Then did she hear
The sound of horse-hoofs swiftly drawing near,
And started up, and cried, "That shall be Guest,
Riding, as still his wont is, from the west
Unto the Thing, and this is just the day
When he is wont at Bathstead to make stay."
Then to the door she went, and with slim hand
Put it aback, and 'twixt the posts did stand,
And saw therewith a goodly company
Ride up the grey slopes leading from the sea.

That spring was she just come to her full height;
Low-bosomed yet she was, and slim and light,

Yet scarce might she grow fairer from that day;
Gold were the locks wherewith the wind did play,
Finer than silk, waved softly like the sea
After a three days' calm, and to her knee
Well-nigh they reached; fair were the white hands laid
Upon the door-posts where the dragons played;
Her brow was smooth now, and a smile began
To cross her delicate mouth, the snare of man;
For some thought rose within the heart of her
That made her eyes bright, her cheeks ruddier
Than was their wont, yet were they delicate
As are the changing steps of high heaven's gate;
Bluer than grey her eyes were; somewhat thin
Her marvellous red lips; round was her chin,
Cloven, and clear-wrought; like an ivory tower
Rose up her neck from love's white-veiled bower.
But in such lordly raiment was she clad,
As midst its threads the scent of southlands had,
And on its hem the work of such-like hands
As deal with silk and gold in sunny lands.
Too dainty seemed her feet to come anear
The guest-worn threshold-stone. So stood she there,
And rough the world about her seemed to be,
A rude heap cast up from the weary sea.

But now the new-come folk, some twelve in all,
Drew rein before the doorway of the hall,
And she a step or two across the grass
Unto the leader of the men did pass,
A white-haired elder clad in kirtle red:
"Be welcome here, O Guest the Wise!" she said,
"My father honours me so much that I
Am bid to pray thee not to pass us by,
But bide here for a while; he says withal
That thou and he together in the hall
Are two wise men together, two who can
Talk cunningly about the ways of man."

Guest laughed, and leapt from off his horse, and said:
"Fair words from fair lips, and a goodly stead,
But unto Thickwood must I go to-night
To give my kinsman Armod some delight;
Nevertheless here will we rest a while,
And thou and I with talk an hour beguile,
For so it is that all men say of thee,
'Not far off falls the apple from the tree,'
That 'neath thy coif some day shall lie again
When he is dead, 'the wise old Oswif's brain."
With that he took her hand, and to the hall
She led him, and his fellows one and all
Leapt to the ground, and followed clattering

In through the porch, and many a goodly thing
There had they plenteously; but mid the noise
And rattling horns and laughter, with clear voice
Spake Gudrun unto Guest, and ever he
Smiled at her goodly sayings joyfully,
And yet at whiles grew grave; yea, and she too,
Though her eyes glistened, seemed as scarce she knew
The things she said. At last, amid their speech,
The old man stayed his hand as it did reach
Out to the beaker, and his grey eyes stared
As though unseen things to his soul were bared;
Then Gudrun waited trembling, till he said:

"Liest thou awake at midnight in thy bed,
Thinking of dreams dreamed in the winter-tide,
When the north-east, turned off the mountain-side,
Shook the stout timbers of the hall, as when
They shook in Norway ere the upland men
Bore axe against them?"

She spake low to him:
"So is it, but of these the most wax dim
When daylight comes again; but four there are—
Four dreams in one—that bring me yet great care,
Nor may I soon forget them, yea, they sink
Still deeper in my soul—but do thou drink,
And tell me merry tales; of what avail
To speak of things that make a maiden pale
And a man laugh?"
"Speak quick," he said, "before
This glimmer of a sight I have is o'er."

Then she delayed not, but in quick words said:
"Methought that with a coif upon my head
I stood upon a stream-side, and withal
Upon my heart the sudden thought did fall
How foul that coif was, and how ill it sat,
And though the folk beside me spoke 'gainst that,
Nevertheless, from off mine head I tore
The cursed thing, and cast it from the shore;
And glad at heart was I when it was gone,
And woke up laughing."
"Well, the second one,"
Said Guest; "Make good speed now, and tell me all!"

"This was the dream," she said, "that next did fall:
By a great water was I; on mine arm
A silver ring, that more my heart did charm
Than one might deem that such a small thing might;
My very own indeed seemed that delight,
And long I looked to have it; but as I

Stood and caressed the dear thing, suddenly
It slipped from off my arm, and straightway fell
Into the water: nor is more to tell
But that I wept thereat, and sorrowed sore
As for a friend that I should see no more."

"As great," said Guest, "is this thing as the last,
What follows after?"
"O'er the road I passed
Nigh Bathstead," said she, "in fair raiment clad,
And on mine arm a golden ring I had;
And seemly did I deem it, yet the love
I had therefor was not so much above
That wherewithal I loved the silver ring,
As gold is held by all a dearer thing
Than silver is; now, whatso worth it bore,
Methought that needs for longer than before
This ring should give me what it might of bliss;
But even as with foolish dreams it is
So was it now; falling I seemed to be,
And spread my arms abroad to steady me;
Upon a stone the ring smote, and atwain
It broke; and when I stooped the halves to gain,
Lo, blood ran out from either broken place;
Then as I gazed thereon I seemed to trace
A flaw within the craftsman's work, whereby
The fair thing brake; yea, withal presently
Yet other flaws therein could I discern;
And as I stood and looked, and sore did yearn,
Midst blind regrets, rather than raging pain,
For that fair thing I should not see again,
My eyes seemed opened, to my heart it came,
Spite of those flaws, that on me lay the blame
Why thus was spoiled that noble gift and rare,
Because therewith I dealt not with due care:
So with a sigh I woke."
"Ill fare," said Guest,
"Three of thy dreams, tell now about the rest."

"This is the last of the four dreams," she said;
"Methought I had a helm upon my head,
Wrought all of gold, with precious gems beset,
And pride and joy I had therein, and yet,
So heavy was it, that I scarce might hold
My head upright for that great weight of gold;
Yet for all that I laid no blame or wrong
Upon it, and I fain had kept it long;
But amid this, while least I looked therefor,
Something, I knew not what, the fair helm tore
From off mine head, and then I saw it swept
Into the firth, and when I would have wept

Then my voice failed me, and mine eyes were dry
Despite my heart; and therewith presently
I woke, and heard withal the neat-herd's song
As o'er the hard white snow he went along
Unto the byre, shouldering his load of hay;
Then knew I the beginning of the day,
And to the window went and saw afar
The wide firth, black beneath the morning-star,
And all the waste of snow, and saw the man
Dark on the slope; 'twixt the dead earth and wan,
And the dark vault of star-besprinkled sky,
Croaking, a raven toward the sea did fly—
With that I fell a yearning for the spring,
And all the pleasant things that it should bring,
And lay back in my bed and shut my eyes,
To see what pictures to my heart would rise,
And slept, but dreamed no more; now spring is here—
Thou knowst perchance, made wise with many a year,
What thing it is I long for; but to me
All grows as misty as the autumn sea
'Neath the first hoar-frost, and I name it not,
The thing wherewith my wondering heart is hot"

Then Guest turned round upon her, with a smile
Beholding her fair face a little while,
And as he looked on her she hid her eyes
With slim hands, but he saw the bright flush rise,
Despite of them, up to her forehead fair;
Therewith he sighed as one who needs must bear
A heavy burden.

                    "Since thou thus hast told
Thy dreams," he said, "scarce may I now withhold
The tale of what mine eyes have seen therein;
Yet little from my foresight shalt thou win,
Since both the blind, and they who see full well,
Go the same road, and leave a tale to tell
Of interwoven miseries, lest they,
Who after them a while on earth must stay,
Should have no pleasure in the winter night,
When this man's pain is made that man's delight."

He smiled an old man's smile, as thus he spake,
Then said, "But I must hasten ere it break
The thin sharp thread of light that yet I see—
Methinks a stirring life shall hap to thee.
Thou shalt be loved and love; wrongs shalt thou give,
Wrongs shalt thou take, and therewithal outlive
Both wrongs, and love, and joy, and dwell alone
When all the fellows of thy life are gone.
Nay, think not I can tell thee much of this,

How it shall hap, the sorrow or the bliss
Only foreshadowing of outward things,
Great, and yet not the greatest, dream-lore brings.

"For whereas of the ill coif thou didst dream,
That such a husband unto me doth seem
As thou shalt think mates thee but ill enow,
Nor shall love-longings bind thee; so shalt thou
By thine own deed shake off this man from thee.

"But next the ring of silver seems to me,
Another husband, loved and loving well;
But even as the ring from off thee fell
Into the water, so it is with him,
The sea shall make his love and promise dim.

"But for the gold ring; thou shalt wed again,
A worthier man belike—yet well-nigh vain
My strivings are to see what means the gold
Thou lovedst not more than silver: I am old
And thou art very young; hadst thou my sight,
Perchance herein thou wouldst have more of might.
But my heart says, that on the land there comes
A faith that telleth of more lovesome homes
For dead men, than we deemed of heretofore,
And that this man full well shall know that lore.
But whereas blood from out the ring did run,
By the sword's edge his life shall be foredone:
Then for the flaws—see thou thyself to these!
Thou knowest how a thing full well may please,
When first thou hast it in thine hold, until
Up to the surface float the seeds of ill,
And vain regret o'er all thy life is spread.

"But for the heavy helm that bowed thine head—
This, thy last husband, a great chief shall be
And hold a helm of terror over thee
Though thou shalt love him: at the end of life
His few last minutes shall he spend in strife
With the wild waves of Hwammfirth, and in vain,
For him too shall the white sea-goddess gain.

"So is thy dream areded; but these things
Shall hang above thee, as on unheard wings
The kestrel hangs above the mouse; nor more
As erst I said shalt thou gain by my lore
Than at the end of life, perchance, a smile
That fate with sight and blindness did beguile
Thine eyes in such sort—that thou knewst the end,
But not the way whereon thy feet did wend
On any day amid the many years,

Wherethrough thou waitedst for the flood of tears,
The dreariness that at some halting-place,
Waited in turn to change thy smiling face.
Be merry yet! these things shall not be all
That unto thee in this thy life shall fall."

Amid these latter words of his, the may
From her fair face had drawn her hands away,
And sat there with fixed eyes, and face grown pale,.
As one who sees the corner of the veil,
That hideth strange things, lifted for a while;
But when he ceased, she said with a faint smile
And trembling lips:
"Thanked be thou; well it is!
From thee I get no promise of vain bliss,
And constant joy; a tale I might have had
From flattering lips to make my young heart glad—
Yea, have my thanks!—yet wise as thou mayst be,
Mayst thou not dimly through these tangles see?"

He answered nought, but sat awhile with eyes
Distraught and sad, and face made over wise
With many a hard vain struggle; but at last
As one who from him a great weight doth cast,
He rose and snake to her:
"Wild words, fair may,
Now time it is that we were on our way."
Then unto him her visage did she turn,
In either cheek a bright red spot did burn,
Her teeth were set hard, and her brow was knit
As though she saw her life and strove with it.
Yet presently but common words she spake,
And bid him bide yet for her father's sake,
To make him joyful when the boards were laid;
But certainly, whatever words she said,
She heeded little, only from her tongue
By use and wont clear in his ears they rung.
Guest answered as before, that he would ride,
Because that night at Thickwood must he bide;
So silent now with wandering weary eyes
She watched his men do on their riding guise,
Then led him from the hall but listlessly,
As though she heeded nought where she might be.
So forth he rode, but turned and backward gazed
Before his folk the garth-gate latch had raised,
And saw her standing yet anigh the hall,
With her long shadow cast upon its wall,
As with her eyes turned down upon the ground
A long lock of her hair she wound and wound
About her hand. Then turning once again,
He passed the gate and shook his bridle-rein.

Now but a short way had he gone ere he
Beheld a man draw nigh their company,
Who, when they met, with fair words Guest did greet,
And said that Olaf Peacock bade him meet
Him and his men, and bid them to his stead:
"And well ye wot, O Goodman Guest," he said,
"That all day long it snoweth meat and drink
At Herdholt, and the gurgle and the clink
Of mead and horns, the harp alone doth still."
Guest laughed, and said, "Well, be that as it will,
Get swiftly back, and say that I will come
To look upon the marvels of his home
And hear his goodly voice; but may not bide
The night through, for to Thickwood must I ride."
Then the man turned and smote his horse; but they
Rode slowly by the borders of the bay
Upon that fresh and sunny afternoon,
Noting the sea-birds' cry and surf's soft tune,
Until at last into the dale they came,
And saw the gilt roof-ridge of Herdholt flame
In the bright sunlight over the fresh grass,
O'er which the restless white-woolled lambs did pass
And querulous grey ewes; and wide around,
Near and far up the dale, they heard the sound
Of lowing kine, and the blithe neat-herd's voice,
For in those days did all things there rejoice.
Now presently from out the garth they saw
A goodly company unto them draw,
And thitherward came Olaf and his men;
So joyous greeting was betwixt them when
They met, and side by side the two chiefs rode,
Right glad at heart unto the fair abode.

Great-limbed was Olaf Hauskuldson, well knit,
And like a chief upon his horse did sit;
Clear-browed and wide-eyed was he, smooth of skin
Through fifty rough years; of his mother's kin,
The Erse king's daughter, did his short lip tell,
And dark-lashed grey-blue eyes; like a clear bell
His voice was yet, despite of waves and wind,
And such a goodly man you scarce might find,
As for his years, in all the northern land.
He held a gold-wrought spear in his right hand,
A chief's gold ring his left arm did upbear,
And as a mighty king's was all his gear,
Well shaped of Flanders' cloth, and silk and gold.
Thus they their way up to the garth did hold,
And Thord the Short, Guest's son, was next thereby,
A brisk man and a brave; so presently
They passed the garth-wall, and drew rein before

The new-built hall's well-carven, fair porch-door,
And Guest laughed out with pleasure, to behold
Its goodly fashion, as the Peacock told
With what huge heed and care the place was wrought,
And of the Norway earl's great wood, he brought
Over the sea; then in they went and Guest
Gazed through the cool dusk, till his eyes did rest
Upon the noble stories, painted fair
On the high panelling and roof-boards there;
For over the high-seat, in his ship there lay
The gold-haired Baldur, god of the dead day,
The spring-flowers round his high pile, waiting there
Until the Gods thereto the torch should bear;
And they were wrought on this side and on that,
Drawing on towards him. There was Frey, and sat
On the gold-bristled boar, who first they say
Ploughed the brown earth, and made it green for Frey.
Then came dark-bearded Niörd; and after him
Freyia, thin-robed, about her ankles slim
The grey cats playing. In another place
Thor's hammer gleamed o'er Thor's red-bearded face;
And Heimdall, with the gold horn slung behind,
That in the God's-dusk he shall surely wind,
Sickening all hearts with fear; and last of all
Was Odin's sorrow wrought upon the wall,
As slow-paced, weary-faced, he went along,
Anxious with all the tales of woe and wrong
His ravens, Thought and Memory, bring to him.

Guest looked on these until his eyes grew dim,
Then turned about, and had no word to praise,
So wrought in him the thought of those strange days
Done with so long ago. But furthermore
Upon the other side, the deeds of Thor
Were duly done; the fight in the far sea
With him who rings the world's iniquity,
The Midgard Worm; strife in the giants' land,
With snares and mockeries thick on either hand,
And dealings with the Evil One who brought
Death even amid the Gods—all these well wrought
Did Guest behold, as in a dream, while still
His joyous men the echoing hall did fill
With many-voiced strange clamour, as of these
They talked, and stared on all the braveries.
Then to the presses in the cloth-room there
Did Olaf take him, and showed hangings fair
Brought from the southlands far across the sea,
And English linen and fair napery,
And Flemish cloth; then back into the hall
He led him, and took arms from off the wall,
And let the mail-coat rings run o'er his hands,

And strung strange bows brought from the fiery lands.
Then through the butteries he made him pass,
And, smiling, showed what winter stock yet was;
Fish, meal, and casks of wine, and goodly store
Of honey, that the bees had grumbled o'er
In clover fields of Kent. Out went they then
And saw in what wise Olaf's serving-men
Dealt with the beasts, and what fair stock he had,
And how the maids were working blithe and glad
Within the women's chamber. Then at last,
Guest smiled, and said;
"Right fair is all thou hast,
A noble life thou livest certainly,
And in such wise as now, still may it be,
Nor mayst thou know beginning of ill days!
Now let it please thee that we go our ways,
E'en as I said, for the sun falleth low."

"So be it then," said he. "Nor shalt thou go
Giftless henceforth; and I will go with thee
Some little way, for we my sons may see;
And fain I am to know how to thine eyes
They seem, because I know thee for most wise,
And that the cloud of time from thee hides less
Than from most men, of woe or happiness."

With that he gave command, and men brought forth
Two precious things; a hat of goodly worth,
Of fur of Russia, with a gold chain wound
Thrice round it, and a coin of gold that bound
The chain's end in the front, and on the same
A Greek king's head was wrought, of mighty fame
In olden time; this unto Guest he gave,
And smiled to see his deep-set eyes and grave
Gleam out with joy thereover: but to Thord,
Guest's son, he gave a well-adorned sword
And English-'broidered belt; and then once more
They mounted by the goodly carven door,
And to their horses gat all Guest's good men,
And forth they rode toward Laxriver: but when
They had just overtopped a low knoll's brow,
Olaf cried out, "There play hot hearts enow
In the cold waves!" Then Guest looked, and afar
Beheld the tide play on the sandy bar
About the stream's mouth, as the sea waves rushed
In over it and back the land-stream pushed;
But in the dark wide pool mid foam-flecks white,
Beneath the slanting afternoon sunlight,
He saw white bodies sporting, and the air
Light from the south-west up the slopes did bear
Sound of their joyous cries as there they played.

Then said he, "Goodman, thou art well apaid
Of thy fair sons, if they shall deal as well
With earth as water."
"Nought there is tell
Of great deeds at their hands as yet," said he;
"But look you, how they note our company!"

For waist-high from the waves one rose withal,
And sent a shrill voice like a sea-mew's call
Across the river, then all turned toward land,
And beat the waves to foam with foot and hand,
And certes kept no silence; up the side
They scrambled, and about the shore spread wide
Seeking their raiment, and the yellowing sun
Upon the line of moving bodies shone,
As running here and there with laugh and shout
They flung the linen and grey cloth about,
Yet spite of all their clamour clad them fast.
So Guest and Olaf o'er the green slopes passed
At sober pace, the while the other men
Raced down to meet the swimmers.
"Many then
There are, who have no part or lot in thee
Among these lads," said Guest.
"Yea, such there be,"
Said Olaf, "sons of dale-dwellers hereby;
But Kiartan rules the swimming."
Earnestly
Guest gazed upon the lads as they drew near,
And scarcely now he seemed the words to hear
That Olaf spake, who talked about his race
And how they first had dwelling in that place;
But at the last Guest turned his horse about
Up stream, and drew rein, yet, as one in doubt,
Looked o'er his shoulder at the youths withal;
But nought said Olaf, doubting what should fall
From those wise lips.
Then Guest spake, "Who are these?
Tell me their names; yon lad upon his knees,
Turning the blue cloak over with his hands,
While over him a sturdy fellow stands,
Talking belike?"
"Hauskuld, my youngest son,"
Said Olaf, "kneels there, but the standing one
Is An the Black, my house-carle, a stout man."

"Good," Guest said; "name the one who e'en now ran
Through upraised hands a glittering silver chain,
And, as we look now, gives it back again
Unto a red-haired youth, tall, fair, and slim."

"Haldor it was who gave the chain to him,
And Helgi took it," Olaf said.
Then Guest:
"There kneeleth one in front of all the rest,
Less clad than any there, and hides from me
Twain who are sitting nigher to the sea?"

Then Olaf looked with shaded eyes and said:
"Steinthor, the sluggard, is it, by my head
He hideth better men! nay, look now, look!"

Then toward the stream his spear-butt Olaf shook,
As Steinthor rose, and gat somewhat aside,
And showed the other twain he first did hide.
On a grey stone anigh unto the stream
Sat a tall youth whose golden head did gleam
In the low sun; half covered was his breast,
His right arm bare as yet, a sword did rest
Upon his knees, and some half-foot of it
He from the sheath had drawn; a man did sit
Upon the grass before him; slim was he,
Black-haired and tall, and looked up smilingly
Into the other's face, with one hand laid
Upon the sword-sheath nigh the broad grey blade,
And seemed as though he listened.
Then spake Guest:
"No need, O friend, to ask about the rest,
Since I have seen these; for without a word
Kiartan I name the man who draws the sword
From out the sheath, and low down in the shade
Before him Bodli Thorleikson is laid.
But tell me of that sword, who bore it erst?"

Then Olaf laughed, "Some call that sword accursed;
Bodli now bears it, which the Eastlander
Geirmund, my daughter's husband, once did wear,
Hast thou not heard the tale? he won the maid
By my wife's word, wherefor with gold he paid,
Or so I deemed; but whereas of good kin
The man was, and the women hot herein,
I stood not in the way; well, but his love,
Whate'er it was, quenched not his will to rove;
He left her, but would nowise leave the sword,
And so she helped herself, and for reward
Got that, and a curse with it, babblers say.
Let see if it prevail 'gainst my good day!"

Guest answered nought at all, his head was turned
Eastward, away from where the low sun burned
Above the swimmers. Olaf spake once more:

"Wise friend, thou thus hast heard their names told o'er,
How thinkest thou? hast thou the heart to tell
Which in the years to come shall do right well?"

Guest spake nought for a while, and then he said,
But yet not turning any more his head:
"Surely of this at least thou wouldst be glad,
If Kiartan while he lived more glory had
Than any man now waxing in the land."

Then even as he spoke he raised his hand
And smote his horse, and rode upon his way
With no word more; neither durst Olaf stay
His swift departing, doubting of his mood;
For though indeed the word he spake was good,
Yet some vague fear he seemed to leave behind,
And Olaf scarce durst seek, lest he should find
Some ill thing lurking by his glory's side.
But after Guest his son and men did ride,
And forth to Thickwood with no stay they went.
But now, the journey and the day nigh spent,
Unto his father as they rode turned Thord,
With mind to say to him some common word,
But stared astonished, for the great tears ran
Over the wrinkled cheeks of the old man,
Yea, and adown his beard, nor shame had he
That Thord in such a plight his face should see,
At last he spake:
"Thou wonderest, O my son,
To see the tears fall down from such an one
As I am—folly is it in good sooth
Bewraying inward grief; but pain and ruth
Work in me so, I may not hold my peace
About the woes, that as thy years increase
Thou shalt behold fall on the country-side—
—But me the grey cairn ere that day shall hide—
Fair men and women have I seen to-day,
Yet I weep not because these pass away,
Sad though that is, but rather weep for this,
That they know not upon their day of bliss
How their worn hearts shall fail them ere they die,
How sore the weight of woe on them shall lie,
No sighing eases, wherewithal no hope,
No pride, no rage, shall make them fit to cope.
Remember what folk thou this day hast seen,
And in what joyous steads thy feet have been,
Then think of this!—that men may look to see
Love slaying love, and ruinous victory,
And truth called lies, and kindness turned to hate,
And prudence sowing seeds of all debate!
Son, thou shalt live to hear when I am dead

Of Bodli standing over Kiartan's head,
His friend, his foster-brother, and his bane,
That he in turn e'en such an end may gain.
Woe worth the while! forget it, and be blind!
Look not before thee! the road left behind,
Let that be to thee as a tale well told
To make thee merry when thou growest old!"

So spake he; but by this time had they come
Unto the wood that lay round Armod's home,
So on the tree-beset and narrow way
They entered now, and left behind the day;
And whatso things thenceforth to Guest befell,
No more of him the story hath to tell.

Gudrun Twice Wedded, Widowed, and Wooed of Kiartan

So wore the time away, nor long it was
Ere somewhat of Guest's forecast came to pass.
Drawn by her beauty, Thorvald wooed Gudrun;
Saying withal that he was such an one
As fainer was to wed a wife than lands,
Readier by far to give forth from his hands
That which he had, than take aught of her kin.
And in such wise he did not fail to win
His fond desire, and, therewith, wretched life.
For she who deemed nought worth so much of strife
As to say 'no' for ever, being wed, found
How the chain galled whereto she now was bound,
And more and more began to look on him
With hate that would be scorn, with eyes grown dim
With hope of change that came not, and lips set
For ever with the stifling of regret.
Coarse Thorvald was, and rough and passionate,
And little used on change of days to wait;
And as she ever Bloomed before his eyes,
Rage took the place of the first grieved surprise,
Wherewith he found that he who needs must love
Could get no love in turn, nay, nor e'en move
Her heart to kindness: then as nothing strange
Still with sad loathing looks she took the change
She noted in him, as if all were done
Between them, and no deed beneath the sun
That he could do would now be worse to her.
Judge if the hot heart of the man could bear
Such days as these! Upon a time it fell
That he, most fain indeed to love her well,
Would she but turn to him, had striven sore
To gain her love, and yet gat nothing more

Than a faint smile of scorn, 'neath eyes whose gaze
Seemed fixed for ever on the hoped-for days,
Wherein he no more should have part or lot;
Then mingled hate with love in him, and hot
His heart grew past all bearing; round about
He stared, as one who hears the eager shout
Of closing foes, when he to death is brought;
In his fierce heart thought crowded upon thought,
Till he saw not and heard not, but rose up
And cast upon the floor his half-filled cup,
And crying out, smote her upon the face;
Then strode adown the hushed and crowded place,
For meal-time was it, till he reached the door;
Then gat his horse, and over hill and moor,
Scarce knowing where he went, rode furiously.

But in the hall, folk turned them round to see
What thing Gudrun would do, who for a while
Sat pale and silent, with a deadly smile
Upon her lips; then called to where she sat
Folk from the hall, and talked of this and that
Gaily, as one who hath no care or pain:
Yea, when the goodman gat him back again
She met him changed, so that he well-nigh thought
That better days his hasty blow had brought.
And still as time wore on, day after day
Wondering, he saw her seeming blithe and gay;
So he, though sore misdoubting him of this,
Took what he might of pleasure and of bliss,
And put thought back. So time wore till the spring,
And then the goodman rode unto the Thing,
Not over light of heart, or free from fear,
Though his wife's face at parting was all clear
Of frown or sullenness; but he being gone,
Next morn Gudrun rode with one man alone
Forth unto Bathstead; there her tale she told,
And as in those days law strained not to hold
Folk whom love held not, or some common tie,
So her divorce was set forth speedily,
For mighty were her kin.

And now once more
At Bathstead did she dwell, free as before,
And, smiling, heard of how her husband fared
When by the Hill of Laws he stood and heard
The words, that he belike half thought to hear,
Which took from him a thing once held so dear,
That all was nought thereby.

Now wise ones tell
That there was one who used to note her well

Within her husband's hall, and many say
That talk of love they had before the day
That she went back to Bathstead; how that was
I know not surely; but it came to pass
That scarcely had abated the first rage
Of her old mate, and scarce less like a cage
Of red-hot iron 'gan to feel his life,
Ere this man, Thord, had won Gudrun to wife;
So, since the man was brisk and brave and fair,
And she had known him when her days were drear,
And turned with hope and longing to his eyes,
Kind amid hard things, in most joyous wise
Their-life went, and she deemed she loved him well;
And the strange things that Guest did once foretell,
Which morn and noon and eve she used to set
Before her eyes, she now would fain forget;
Alas! forgotten or remembered, still
Midst joy or sorrow fate shall work its will;
Three months they lived in joy and peace enow,
Till on a June night did the south-west blow
The rainy rack o'er Gudrun's sleeping head,
While in the firth was rolled her husband dead
Toward the black cliffs; drowned was he, says my tale,
By wizard's spells amidst a summer gale.

Then back to Bathstead Gudrun came again,
To sit with fierce heart brooding o'er her pain,
While life and time seemed made to torture her,
That she the utmost of all pain might bear,
To please she knew not whom; and yet mid this,
And all her raging for the vanished bliss,
Would Guest's words float up to her memory,
And quicken cold life; then would she cast by
As something vile the comfort that they brought,
Yet, none the less, still stronger grew that thought,
Unheeded, and unchidden therefore, round
The weary wall of woe, her life that bound.

So wore the months; spring with its longings came,
And now in every mouth was Kiartan's name,
And daily now must Gudrun's dull ears bear
Tales of the prowess of his youth to hear,
While in his cairn forgotten lay her love.
For this man, said they, all men's hearts did move,
Nor yet might envy cling to such an one,
So far beyond all dwellers 'neath the sun;
Great was he, yet so fair of face and limb
That all folk wondered much, beholding him,
How such a man could be; no fear he knew,
And all in manly deeds he could outdo;
Fleet-foot, a swimmer strong, an archer good,

Keen-eyed to know the dark waves' changing mood;
Sure on the crag, and with the sword so skilled,
That when he played therewith the air seemed filled
With light of gleaming blades; therewith was he
Of noble speech, though says not certainly
My tale, that aught of his be left behind
With rhyme and measure deftly intertwined;
Well skilled was he, too, in the craftsman's lore
To deal with iron mid the stithy's roar,
And many a sword-blade knew his heavy hand.
Shortly, if he amid ten kings should stand,
All men would think him worthier man than they;
And yet withal it was his daily way
To be most gentle both of word and deed,
And ever folk would seek him in their need,
Nor was there any child but loved him well.

Such things about him ever would men tell,
Until their hearts swelled in them as they thought
How great a glory to their land was brought,
Seeing that this man was theirs. Such love and praise
Kiartan's beginning had in those fair days,
While Gudrun sat sick-eyed, and hearkened this,
Still brooding on the late-passed days of bliss,
And thinking still how worthless such things were.

But now when midsummer was drawing near,
As on an eve folk sat within the hall,
Man unto man far off did they hear call,
And then the sound of horse-hoofs; Oswif rose,
And went into the porch to look for those
Who might be coming, and at last folk heard,
Close to the porch, the new-come travellers' word,
And turned to meet them; Gudrun sat alone
High on the dais when all folk were gone,
And playing with her golden finger-rings,
Set all her heart to think of bygone things,
Till hateful seemed all hopes, all thoughts of men.

Yet did she turn unto their voices, when
Folk back again into the hall did crowd,
Torch-litten now, laughing and talking loud,
Then as the guests adown the long hall drew,
Olaf the Peacock presently she knew,
Hand in hand with her father; but behind
Came two young men; then rose up to her mind,
Against her will, the tales of Kiartan told,
Because she deemed the one, whose hair of gold
In the new torch-light gleamed, was even he,
And that the black-haired high-browed one must be
Bodli, the son of Thorleik; but with that

Up to the place where listlessly she sat,
They came, and on her feet she now must stand
To welcome them; then Olaf took her hand,
And looked on her with eyes compassionate,
And said:
"O Gudrun, ill has been thy fate,
But surely better days shall soon be thine,
For not for nought do eyes like thine eyes shine
Upon the hard world; thou shalt bless us yet
In many a wise and all thy woes forget."

She answered nought, but drew her hand away,
And heavier yet the weight upon her lay
That thus men spake of her. But, turning round,
Kiartan upon the other hand she found,
Gazing upon her with wide hungry eyes
And parted lips; then did strange joy surprise
Her listless heart, and changed her old world was;
Ere she had time to think, all woe did pass
Away from her, and all her life grew sweet,
And scarce she felt the ground beneath her feet,
Or knew who stood around, or in what place
Of heaven or earth she was; soft grew her face;
In tears that fell not yet, her eyes did swim,
As, trembling, she reached forth her hand to him,
And with the shame of love her smooth cheeks burned,
And her lips quivered, as if sore they yearned
For words they had not learned, and might not know
Till night and loneliness their form should show.

But Kiartan's face a happy smile did light,
Kind, loving, confident; good hap and might
Seemed in his voice as now he spake, and said:
"They say the dead for thee will ne'er be dead,
And on this eve I thought in sooth to have
Labour enow to draw thee from the grave
Of the old days; but thou rememberest,
Belike, days earlier yet, that men call best
Of all days, when as younglings erst we met.
Thou thinkest now thou never didst forget
This face of mine, since now most certainly
The eyes are kind wherewith thou lookst on me."

A shade came o'er her face, but quickly passed,
"Yea," said she, "if such pleasant days might last,
As when we wandered laughing hand in hand
Along the borders of the shell-strewn strand."

She wondered at the sound of her own voice,
She chid her heart that it must needs rejoice,
She marvelled why her soul with fear was filled;

But quickly every questioning was stilled
As he sat down by her.
Old Oswif smiled
To see her sorrow in such wise beguiled,
And Olaf laughed for joy, and many a thought
Of happy loves to Bodli's heart was brought
As by his friend he sat, and saw his face
So bright with bliss; and all the merry place
Ran over with goodwill that sight to see,
And the hours passed in great festivity.
At last beneath the glimmer of the moon,
Fanned by the soft sea-wind that tempers June,
Homeward they rode, sire, son and foster-son,
Kiartan half joyful that the eve was done,
And he had leisure for himself to weave
Tales of the joyful way that from that eve
Should lead to perfect bliss; Bodli no less
Rejoicing in his fellow's happiness,
Dreaming of such-like joy to come to him,
And Olaf, thinking how that nowise dim
The glory of his line through these should grow.

But while in peace these through the night did go,
Vexed by new thoughts and old thoughts, Gudrun lay
Upon her bed: she watched him go away,
And her heart sank within her, and there came,
With pain of that departing, pity and shame,
That struggling with her love yet made it strong,
That called her longing blind, yet made her long
Yet more for more desire, what seeds soe'er
Of sorrow hate and ill were hidden there.
So with her strong heart wrestled love, till she
Sank 'neath the hand of sleep, and quietly
Beneath the new-risen sun she lay at rest,
The bed-gear fallen away from her white breast,
"One arm deep buried in her hair, one spread
Abroad, across the 'broideries of the bed,
A smile upon her lips, and yet a tear,
Scarce dry, but stayed anigh her dainty ear—
How fair, how soft, how kind she seemed that morn,
Ere she anew to love and life was born.

A little space to part these twain indeed
Was seven short miles of hill and moor and mead,
And soon the threshold of the Bathstead hall
Knew nigh as much of Kiartan's firm footfall
As of the sweep of Gudrun's kirtle-hem,
And sweet past words to tell life grew to them;
Sweet the awaking in the morn, when lay
Below the hall the narrow winding way,
The friend that led, the foe that kept apart;

And sweet the joyful flutter of the heart
Anigh the door, ere clinging memory
Gave place to rapturous sight, and eye met eye;
Sweet the long hours of converse when each word
Like fairest music still seemed doubly heard,
Caught by the ear and clung to by the heart;
Yea, even most sweet the minute they must part,
Because the veil, that so oft time must draw
Before them, fell, and clear without a flaw,
Their hearts saw love, that moment they did stand
Ere lip left lip, or hand fell down from hand;
Yea, that passed o'er, still sweet and bitter sweet
The yearning pain that stayed the lingering feet
Upon the threshold, and the homeward way;
And silent chamber covered up from day
For thoughts of words unsaid—ah, sweet the night
Amidst its dreams of manifold delight!

And yet sometimes pangs of perplexed pain
Would torture Gudrun, as she thought again
On Guest and his forecasting of her dream;
And through the dark of days to come would gleam
.Fear, like a flame of hell shot suddenly
Up through spring meadows 'twixt fair tree and tree,
Though little might she see the flaws, whereof
That past dream warned her, midst her dream of love;
And whatso things her eyes refused to see,
Made wise by fear, none others certainly
Might see in love so seeming smooth as this,
That looked to all men like the door of bliss
Unto the twain, and to the country-side
Good hope and joy, that thus so fast were tied
The bonds 'twixt two such houses as were these,
And folk before them saw long years of peace.

Of Bodli Thorleikson the story says,
That he, o'ershadowed still by Kiartan's praise,
Was second but to him; although, indeed,
He, who perchance the love of men did need
More than his fellow, less their hearts might move;
Yet fair to all men seemed the trust and love
Between the friends, and fairer unto none
Than unto Olaf, who scarce loved his son
More than his brother's son; now seemed it too,
That this new love closer the kinsmen drew
Than e'en before, and whatso either did
The other knew, and scarce their thoughts seemed hid,
One from the other.

So as day by day
Went Kiartan unto Bathstead, still the way

Seemed shorter if his friend beside him rode;
Then might he ease his soul of that great load
Of love unsatisfied, by words, and take
Mockeries in turn, grown sweet for that name's sake
They wrapped about, or glow with joy to hear
The praises of the heart he held so dear,
And laugh with joy and pleasure of his life,
To note how Bodli's heart withal, seemed rife
With love that his love kindled, though as yet
It wandered, on no heart of woman set.
So Bodli, nothing loth, went many a day,
Whenso they would, to make the lovers gay,
Whenso they would, to get him gone, that these
E'en with such yearning words their souls might please
As must be spoken, but sound folly still
To aught but twain, because no tongue hath skill
To tell their meaning: kinder, Kiartan deemed,
Grew Bodli day by day, and ever seemed
Well-nigh as happy as the loving twain,
And unto Bodli life seemed nought but gain,
And fair the days were.

On a day it fell
As the three talked, they 'gan in sport to tell
The names o'er of such women good and fair,
As in the land that tide unwedded were,
Naming a mate for Bodli, and still he
Must laugh and shake his head;
"Then over sea,"
Quoth Kiartan, "mayhap such an one there is
That thou mayst deem the getting of her bliss;
Go forth and win her with the rover's sword!"

Then Bodli laughed, and cast upon the board
The great grey blade and ponderous iron hilt,
All unadorned, the yoke-fellow of guilt,
And said, "Go, sword, and fetch me home a bride!
But here in Iceland have I will to bide
With those that love me, till the fair days change."

Then Gudrun said, "Things have there been more strange,
Than that we three should sit above the oars,
The while on even keel 'twixt the low shores
Our long-ship breasts the Thames flood, or the Seine.
Methinks in biding here is little gain,
Cooped up in this cold corner of the world."

Then up sprang Kiartan, seized the sword, and hurled
Its weight aloft, and caught it by the hilt
As down it fell, and cried, "Would that the tilt
Were even now being rigged above the ship!

Would that we stood to see the oars first dip
In the green waves! nay, rather would that we
Above the bulwarks now saw Italy,
With all its beacons flaring! Sheathe thy sword,
Fair foster-brother, till I say the word
That draws it forth; and, Gudrun, never fear
That thou a word or twain of me shalt hear,
E'en if the birds must bear them o'er the sea."

Her eyes were fixed upon him lovingly
As thus he spake, and Bodli smiling saw
Her hand to Kiartan's ever nigher draw;
Then he rose up and sheathed the sword, and said,
"Nay, rather if I be so hard to wed,
I yet must think of roving, so I go
To talk to Oswif, all the truth to know
About the news the chapmen carried here,
That Olaf Tryggvison his sword doth rear
'Gainst Hacon and his fortune."
Therewithal
He laughed, and gat him swiftly from the hall,
And found the old man, nor came back again
Until through sun and shadow had the twain
Sat long together, and the hall 'gan fill.
Then did he deem his friend sat somewhat still,
And something strange he saw in Gudrun's eyes
As she gazed on him; nor did fail to rise
In his own heart the shadow of a shade,
That made him deem the world less nobly made,
And yet was like to pleasure. On the way
Back home again, not much did Kiartan say,
And what he spake was well-nigh mockery
Of speech, wherewith he had been wont to free
His heart from longings grown too sweet to bear.
But time went on, and still the days did wear
With little seeming change; if love grew cold
In Kiartan's heart one day, the next o'er bold,
O'er frank, he noted not who might be by,
When he unto his love was drawing nigh;
Gudrun gloomed not; as merry as before
Did Bodli come and go 'twixt dais and door.
Only perchance a little oftener they
Fell upon talk of the fair lands that lay
Across the seas, and sometimes would a look
Cross Gudrun's face that seemed a half rebuke
To Kiartan, as all over-eagerly
He talked about the life beyond the sea,
As thereof he had heard the stories tell.
Then Bodli sometimes into musings fell,
So dreamlike, that he might not tell his thought
When he again to common life was brought.

So passed the seasons, but in autumn-tide
The foster-brothers did to Burgfirth ride,
Unto a ship new come to White-river;
Talk with the outland chapmen had they there,
And Kiartan bade the captain in the end
p Back unto Herdholt as his guest to wend,
And nothing loth he went with him; and now
Great tidings thereupon began to show
Of Hacon slain, his son thrust from the land,
And Norway in fair peace beneath the hand
Of Olaf Tryggvison; nor did he fail
To tell about the king full many a tale,
And praise him for the noblest man, that e'er
Had held the tiller, or cast forth the spear:
And Kiartan listened eagerly, yet seemed
As if amid the tale he well-nigh dreamed;
And now withal, when he to Bathstead went,
Less than before would talk of his intent
To see the outlands, to his listening love;
And when at whiles she spake to him thereof
Lightly he answered her, and smile or kiss
Would change their talk to idle words of bliss:
Less of her too to Bodli now he spake,
Although this other, (for her beauty's sake
He told himself) to hear of her was fain;
And he, for his part, sometimes felt a pain,
As though the times were changing over fast,
When Kiartan let the word of his go past
Unnoted, that in other days belike
Had nowise failed from out his heart to strike
The sparks of lovesome praise.

But now Yule-tide
Was come at last, and folk from far and wide
Went to their neighbours' feasts, and as wont was
All Bathstead unto Herdholt hall did pass,
And the feast lasted long, and all folk gat
Things that their souls desired, and Gudrun sat
In the high-seat beside the goodwife there.

But ever now her wary ears did hear
The new king's name bandied from mouth to mouth,
And talk of those new-comers from the south;
And through her anxious heart a sharp pain smote
As Kiartan's face she eagerly 'gan note
And sighed; because, leaned forward on the board,
He sat, with eager face hearkening each word,
Nor speaking aught; then long with hungry eyes
She sat regarding him, nor yet would rise
A word unto her lips: and all the while

Bodli gazed on them with a fading smile
About his lips, and eyes that ever grew
More troubled still, until he hardly knew
What folk were round about.

So passed away
Yule-tide at Herdholt, cold day following day,
Till spring was gone, and Gudrun had not failed
To win both many days where joy prevailed,
And many a pang of fear; till so it fell
That in the summer, whereof now we tell,
Upon a day in blithe mood Kiartan came
To Bathstead, not as one who looks for blame,
And Bodli with him, sad-eyed, silent, dull,
Noted of Gudrun, who no less was full
Of merry talk, yea, more than her wont was.
But as the hours toward eventide did pass,
Said Kiartan:
"Love, make we the most of bliss,
For though, indeed, not the last day this is
Whereon we twain shall meet in such a wise,
Yet shalt thou see me soon in fighting guise,
And hear the horns blow up our Loth to go,
For in White-River—"
"Is it even so,"
She broke in, "that these feet abide behind?
Men call me hard, but thou hast known me kind;
Men call me fair, my body give I thee;
Men call me dainty, let the rough salt sea
Deal with me as it will, so thou be near!
Let me share glory with thee, and take fear
That thy heart throws aside!"
Hand joined to hand,
As one who prays, and trembling, did she stand
With parted lips, and pale and weary-faced.
But up and down the hall-floor Bodli paced
With clanking sword, and brows set in a frown,
And scarce less pale than she. The sun low down
Shone through the narrow windows of the hall,
And on the gold upon her breast did fall,
And gilt her slim clasped hands.

There Kiartan stood
Gazing upon her in strange wavering mood,
Now longing sore to clasp her to his heart,
And pray her, too, that they might ne'er depart,
Now well-nigh ready to say such a word
As cutteth love across as with a sword;
So fought love in him with the craving vain
The love of all the wondering world to gain,
Though such he named it not. And so at last

His eyes upon the pavement did he cast,
And knit his brow as though some word to say;
Then fell her outstretched hands, she cried:
"Nay, nay!
Thou need'st not speak, I will not ask thee twice
To take a gift, a good gift, and be wise;
I know my heart, thou know'st it not; farewell,
Maybe that other tales the Skalds shall tell
Than of thy great deeds."
Still her face was pale,
As with a sound betwixt a sigh and wail,
She brushed by Bodli, who, aghast, did stand
With open mouth, and vainly stretched-out hand;
But Kiartan followed her a step or two,
Then stayed, bewildered by his sudden woe;
But even therewith, as nigh the door she was,
She turned back suddenly, and straight did pass,
Trembling all over, to his side, and said,
With streaming eyes:
"Let not my words be weighed
As a man's words are! O, fair love, go forth
And come thou back again, made no more worth
Unto this heart; but worthier it may be
To the dull world thy worth that cannot see.
Go forth, and let the rumour of thee run
Through every land that is beneath the sun;
For know I not, indeed, that everything
Thou winnest at the hands of lord or king,
Is surely mine, as thou art mine at last?"

Then round about his neck her arms she cast,
And wept right sore, and touched with love and shame,
Must Kiartan offer to leave hope of fame,
And noble life; but midst her tears she smiled,
"Go forth, my love, and be thou not beguiled
By woman's tears, I spake but as a fool,
We of the north wrap not our men in wool,
Lest they should die at last; nay, be not moved,
To think that thou a faint-heart fool hast loved!"

For now his tears fell too, he said: "My sweet,
Ere the ship sails we yet again shall meet
To say farewell, a little while, and then,
When I come back to hold my place mid men,
With honour won for thee—how fair it is
To think on now, the sweetness and the bliss!"

Some little words she said no pen could write,
Upon his face she laid her fingers white,
And, midst of kisses, with his hair did play;
Then, smiling through her tears, she went away.

Nor heeded Bodli aught—
Men say the twain,
Kiartan and Gudrun, never met again
In loving wise; that each to each no more
Their eyes looked kind on this side death's dark shore,
That midst their tangled life they must forget,
Till they were dead, that ere their lips had met.

For ere the day that Kiartan meant to come
And kiss his love once more within her home,
The south-east wind, that had stayed hitherto
Their sailing, changed, and northwest now it blew;
And Kálf, the captain, urged them to set forth,
Because that tide the wind loved not the north,
And now the year grew late for long delay.
Night was it when he spake; at dawn next day,
Before the door at Herdholt might men see,
Armed, and in saddle, a goodly company.
Kiartan, bright-eyed and flushed, restless withal,
As on familiar things his eyes did fall,
Yet eager to be gone, and smiling still,
For pride and hope and love his soul did fill,
As of his coming life he thought, and saw
In all the days that were to be, no flaw.
About him were his fellows, ten such men
As in the land had got no equals then;
By him his foster-brother sat, as true
As was the steel the rover's hand erst drew;
There stood his father, flushed with joy and pride,
By the fair-carven door that did abide,
Till he fulfilled of glory came again
To take his bride before the eyes of men.

Now skipper Kálf, clad in the Peacock's gift,
Unto the south his gold-wrought spear did lift,
And Kiartan stooped and kissed his sire. A shout
Rose from the home-men, as they turned about,
And trotted jingling down the grassy knoll.
Silent awhile rode Kiartan, till his soul,
Filled with a many thoughts, in speech o'erflowed,
And unto Bodli, who beside him rode,
He fell to talk of all that they should do
In the fair countries that they journeyed to.
Not Norway only, or the western lands,
In time to come, he said, might know their hands,
But fairer places, folk of greater fame,
Where 'neath the shadow of the Roman name
Sat the Greek king, gold-clad, with bloodless sword.
But as he spoke Bodli said here a word
And there a word, and knew not what he said,
Nay, scarcely knew what wild thoughts filled his head,

What longings burned, like a still quickening flame,
Within his sad heart.

So that night they came
To Burg-firth and the place upon the strand
Where by the ready ship the tents did stand,
And there they made good cheer, and slept that night,
But on the morrow, with the earliest light,
They gat a ship-board, and, all things being done,
Upon a day when low clouds hid the sun,
And 'neath the harsh north-west down drave the rain,
They drew the gangway to the ship again,
And ran the oars out. There did Kiartan stand
By Kálf, who took the tiller in his hand
And conned the rising bows; but when at last
Toward the grey sky the wet oar-blades were cast,
And space 'twixt stern and land 'gan widen now,
Kiartan cried out and ran forth to the prow,
While rope and block yet beat confusedly,
And shook his drawn sword o'er the dark grey sea;
And step for step behind him Bodli went,
And on his sword-hilt, with a like intent,
He laid his hand, and half drew from its sheath
The rover's sword; then with a deep-drawn breath,
Most like a sigh, he thrust it back again,
His face seemed sharpened with a sudden pain.
He turned him round the driving scud to face,
His breast heaved, and he staggered in his place,
And stretched his strong arms forth with a low moan
Unto the hidden hills, 'neath which alone
Sat Gudrun—sat his love—and therewithal
Down did the bows into the black trough fall,
Up rose the oar-song, through the waters grey,
Unto the south the good ship took her way.

The Dealings of King Olaf Tryggvison with the Icelanders

Now tells the tale that safe to Drontheim came
Kiartan with all his folk, and the great fame
Of Olaf Tryggvison then first they knew,
When thereof spake the townsmen to the crew,
But therewithal yet other news they heard,
Which seemed to one and all a heavy word;
How that the king, from the old customs turned,
Now with such zeal toward his new faith burned,
That thereby nothing else to him was good
But that all folk should bow before the Rood.
When Kiartan's coming thitherward betid
Three ships of Iceland lay there in the Nid,

Manned by stout men enow; downcast were these
Who had been glad enow the king to please;
And save their goods, and lives, perchance, withal,
But knew not how their forefathers to call
Souls damned for ever and ever; yet they said
That matters drew so swiftly to a head,
That when they met the king he passed them by
With head turned round, or else with threatening eye
Scowled on them; "And when Yule-tide comes," said they,
"We look to have from him a settled day
When we must change our faith or bide the worst."

"Well," Kiartan said, "this king is not the first
To think the world is made for him alone;
Who knows how things will go ere all is done?
God wot, I wish my will done even as he;
I hate him not."
And therewith merrily
From out the ship the men of Herdholt went;
A bright eve was it, and the good town sent
Thin smoke and blue straight upward through the air,
For it had rained of late, and here and there
Sauntered the townsfolk, man and maid and child;
Where street met quay a fiddle's sound beguiled
A knot of listening folk, who no less turned
And stared hard as the westering sunbeams burned
Upon the steel and scarlet of that band,
Whom, as ye well may wot, no niggard hand
Had furnished forth; so up the long street then,
Gazing about, well gazed at, went the men,
A goodly sight. But e'en as they would wend
About the corner where that street had end,
High up in air nearby 'gan ring a chime
Whose sweetness seemed to bless e'en that sweet time
With double blessing. Kiartan stayed his folk
When first above his head that sound outbroke,
And listened smiling, till he heard a sigh
Close by him, and met Bodli's wandering eye
That fell before his.

Softly Kiartan spake:
"Now would Gudrun were here e'en for the sake
Of this sweet sound! nought have I heard so sweet."

So on they passed, and turned about the street,
And saw the great church cast its shadow down
Upon the low roofs of the goodly town,
And yet awhile they stayed there marvelling;
But therewith heard behind them armour ring,
And turning, saw a gallant company
Going afoot, and yet most brave to see,

Come toward the church, and nigher as they drew
It was to Kiartan even as if he knew
One man among them, taller by the head
Than any there, and clad in kirtle red,
Girt with a sword, with whose gold hilt he played
With his left hand, the while his right did shade
His eyes from the bright sun that 'gainst him blazed,
As on the band of Icelanders he gazed;
Broad-shouldered was he, grand to look upon,
And in his red beard tangled was the sun
That lit his bright face up in wrathful wise,
That fiercer showed his light-grey eager eyes.
Now ere he came quite close, sidelong he bent
Unto a man who close beside him went,
Then turned, and gazed at Kiartan harder yet,
As he passed by, and therewith their eyes met,
And Kiartan's heart beat, and his face grew bright,
His eyes intent as if amidst a fight,
Yet on his lips a smile was, confident,
Devoid of hate, as by him the man went.
But Bodli said, "Let us begone ere day
Is fully passed, if even yet we may;
This is the king, and what then may we do
'Gainst such a man, a feeble folk and few?"

But Kiartan turned upon him loftily,
And said, "Abide! I do not look to die
Ere we get back to Iceland; one there is,
Thou knowst, therein, to hold through woe and bliss
My soul from its departing; go we then
And note the way of worship of these men."

So on that eve about the church they hung,
And through the open door heard fair things sung,
And sniffed the incense; then to ship they went.

But the next morn the king to Kiartan sent
To bid him come unto the royal hall,
Where nought but good to him and his should fall;
Close by the ship upon the sunny quay
Was Kiartan, when the man these words did say,
Amid a ring of Icelanders, who sat
Upon the bales of unshipped goods: with that
Kiartan stood up and said unto the man:

"Undo thy kirtle if thy worn hands can!
Show us thy neck where the king's chain has galled;
But tell us not whereby thy sire was called
Lest some of these should blush—go tell the king
That I left Iceland for another thing
Than to curse all the dead men of my race,

To make him merry—lengthen not thy face,
For thou shalt tell him therewithal, that I
Will do him service well and faithfully
As a free man may do; else let him take
What he can get of me for his God's sake."

Silence there was about him at this word,
Except that Bodli muttered in his beard:
"Now certainly a good reward we have,
In that we cast away what fortune gave,
Yet doubtless shall our names be bruited far
When we are dead—then, too, no longings are
For what we may not have."
So as he came
The man went, and e'en Kiartan now had blame
For his rash word. "What will ye, friends?" he said,
"The king is wise; his wrath will well be weighed;
He knoweth that we shall not fall for nought.
Should I speak soft?—why then should we be brought,
Unarmed belike, and helpless, one by one
Up to the bishop when the feast was done—
What, Kálf! thou say'st, aboard, and let us weigh?
Yes, and be overhauled ere end of day
By the king's longships—nay, friends, all is well;
And at the worst shall be a tale to tell
Ere all is o'er."
They hearkened, and cast fear
Aside awhile; for death had need be near
Unto such men for them to heed him aught.
So the time passed, and the king harmed them nought
And sent no message more to them, and they
Were lodged within the town, and day by day
Went here and there in peace, till Yule drew nigh.
And now folk said the feast would not pass by
Without some troubling of the ancient faith
At the king's hands, and war and ugly death
Drew round the season of the peace on earth
The angels sang of at that blessed birth.
Put whoso gloomed at tidings men might show,
It was not Kiartan; wary was he though,
And weighed men's speech well; and upon a day
He, casting up what this and that might say,
All Iceland folk into one place did call,
And when they were assembled in the hall,
Spake on this wise:
"Fair fellows, well ye know,
The saw that says, the wise saves blow by blow;
This king who lies so heavy on us here
Is a great man; his own folk hold him dear,
For he spares nought to them. Yet ye know well
That when his might on Hacon's fortune fell,

Great foes he left alive, and still they live.
Noble the man is; but yet who can give
Good fortune to his foe? and he must be,
Despite our goodwill, still our enemy.
I grudge it not, for noble seems the chance
The fortunes of a fair name to advance.
And so it may be, friends, that we shall free
The land this tide of the long tyranny
That Harald Fair-hair laid on it, and give
Unto all folk beneath just laws to live,
As in the old days—shortly let us go,
When time shall serve, and to king Olaf show
That death breeds death; I say not this same night,
But hold ye ever ready for the fight,
And shun the mead-horn: Yule is close anigh
And the king's folk will drink abundantly;
Then light the torch and draw the whetted sword!

A great man certes—yet I marked this word
Said by his bishop—many words he made
About a matter small if rightly weighed—
To die is gain—this king and I, and ye
Are young for that, yet so it well may be:
Some of us here are deemed to have done well;
How shall it be when folk our story tell
If we die grey-haired? honour fallen away,
Good faith lost, kindness perished—for a day
Of little pleasure mingled with great pain—
So will we not unto the Gods complain
Or draw our mouths awry with foolish hate,
This king and I, if 'neath the hand of fate
Sword to sword yet we meet: hearken once more—
It seems the master of this new-found lore
Said to his men once, Think ye that I bring
Peace upon earth? nay but a sword—O king,
Behold the sword ready to meet thy sword!"

Out sprang his bright steel at that latest word,
And bright the weapons glittered round about,
And the roof shook again beneath their shout;
But only Bodli, silent, pensive, stood,
As though he heeded nought of bad or good
In word or deed. But Kiartan, flushed and glad,
Noted him not, for whatso thought he had,
He deemed him ever ready in the end
To follow after as himself should wend.
Howso that was, now were these men at one,
That e'en as Kiartan bade it should be done,
And the king set on, ere on them he fell;
So then to meat they gat and feasted well;
But the next morn espial should be made

How best to do the thing that Kiartan bade.

The next morn came, and other news withal,
For by a messenger the king did call
The Icelanders to council in his house,
Bidding them note, that howso valorous
They might be, still but little doubt there was
That lightly he might bring their end to pass
If need should drive him thereto. "Yet," said he,
"Fain would I give you peace, though certainly
This tide but one of two things must ye choose,
Either nought else but life itself to lose,
Or else to come and hearken to my words
In the great hall whereas I see my lords."

Kiartan gazed round about when this was said,
Smiling beneath a frown, his face flushed red
With wrath and shame. "Well," said he, "we are caught—
The sluggards' counsel morning brings to nought.
What say ye, shall we hold the feast at home?
Hearken, the guests get ready! shall they come?"

For as he spake upon the wind was borne
Unto their ears the blast of a great horn,
And smiled the messenger, and therewithal
Down from the minster roar of bells did fall,
Rung back and clashing; thereon Bodli spake:

"Thou and I, cousin, for our honour's sake,
May be content to die; but what of these?
Thy part it is to bring us unto peace
If it may be; then, if the worst befall,
There can we die too, as in Atli's Hall
The Niblungs fell; nor worser will it sound
That thus it was, when we are underground,
And over there our Gudrun hears the tale."

Silent sat Kiartan, gazing on the pale
Set face of Bodli for a while, then turned
Unto his silent folk, and saw they yearned
For one chance more of life.
"Go, man," he said,
And tell thy king his will shall be obeyed
So far as this, that we will come to him;
But bid him guard with steel, head, breast, and limb,
Since as we come, belike, we shall not go,
And who the end of words begun can know.
Ho, friends! do on your war-gear! Fear ye not,
Since two good things to choose from have ye got:
Peace, or a famed death!"
Then with both his ears

Ringing with clink of mail and clash of spears
The messenger went forth upon his way;
And the king knew by spies, the wise ones say,
What counsel Kiartan gave his folk that eve,
And had no will in such great hands to leave
His chance of life or death. Now, armed at last,
The men of Iceland up the long street passed,
And saw few men there; wives and children stood
Before the doors to gaze, or in his hood
An elder muttered, as they passed him by,
Or sad-eyed maids looked on them longingly.
So came they to the great hall of the king,
And round about the door there stood a ring
Of tall men armed, and each a dreaded name;
These opened to them as anigh they came,
And then again drew close, and hemmed them in,
Nor spared they speech or laughter, and the din
Was great among them as all silently
The men of Herdholt passed the door-posts by.
Then through the hall's dusk Kiartan gazed, and saw
Small space whereby his company might draw
Nigh to the king, for there so thick men stood
That their tall spears were like a wizard's wood.
Now some way from the daïs must they stand
Where sat the king, and close to his right hand
The German bishop, but no heed at all
The king gave to our folk, as down the hall
His marshal cried for silence, and the din
Being quite appeased, in a clear voice and thin
The holy man 'gan to set forth the faith;
But for these men brought nigh the gate of Death,
Hard was it now to weigh the right and wrong
Of what he said, that seemed both dull and long.
So when at last he came unto an end,
Uprose the king, and o'er the place did send
A mighty voice: "Now have ye heard the faith,
And what the High God through his servant saith;
This is my faith: what say ye to it, then?"

Uprose a great shout from King Olaf's men,
And clash of tossing spears, and Bodli set
His hand upon his sword, while Kiartan yet
Stood still, and, smiling, eyed the king: and he
Turned on him as the din fell:
"What say ye,
What say ye, Icelanders? thou specially?
I call thee yet a year too young to die,
Son of my namesake; neither seem'st thou such
As who would trust in Odin overmuch,
Or pray long prayers to Thor, while yet thy sword
Hangs by thy side."

Now at the king's first word
Down Kiartan stooped, and 'gan his shoe to lace,
And a dumb growl went through the crowded place
Like the far thunder while the sky is bright;
But when he rose again and stood upright
The king cried out:
"Which man of these is he
Who counselled you to slay no man but me
Amid my guards?"
Kiartan stood forth a space;
And said: "E'en so, O king, thou biddst him face
Of his own will, the thing that all men fear,
Swift death and certain—king, the man is here,
And in his own land, Kiartan Olafson
Men called him—pity that his days are done,
For fair maids loved him."
As he said the word
From out its sheath flamed forth the rover's sword,
And Bodli was beside him, and the hall
Was filled with fury now from wall to wall,
And back to back now stood the Herdholt band,
Each with his weapon gleaming in his hand.

Then o'er the clamour was the king's voice heard;
"Peace, men of mine, too quickly are ye stirred!
Do ye not see how that this man and I
Alone of men still let our sharp swords lie
Within their sheaths? Wise is the man to know
How troublous things among great men will go.
Speak, Kiartan Olafson! I offer thee
That in my court here thou abide with me,
Keeping what faith thou wilt; but let me deal
To these thy fellows either bane or weal,
As they shall do my bidding."
"Kinglike then,"
Said Kiartan, "dost thou speak about these men;
Yea, like a fool, who knowest not the earth,
And what things thereon bring us woe or mirth;
No man there is of these but calls me friend;
Yea, and if all truth but this truth should end,
And sire, and love, and all were false to me,
Still should I look on my right hand to see
Bodli the son of Thorleik—Come, then, death,'
Thy yokefellow am I."
Then from his sheath
Outsprang his sword, and even therewithal
Clear rang the Iceland shout amidst the hall,
And in a short space had the tale been o'er,
But therewith Olaf stilled the noise once more,
And smiling said;
"Thou growest angry, man!

Content thee, thou it was the strife began,
And now thou hast the best of it; come, then,
And sit beside me; thou and thy good men
Shall go in peace—only, bethink thee how
In idle poet's lies thou needst must trow—
Make no delay to take me by the hand,
Not meet it is that 'neath me thou shouldst stand."

To Kiartan's face, pale erst with death, there rose
A sudden flush, and then his lips, set close,
And knitted brow, grew soft, and in his eyes
There came at first a look of great surprise,
Then kind they grew, and with shamefaced smile
He looked upon the king a little while,
Then slowly sank his sword, and, taking it
By the sharp point, to where the king did sit
He made his way, and said:
"Nay, thou hast won;
Do thou for me what no man yet has done,
And take my sword, and leave me weaponless:
And if thy Christ is one who e'en can bless
An earthly man, or heed him aught at all,
On me too let his love and blessing fall;
But if nor Christ, nor Odin help, why, then
Still at the worst are we the sons of men,
And will we, will we not, yet must we hope,
And after unknown happiness must grope,
Since the known fails us, as the elders say;
Though sooth, for me, who know no evil day,
Are all these things but words."
"Put back thy blade,"
The king said, "thereof may I be apaid,
With thee to wield it for me; and now, come,
Deem of my land and house e'en as thy home,
For surely now I know that this thy smile
The heart from man or maid can well beguile."

As the king spake, drew Bodli nigh the place,
And a strange look withal there crossed his face;
It seemed he waited as a man in dread
What next should come; but little Kiartan said
Save thanks unto the king, and gayer now
Than men had seen him yet, he 'gan to grow.
Then gave the king command, and presently
All strife was swallowed of festivity,
And in all joyance the time slipped away,
And a fair ending crowned a troublous day.

Great love there grew 'twixt Kiartan and the king
From that time forth, and many a noble thing
Was planned betwixt them; and ere Yule was o'er

White raiment in the Minster, Kiartan bore,
And he and his were hallowed at the font.

Now so I deem it is, that use and wont,
The lords of men, the masks of many a face,
Raising the base perchance, somewhat abase
Those that are wise and noble; even so
O'er Kiartan's head as day by day did go,
Worthier the king's court, and its ways 'gan seem
Than many a thing whereof he erst did dream,
And gay he grew beyond the wont of men.
Now with the king dwelt Ingibiorg as then,
His sister; unwed was she, fair of face,
Beloved and wise, not lacking any grace
Of mind or body: Often it befell
That she and Kiartan met, and more than well
She 'gan to love him; and he let her love,
Saying withal, that nought at all might move
His heart from Gudrun; and for very sooth
He might have held that word; but yet for ruth.
And a soft pleasure that he would not name
All unrebuked he let her soft eyes claim
Kindness from his; and surely to the king
This love of theirs seemed a most happy thing,
And to himself he promised merry days,
And had in heart so Kiartan's state to raise
That he should be a king too.
But meanwhile,
Silent would Bodli go, without a smile
Upon his sad changed face from morn to eve;
And often now the thronged hall would he leave
To wander by the borders of the sea,
Waiting, half dreading, till some news should free
The band of Icelanders; most wearily
Month after month to him the days dragged by.

For ye shall know that the king looked for news
Whether the folk of Iceland would refuse,
At the priest Thangbrand's word, to change their faith.
A man of violence, the story saith,
A lecher, and a manslayer—tidings came
While yet the summer at its height did flame,
And Thangbrand brought it; little could he do,
Although indeed two swordsmen stout he slew,
Unto the holy faith folk's hearts to turn.
Hall of the Side, as in the tale we learn,
Gizur the White, and Hialti Skeggison,
With some few others, to the faith were won,
The most of men little these things would heed,
And some were furious heathens; so, indeed,
To save his life he had to flee away.

Wroth was the king hereat, and now would stay
The Iceland ships from sailing; little fain
Was Kiartan yet to get him back again,
Since he, forgetting not the former days—
It might be—passed his life fulfilled of praise,
And love, and glory. So the time went on,
Gizur the White and Hialti Skeggison,
Fleeing from Iceland, in the autumn-tide
Came out to Norway with the king to bide
Until the summer came, when they should go
Once more the truth of Christ's fair lore to show.
Long ago now of Gudrun and her ways,
And of the coming of those happy days
That were to be, had Kiartan ceased to speak
Unto his friend; who sullen now and weak,
Weary with waiting, faint with holding back
He scarcely knew from what, did surely lack
Some change of days if yet he was to live.
Tidings the new comers to him did give
From Laxdale, speaking lightly of the thing
That like a red-hot iron hand did wring
His weary heart; Gudrun was fair and well,
And still at Bathstead in good hope did dwell
Of Kiartan's swift return. That word or two,
That name, wrought in him, that at last he knew
His longing, and intent; and desolate
The passing of the days did he await,
Torn by remorse, tortured by fear, lest yet
Kiartan the lapse of strange days should forget,
And take to heart the old familiar days,
And once more turn him to the bygone ways
Where they were happy—but his fear was vain,
For if his friend of Iceland had been fain
Scarce had he gone; the king would keep him there
A pledge with other three, till he should hear
What thing the Icelanders this time would do,
Nor, as we said, had he good will to go
Whatso his power was: for so far things went
With Ingibiorg, that folk with one consent
Named her his bride that was to be, and said,
That sure a nobler pair were never wed.

And so the time passed, till the day came round
When at the quay the ships lay Iceland-bound,
And Bodli went to bid his friend farewell,
Flushed and bright-eyed, for wild hope, sooth to tell,
Had striven with shame, and cast its light on love,
Until a fairer sky there seemed above,
A fairer earth about, and still most fair
The fresh green sea that was to bring him there,
Whereon his heart was set.

"O gay! O gay!"
Said Kiartan, "thou art glad to go away;
This is the best face I have seen on thee
Since first our black oars smote the Burgfirth sea."

But as he spake a dark flush and a frown
Swallowed up Bodli's smile; he cast adown
His eager eyes: "Thou art as glad to stay,
Belike," he said, "as I to go away.
What thinkest thou I plot against thee then?"

"Thou art the strangest of the sons of men,"
Said Kiartan, with a puzzled look. "Come now,
Leave off thy riddles, clear thy troubled brow,
And let me think of thee as in time past,
When ever a most merry lad thou wast!
Why talkest thou of plotting? True and leal
I deem thee ever as the well-tried steel
That hangs beside thee; neither cross at all
Our fond desires. Though whatso thing may fall
Still shall I trust thee."
His own face grew grave
As o'er his heart there swept a sudden wave
Of the old thoughts. But Bodli said, "O friend,
Forgive my face fair looks and foul; I wend
Back to our kin and land, that gladdens me.
I leave thee here behind across the sea,
That makes me sad and sour."
He did not raise
His eyes up midst his words, or meet the gaze
Kiartan bent on him, till again he said:
"Olaf shall hear of all the goodlihead
Thou gainest here. Thy brethren shall be glad
That thou such honour from all men hast had.
Oswif the Wise no doubt I soon shall see—
What shall I say to him?"
Then steadily
Gazed Kiartan on him. "Tell Gudrun all this
Thou knowest of, my honour and my bliss;
Say we shall meet again!"
No more they spake,
But kissed and parted; either's heart did ache
A little while with thought of the old days;
Then Bodli to the future turned his gaze,
Unhappy and remorseful, knowing well
How ill his life should go whate'er befell.
But Kiartan, left behind, being such a man
As through all turns of fortune never can
Hold truce with fear or sorrow, lived his life
Not ill content with all the change and strife.

Fair goes the ship that beareth out Christ's truth,
Mingled of hope, of sorrow, and of ruth,
And on the prow Bodli the Christian stands,
Sunk deep in thought of all the many lands
The world holds, and the folk that dwell therein,
And wondering why that grief and rage and sin
Was ever wrought; but wondering most of all
Why such wild passion on his heart should fall.

Bodli Brings Tidings to Bathstead

Now so it chanced, on a late summer day,
Unto the west would Oswif take his way
With all his sons, and Gudrun listlessly
Stood by the door their going forth to see,
Until the hill's brow hid them; then she turned,
And long she gazed, the while her full heart yearned
Toward Herdholt and the south.
"Late grows the year,"
She said, "and winter cometh with its fear
And dreams of dying hopes. Ah me, I change,
And my heart hardens! Will he think me strange
When he beholds this face of mine at last,
Or shall our love make nought of long days past,
Burn up the sights that we apart have seen,
And make them all as though they had not been?
Ah, the hard world! I, who in hope so sure
Have waited, scarcely may the days endure.
How has it been with those who needs must wait
With dying hope and lingering love, till hate,
The seed of ill lies, told and hearkened to,
The knot of loving memories shall undo,
Break the last bonds of love, and cast them forth
With nothing left to them of joy or worth?

"O love, come back, come back, delay no more
To ease thine aching heart that yearneth sore
For me, as mine for thee! Leave wealth and praise
For those to win who know no happy days.
Come, though so true thou art, thou fearest not
Yet to delay! Come, my heart waxes hot
For all thy lonely days to comfort thee."

So spake she, and awhile stood quietly,
Still looking toward the south, her wide grey eyes
Made tenderer with those thronging memories,
Until upon the wind she seemed to hear
The sound of horse-hoofs, and 'twixt hope and fear
She trembled, as more clear the far sounds grew,

And thitherward it seemed from Herdholt drew;
So now at last to meet that sound she went,
Until her eyes, on the hill's brow intent,
Beheld a spear rising against the sky
O'er the grey road, and therewith presently
A gilded helm rose up beneath the spear,
And then her trembling limbs no more might bear
Her body forward; scarce alive she stood,
And saw a man in raiment red as blood
Rise o'er the hill's brow, who when he did gain
The highest part of the grey road, drew rein
To gaze on Bathstead spreading 'neath him there,
Its bright vanes glittering in the morning air.,
She stared upon him panting, and belike
He saw her now, for he his spurs did strike
Into his horse, and, while her quivering face
Grew hard and stern, rode swiftly to the place
Whereas she stood, and clattering leapt adown
Unto the earth, and met her troubled frown
And pale face, with the sad imploring eyes
Of Bodli Thorleikson.

Then did there rise
A dreadful fear within her heart, for she
No look like that in him was wont to see;
Scarce had she strength to say:
"How goes it then,
With him—thy kinsman, mid the Eastland men?"

Then, writhen as with some great sudden sting
Of pain, he spake; "Fear not, Gudrun, I bring
Fair news of his well-doing—he is well."

"Speak out," she said, "what more there is to tell!
Is he at Herdholt? will he come to-day?"

And with that word she turned her face away,
Shamed with the bitter-sweet of yearning pain,
And to her lips the red blood came again;
But he a moment made as he would reach
His hand to hers, his sad eyes did beseech
Some look from hers, so blind to him, so blind!
And scarce his story might he call to mind,
Until he deemed he saw her shoulders heave
As with a sob.

Then said he, "We did leave
Kiartan in Norway, praised of all men there;
He bade me tell thee that his life was fair
And full of hope—and that he looked to see
Thy face again.—So God be good to me,

These were the words he spake!"
For now she turned
Tearless upon him, and great anger burned
Within her eyes: "O trusty messenger,
No doubt through thee his very voice I hear!
Sure but light thought and stammering voice he had
To waste on one, who used to make him glad!
Thou art a true friend! Ah, I know thee, then,
A follower on the footsteps of great men,
To reap where they have sowed. Alive and well!
And doing deeds whereof the skalds shall tell!
Ah, what fair days he heapeth up for me!
Come now, unless thine envy stayeth thee,
Speak more of him, and make me glad at heart!"

Then Bodli said, "Nay, I have done my part,
Let others tell the rest "—and turned to go,
Yet lingered, and she cried aloud:
"No, no,
Friend of my lover! if ill words I spake
Yet pardon me! for sore my heart doth ache
With pent-up love."
She reached her hand to him,
He turned and took it, and his eyes did swim
With tears for him and her; a while it seemed,
As though the dream so many a sweet night dreamed,
Waked from with anguish on so many a morn,
Were come to pass, that he afresh was born
To happy life, with heavens and earth made new;
But slowly from his grasp her hand she drew,
And stepped aback, and said:
"Speak, I fear not,
Because so true a heart my love hath got
That nought can change it; speak, when cometh he?
Tell me the sweet words that he spake of me,
Did he not tell me in the days agone,
That oft he spake of me to thee alone?
Nay, tell me of his doings, for indeed
Of words 'twixt him and me is little need."

Then Bodli 'gan in troubled voice to tell
True tidings of the things that there befell,
Saving of Ingibiorg, and Gudrun stood
And hearkened, trembling:
"Good, yea, very good,"
She said, when he had done, "and yet I deem
All this thou say'st as if we dreamed a dream
Nor cam'st thou here to say but this to me—
Why tarrieth Kiartan yet beyond the sea?"

Bodli flushed red, and, trembling sorely, spake:

"O Gudrun, must thou die for one man's sake,
So heavenly as thou art? What shall I say?
Thou mayst live long, yet never see the day
That bringeth Kiartan back unto this land."

He looked at her, but moveless did she stand,
Nor spake a word, nor yet did any pain
Writhe her fair face, grown deadly pale again.
Then Bodli stretched his hand forth;
"Yet they lie,
Who say I did the thing, who say that I,
E'en in my inmost heart, have wished for it.
But thou—O, hearken, Gudrun—he doth sit
By Ingibiorg's side ever; day by day,
Sadder his eyes grow when she goes away—
What! know I not the eyes of lovers then?—
Why should I tell thee of the talk of men,
Babbling of how he weds her, is made king,
How he and Olaf shall have might to bring
Denmark and England both beneath their rule.
—Ah, woe, woe, woe, that I, a bitter fool,
Upon one heart all happy life should stake;
Woe is me, Gudrun, for thy beauty's sake!
Ah, for my fool's eyes and my greedy heart
Must all rest henceforth from my soul depart?"

He reached his hand to her, she put it by,
And gathered up her gown-skirts hurriedly,
And in a voice, like a low wailing wind,
Unto the wind she cried:
"Still may he find
A woman worthy of his loveliness;
Still may it be that she his days will bless,
As I had done, had we been wed at last!"

Therewith by Bodli's trembling hands she passed,
Nor gave one look on him; but he gazed still,
E'en when her gown fluttered far down the hill,
With staring eyes upon the empty place
Where last he saw the horror of her face
Changed by consuming anguish; when he turned,
Blind with the fire that in his worn heart burned,
Empty the hill-side was of anyone,
And as a man who some great crime hath done
He gat into his saddle, and scarce knew
Whither he went, until his rein he drew
By Herdholt porch, as in the other days,
When Kiartan by his side his love would praise.

Three days at Herdholt in most black despair
Did Bodli sit, till folk 'gan whisper there

That the faith-changer on the earth was dead,
Although he seemed to live; with mighty dread
They watched his going out and coming in;
On the fourth day somewhat did hope begin
To deal, as its wont is, with agony;
And he, who truly at the first could see
What dreadful things his coming days did wait,
Now, blinded by the hand of mocking fate,
Deeming that good from evil yet might rise,
Once more to pleasure lifted up his eyes.
And now, to nurse his hope, there came that day
A messenger from Gudrun, who did pray
That he would straightly come and see her there.
At whose mazed face a long while did he stare
As one who heard not, and the man must speak
His message thrice, before a smile 'gan break
Over his wan face; neither did he say
A word in answer, but straight took his way
O'er rough and smooth to Bathstead, knowing not
What ground his horse beneath his hoofs had got.

Ah, did he look for pleasure, when he saw
Her long slim figure down the dusk hall draw
Unto his beating heart, as nobly clad
As in the days when all the three were glad?
Did he perchance deem that he might forget
The man across the sea? His eyes were wet
For pity of that heart so made forlorn,
But on his lips a smile, of pleasure born,
Played, that I deem perchance he knew not of,
As he reached out his hand to touch his love
Long ere she drew anigh. But now, when she
Was close to him, and therewith eagerly,
Trembling and wild-eyed, he beheld the face
He deemed e'en then would gladden all the place,
Blank grew his heart, and all hope failed in him,
And e'en the anguish of his love grew dim,
And poor it seemed, a thing of little price,
Before the gathered sorrow of her eyes.

But while, still trembling there, the poor wretch stood,
She spoke in a low voice that chilled his blood,
So worn and far away it seemed; "See now,
I sent for thee, who of all men dost know
The heart of him who once swore troth to me:
Kiartan, I mean, the son of Olaf, he
Who o'er the sea wins great fame as thou say'st—
That thou mayst tell again, why he doth waste
The tale of happy days that we shall have;
For death comes quickly on us, and the grave
Is a dim land whereof I know not aught."

As a grey dove, within the meshes caught,
Flutters a little, then lies still again
Ere wildly beat its wings with its last pain,
So once or twice her passion, as she spake,
Rose to her throat, and yet might not outbreak
Till that last word was spoken; then as stung
By pain on pain, her arms abroad she flung,
And wailed aloud; but dry-eyed Bodli stood
Pale as a corpse, and in such haggard mood,
Such helpless, hopeless misery, as one
Who first in hell meets her he hath undone.
Yet sank her wailing in a little while,
Through dreadful sobs to silence, and a smile,
A feeble memory of the courteous ways,
For which in days agone she won such praise,
Rose to her pale lips, and she spake once more
As if the passionate words, cast forth before,
Were clean forgotten, with that bitter wail:

"O, Bodli Thorleikson, of good avail
Thou ever art to me, and now hast come
Swiftly indeed unto a troubled home:
For ill at ease I am, and fain would hear
From thee who knowst him, why this looked-for year
Lacks Kiartan still."
He knew not what to say,
But she reached out her hand in the old way
And coldly palm met palm: then him she led
Unto a seat, and sat by him, and said:

"Yea, fain am I to hear the tale once more,
The shame and grief, although it hurt me sore;
Yea, from thee, Bodli; though it well may be
That he I trusted, too much trusted thee."

So great a burden on his spirit lay
He heeded not the last words she did say,
But in low measured speech began again
The story of the honour and the gain
That Kiartan had, and how his days went now;
She sat beside him, with her head bent low,
Hearkening, or hearkening not; but now when all
Was done, and he sat staring at the wall
Silent, and full of misery, then she said:

"How know I yet but thou the tale hast made,
Since many a moment do I think of now
In the old time before ye went, when thou
Wouldst look on me, as on him I should gaze
If he were here, false to the happy days?"

"A small thing," said he, "shall I strive with fate
In vain, or vainly pray against thy hate?
Would God I were a liar! that his keel
E'en now the sands of White-river did feel.
O Gudrun, Gudrun, thou shalt find it true!
Ah, God, what thing is left for me to do?"

Therewith he rose, and towards the hall-door went,
Nor heard her voice behind him, as she bent
O'er the tear-wetted rushes of the floor.
Sick-hearted was he when he passed the door,
Weary of all things, weary of his love,
And muttering to himself hard things thereof;
But when he reached the Herdholt porch again,
A heaven long left seemed that morn's bitter pain,
And one desire alone he had, that he
Once more anigh unto his love might be;
Honour and shame, truth, lies, and weal and woe,
Seemed idle words whose meaning none might know;
What was the world to him with all its ways,
If he once more into her eyes might gaze?
Again he saw her, not alone this tide,
But in the hall, her father by her side,
And many folk around: if like a dream
All things except her loveliness did seem,
Yet doubt ye not that evil shades they were;
A dream most horrible for him to bear,
That all his strength was fallen to weakness now,
That he the sweet repose might never know
Of being with her from all the world apart,
Eyes watching eyes, heart beating unto heart.
Cold was her face, not pensive as before,
And like a very queen herself she bore
Among the guests, and courteous was to all,
But no kind look on Bodli's face did fall,
Though he had died to gain it.

So time wore,
And still he went to Bathstead more and more,
And whiles alone, and whiles in company,
With raging heart her sad face did he see,
And still the time he spent in hall and bower
Beside her did he call the evillest hour
Of all the day, the while it dured; but when
He was away, came hope's ghost back again
And fanned his miserable longing, till
He said within himself that nought was ill
Save that most hideous load of loneliness.
Howso the time went, never rest did bless
His heart a moment; nought seemed good to him,

Not e'en the rest of death, unknown and dim.

And Kiartan came not, and what news came out
From Norway was a gravestone on such doubt
As yet might linger in the hearts of men,
That he perchance might see that land again.
And no more now spake Gudrun any word
Of Kiartan, until folk with one accord
Began to say, how that no little thing
It was, those two great strains of men to bring
Into alliance: "Pity though!" they said,
"That she to such a strange man should be wed
As Bodli Thorleikson of late hath grown!"

So sprung the evil crop by evil sown.

Kiartan's Farewell to Norway

Meanwhile to Kiartan far across the sea,
Unto all seeming, life went merrily;
Yet none the less the lapse of days would bring
Unto his frank heart something of a sting,
And Bodli's sad departing face and word,
Not wholly thrust out from his memory, stirred
Doubts of the changing days in Kiartan's mind,
And scarce amid his joyance might he find
The happy days he ever looked to have,
Till he were lying silent in his grave.
And somewhat more distraught now would he take
The gentle words that the king's sister spake,
And look into her eyes less fervently,
And less forget the world when she drew nigh,
And start and look around as her soft hand
Fell upon his, as though a ghost did stand
Anigh him, and he feared to hear it speak.
And Ingibiorg for her part, grown too weak
Against the love she had for him to strive,
Yet knew no less whither the days did drive
Her wasted life; and, seeing him as oft
As she might do, and speaking sweet and soft,
When they twain were together: smiling, too,
Though fast away the lovesome time did go,
Wept long through lonely hours, nor cast away
From out her heart thought of the coming day,
When all should be as it had never been,
And the wild sea should roll its waves between
His grey eyes and her weary useless tears.

But while she brooded o'er the coming years

Empty of love, and snatched what joy there was
Yet left to her, great tidings came to pass;
For late the summer after Bodli sailed,
News came, that now at last had Christ prevailed
In Iceland; that the Hill of Laws had heard
Sung through the clear air many a threatening word,
And seen the weapons gather for the fight;
Till Snorri's wiles, Hall's wisdom, Gizur's might,
And fears of many men, and wavering doubt
On the worse side, had brought it so about
That now Christ's faith was law to everyone:
The learned say, a thousand years agone
Since the cold shepherds in the winter night
Beheld and heard the angels' fresh delight.
King Olaf's heart swelled at such news as these,
Straightway he sent for the four hostages,
And bade them with good gifts to go their ways
If so they would; or stay and gather praise
And plenteous honour there; and as he spake
He glanced at Kiartan, and a smile did break
Across his kingly face, as who would say,
"Thou at the least wilt scarcely go away."
But Kiartan answered not the smile, but stood
Grave with deep thought, and troubled in his mood,
Until he saw his fellows looked that he
Should speak for all; then said he presently:

"Thanks have thou, King, for all that thou hast done
To us, and the great honour I have won
At thine hands here; yet be not angry, King,
If still we thank thee most for this one thing,
That here thou stay'st us not against our will;
Thicker is blood than water, say I still;
This is the third year since I left my kin
And land—and other things that dwell therein."

The king's face fell, and in sharp words and few
He answered: "Well, a gift I gave to you;
And will not take it back—Go, Kiartan, then,
And, if thou canst, find kinder, truer men,
And lovelier maids in thy land than in this!"

But Kiartan said, "King, take it not amiss!
Thou knowest I have ever said to thee,
That I must one day go across the sea;
Belike I shall come back upon a tide,
And show thee such a wonder of a bride
As earth holds not, nay nor the heavens, I deem."

"God send thee a good ending to thy dream;
Yet my heart cries that if thou goest from me,

Thy pleasant face I never more shall see;
Be merry then, while fate will have it so!"

So therewith unto high feast did they go,
And by the king sat Kiartan, and the day
'Twixt merry words and sad thoughts wore away.

Now were the ships got ready, and the wares
Drawn for long months past from the upland fairs
Were laid ashipboard. Kálf was skipper still
Of Kiartan's ship, for never had he will
To leave his side. Now restless Kiartan was,
And longed full sore for these last days to pass,
For in his heart there lurked a spark of fear,
Nor any word of Gudrun might he hear
From those who brought the news of change of faith,
Since nigh the fleet they dwelt, my story saith,
In the south country, and knew nought at all
Of what in Laxdale late had chanced to fall.

Now by their bridges lay the laden ships,
And he now at the last must see the lips
Of Ingibiorg grow pale with their farewell;
And sick at heart he grew, for, sooth to tell,
He feared her sorrow much, and furthermore
He loved her with a strange love very sore,
Despite the past and future. So he went
Sad-eyed amid the hall's loud merriment
Unto her bower on that last morn of all.
Alone she was, her head against the wall
Had fallen; her heavy eyes were shut when he
Stood on the threshold; she rose quietly,
Hearing the clash of arms, and took his hand,
And thus with quivering lips awhile did stand
Regarding him: but he made little show
Of manliness, but let the hot tears flow
Fast o'er his cheeks. At last she spake:
"Weep then!
If thou who art the kindest of all men
Must sorrow for me, yet more glad were I
To see thee leave my bower joyfully
This last time; that when o'er thee sorrow came,
And thought of me therewith, thou mightst not blame
My little love for ever saddening thee.
Love!—let me say love once—great shalt thou be,
Beloved of all, and dying ne'er forgot.
Farewell! farewell! farewell! and think thou not
That in my heart there lingers any hate
Of her who through these years for thee did wait,
A weary waiting—three long, long, long years,
Well over now; nay when of me she hears,

Fain were I she should hate me not. Behold,
Here is a coif, well wrought of silk and gold
By folk of Micklegarth, who had no thought
Of thee or me, and thence by merchants brought
Who perchance loved not. Is Gudrun too fair
To take this thing, a queen might long to wear?
Upon the day when on the bench ye sit,
Hand held in hand, crown her fair head with it,
And tell her whence thou hadst it. Ah, farewell,
Lest of mine eyes thou shouldst have worse to tell
Than now thou hast!"
Therewith she turned from him
And took the coif, wherein the gold was dim
With changing silken threads, the linen white
Scarce seen amid the silk and gold delight.
With hands that trembled little did she fold
The precious thing, and set its weight of gold
Within a silken bag; and then to his
She reached her hands, and in one bitter kiss
Tasted his tears, while a great wave of thought
Of what sweet things the changed years might have brought
Swept over her—and then she knew him gone,
And yet for all that scarcely felt more lone
Than for a many days past she had felt.
So with fixed eyes she drew into her belt
Her kirtle, and to this and that thing turned
With heart that ever for the long rest yearned.

Bearing that gift, but heeding not what thing
He had with him, came Kiartan to the king,
Who in the porch abode him, his great men
Standing around; then said he:
"Welcome then
This last day that I see thee; go we forth,
Fair lords, and see his ship's head greet the north,
For seldom from the north shall any come
Like unto him to greet us in our home."

So forth they went, and all the Iceland men
Gat them aboard, and skipper Kálf by then
Stood midway on the last bridge, while the king
'Gan say to Kiartan:
"Many a treasured thing
Had I laid down, O friend, to keep thee here,
But since the old thing still must be more dear
Than the new thing, to such men as thou art,
Now, with my goodwill, to thy love depart,
And leave me here the coming woes to meet
Without thee. May thy life be fair and sweet,
Nor yet drag on till present days are nought,
And all the past days a tormenting thought!

Take this last gift of me; a noble sword,
Which if thou dost according to my word,
Shall never leave thy side; for who can know
Ere all is o'er, how madly things may go?"

So Kiartan took the sword, and thanked the king,
With no light heart, for that and everything
That at his hands he had, and therewith crossed
The gangway; shoreward were the hawsers tossed,
The long sweeps smote the water, and the crew
Shouted their last farewell; the white sail drew,
'Twixt Norway and the stern, swept in the sea.

There stood the king, and long time earnestly
Looked on the lessening ship; then said at last,
As o'er his knitted brow his hand he passed:
"Go thy ways, Kiartan; great thou art indeed,
And great thy kin are, nathless shalt thou need
Stout heart enough to meet what waiteth thee
If aught mine eyes of things to come may see."

Kiartan Back in Iceland; Refna Comes into the Tale

Kiartan and Kálf in Burgfirth came aland
And raised their tents anigh unto the strand,
As in the summer-tide the fashion was
Of mariners, the while the news did pass
That they were come out, through the country-side,
And there awhile that summer would abide.
Now when to Herdholt did that tidings come,
Olaf and all his sons were gone from home:
So Kiartan saw them not at first, among
The folk that to the newcomers did throng;
Amidst the first of whom, he, none the less,
Noted his friend Gudmund of Asbiornsness,
Who to his sister Thurid now was wed,
And brought her with him; with all goodlihead
He greeted them, yet Kiartan deemed that they
Looked on him strangely; on the self-same day
Kálf's father, Asgeir, came, and brought with him
Refna, his daughter, fair of face and limb,
Dark-haired, great-eyed, and gentle: timidly
She gazed at Kiartan as he drew anigh
And gave her welcome.

Now as he began
To ask them news of this and that good man,
And how he fared, Thurid with anxious face
Came up to him, and drew him from the place,

Saying, "Come, talk with me apart awhile!"
He followed after with a puzzled smile,
Yet his heart felt as something ill drew near.
So, when they came where none their speech might hear,
Thurid turned round about on him, and said,
"Brother, amidst thy speech, I shook with dread
Lest .Gudrun's name from out thy lips should burst;
How was it then thou spak'st not of her first?"

Then Kiartan, trembling, said, "Indeed, I thought
That news of ill unasked would soon be brought—
Sister, what ails thee then—is my love dead?"

"Nay," Thurid stammered, "she is well—and wed."

"What!" cried out Kiartan, "and the Peacock's house?
I used to deem my brothers valorous,
My father a great man—and Bodli's sword,
Where was it midst this shame?"
Scarce was the word
Out of his lips, ere, looking on her face,
He turned and staggered wildly from the place,
Crying aloud, "O blind, O blind, O blind!
Where is the world I used to deem so kind,
So loving to me? O Gudrun, Gudrun,
Here I come back with all the honour won
We talked of, that thou saidst thou knewest well
Was but for thee—to whom then shall I tell
The tale of that well-doing? And thou, friend,
How might I deem that aught but death should end
Our love together? yea, and even now,
How shall I learn to hate thee, friend, though thou
Art changed into a shadow and a lie?
O ill day of my birth, ill earth and sky,
Why was I then bemocked with days of bliss
If still the ending of them must be this?
O wretch, that once wast happy, days a-gone,
Before thou wert so wretched and alone,
How on unhappy faces wouldst thou look
And scarce with scorn and ruth their sorrow brook!
Now then at last thou knowest of the earth,
And why the elders look askance on mirth."

Some paces had he gone from where she stood,
Gazing in terror on his hapless mood,
And now she called his name; he turned about,
And far away he heard the shipmen's shout
And beat of the sea, and from the down there came
The bleat of ewes; and all these, and his name,
And the sights too, the green down 'neath the sun,
The white strand and the far-off hill-sides dun,

And white birds wheeling, well-known things did seem,
But pictures now or figures in a dream,
With all their meaning lost. Yet therewithal
On his vexed spirit did the new thought fall
How weak and helpless and alone he was.
Then gently to his sister did he pass,
And spake:
"Now is the world clean changed for me
In this last minute, yet indeed I see
That still will it go on for all my pain;
Come then, my sister, let us back again;
I must meet folk, and face the life beyond,
And, as I may, walk 'neath the dreadful bond
Of ugly pain—such men our fathers were,
Not lightly bowed by any weight of care."

She smiled upon him kindly, and they went
And found folk gathered in the biggest tent,
And busied o'er the wares, and gay enow
In outward seeming; though ye well may know
Folk dreaded much for all the country's sake
In what wise Kiartan this ill news would take.
Now Kálf had brought the gayest things to show
The women-folk, and by a bale knelt now
That Kiartan knew right well, and close by him
Sat Refna, with her dainty hand and slim
Laid on a broidered bag, her fair head crowned
With that rich coif thereafter so renowned
In Northland story. As he entered there
She raised to him her deep grey eyes, and fair
Half-opened mouth, and blushed blood-red therewith;
And inwardly indeed did Kiartan writhe
With bitter anguish as his eyes did meet
Her bright-flushed gentle face so pure and sweet;
And he thenceforth to have no lot or part
In such fair things; yet struggling with his heart
He smiled upon her kindly. Pale she grew
When the flush passed, as though in sooth she knew
What sickness ailed him.
"Be not wroth," she said,
"That I have got this queen's gift on my head,
I bade them do it not."
Then wearily
He answered: "Surely it beseemeth thee
Right well, and they who set it there did right.
Rich were the man who owned the maiden bright,
And the bright coif together!"
As he spake
Wandered his eyes; so sore his heart did ache
That not for long those matters might he note;
Yet a glad flush again dyed face and throat

Of Refna, and she said, "So great and famed,
So fair and kind! where shall the maid be named
To say no to thine asking?"
Once again
All pale she grew, for stung by sudden pain
Kiartan turned round upon the shrinking maid,
And, laughing wildly, with a scowl he said:
"All women are alike to me—all good—
All blessings on this fair earth by the rood!"

Then silence fell on all, yet he began
Within awhile to talk to maid and man
Mildly as he was wont, and through the days
That they abode together in that place
Seemed little changed; and so his father thought
When he to him at last his greeting brought,
And bade him home to Herdholt. So they rode,
Talking of many things, to his abode,
Nor naming Gudrun aught. Thus Kiartan came
Back to his father's house, grown great of fame,
And tidingless a while day passed by day
What hearts soe'er 'neath sorrow's millstone lay.

Tidings Brought to Bathstead of Kiartan's Coming Back

Yes, there the hills stood, there Lax-river ran
Down to the sea; still thrall and serving-man
Came home from fold and hayfield to the hall,
And still did Olaf's cheery deep voice call
Over the mead horns; danced the fiddle-bow,
And twanged the harp-strings, and still sweet enow
Were measured words, as someone skilled in song
Told olden tales of war, and love, and wrong.
And Bodli's face from hall and board was gone,
And Gudrun's arms were round him, as alone
They lay, all unrebuked that hour, unless
The dawn, that glimmered on the wretchedness
Of Kiartan's lone and sleepless night, should creep
Cold-footed o'er their well-contented sleep,
And whisper, 'Sleep on, lapse of time is here
Death's brother, and the very Death is near!'

Such thoughts might haunt the poor deserted man,
When through the sky dawn's hopeless shiver ran,
And bitterness grew in him, as the day,
Cleared of fantastic half-dreams, cold and grey,
Was bared before him. Yet I deem, indeed,
That they no less of pity had good need.
Yea, had his eyes beheld that past high-tide

At Bathstead, where sat Gudrun as a bride
By Bodli Thorleikson! Her face of yore,
So swift to change, as changing thoughts passed o'er
Her eager heart, set now into a smile
That scarce the fools of mankind might beguile
To deeming her as happy: his, once calm
With dreamy happiness, that would embalm
Into sweet memory things of yesterday,
And show him pictures of things far away,
Now drawn, and fierce, and anxious, still prepared
It seemed, to meet the worst his worn heart feared.
A dismal wedding! every ear at strain
Some sign of things that were to be to gain;
A guard on every tongue lest some old name
Should set the poisoned smouldering pile aflame.
Silent the fierce dull sons of Oswif drank,
And Olaf back into his high seat shrank,
And seemed aged wearily, the while his sons
Glanced doubtfully at Bodli; more than once
Did one of them begin some word to speak,
And catch his father's eye, and then must break
His speech off with a smile not good or kind;
And in meanwhile the wise would fain be blind
To all these things, or cover boisterously
The seeds of ill they could not fail to see.

But if 'neath all folk's eyes things went e'en so,
How would it be then with the hapless two
The morrow of that feast? This know I well,
That upon Bodli the last gate of hell
Seemed shut at last, and no more like a star
Far off perchance, yet bright however far,
Shone hope of better days; yet he lived on,
And soon indeed, the worst of all being won,
And gleams of frantic pleasure therewithal,
A certain quiet on his soul did fall,
As though he saw the end and waited it.
But over Gudrun changes wild would flit,
And sometimes stony would she seem to be;
And sometimes would she give short ecstasy
To Bodli with a fit of seeming love;
And sometimes, as repenting sore thereof,
Silent the live-long day would sit and stare,
As though she knew some ghost were drawing near,
And ere it carne with all the world must break,
That she might lose no word it chanced to speak.

So slowly led the changed and weary days
Unto the gateway of the silent place,
Where either rest or utter change shall be;
But on an eve, when summer peacefully

Yielded to autumn, as men sat in hall
Two wandering churles old Oswif forth did call
Into the porch, and asked for shelter there.
And since unheeded none might make such prayer,
Soon 'mid the boisterous house-carles were they set,
The ugly turns of fortune to forget
In mirth and ease, and still with coarse rude jest
They pleased the folk, and laughed out with the best.
But while the lower hall of mirth was full
More than their wont the great folk there were dull;
Oswif was sunk in thought of other days,
And Gudrun's tongue idly some tale did praise
Her brother Ospak told, the while her heart
Midst vain recurring hopes was set apart;
And Bodli looked as though he still did bide
The coming fate it skilled no more to hide
From his sore wearied heart: no more there were
Upon the dais that eve; but when the cheer
Was over now, old Oswif went his ways,
But Ospak sat awhile within his place
Staring at Bodli with a look of scorn;
For much he grew to hate that face forlorn,
Bowed down with cares he might not understand.

At last midst Gudrun's talk, with either hand
Stretched out did Ospak yawn, and cried aloud
Unto the lower table's merry crowd:
"Well fare ye, fellows! ye are glad to-night;
What thing is it that brings you such delight?
We be not merry here."
Then one stepped forth,
And said: "Sooth, Ospak, but of little worth
Our talk was; yet these wandering churles are full
Of meat and drink, and need no rope to pull
Wild words and gleesome from them."
"Bring them here,"
Said Ospak, "they may mend our doleful cheer."

So from the lower end they came, ill clad,
Houseless, unwashen, yet with faces glad,
If for a while; yet somewhat timorous, too,
With such great men as these to have to do,
Although to fear was drink a noble shield.

"Well, fellows, what fair tidings are afield?"
Said Ospak, "and whence come ye?"
The first man
Turned leering eyes on Bodli's visage wan,
And o'er his face there spread a cunning grin.
But just as he his first word would begin,
The other, drunker, and a thought more wise

Maybe for that, said, screwing up his eyes,
"Say-all-you-know shall go with clouted head."

"Say-nought-at-all is beaten," Ospak said,
"If, with his belly full of great men's meat
He has no care to make his speeches sweet."

"Be not wrath, son of Oswif," said the first;
"Now I am full I care not for the worst
That haps to-night; yet Mistress Gudrun there—"

"Tush!" said the second, "thou art full of care
For a man full of drink. Come, let her say
That as we came so shall we go away,
And all is soon told."
Ospak laughed thereat,
As sprawling o'er the laden board he sat,
His cheek close to his cup; but Gudrun turned
Unto him, pale, although her vexed heart burned
With fresh desire, and a great agony
Of hope strove in her.
"Tell thy tale to me
And have a gift therefor," she said: "behold!
My finger is no better for this gold!
Draw it off swiftly!"
Then she reached her hand
Out to the man, who wondering there did stand
Beholding it, half sobered by her face;
Nor durst he touch the ring.
"Unto this place
From Burgfirth did we come," he said, "and there,
Around a new-beached ship folk held a fair—
Kálf Asgeirson, men said, the skipper was—
But others to and fro did I see pass."

Still Ospak chuckled, lolling o'er his drink,
Nor any whit hereat did Gudrun shrink,
But Bodli rose up, and the hall 'gan pace,
As on the last time when in that same place
Kiartan and he and she together were;
And on this day of anguish and of fear,
Well-nigh his weary heart began to deem
That that past day did but begin a dream
From which he needs must wake up presently,
Those lovers in each other's arms to see,
To feel himself heart-whole and innocent;
"Yea, yea, a many people came and went
About the ship," he heard the first guest say;
"Gudmund and Thurid did I see that day,
And Asgeir and his daughter, and they stood
About a man, whose kirtle, red as blood,

Was fine as a king's raiment."
Ospak here
Put up his left hand slowly to his ear,
As one who hearkens, smiling therewithal,
And now there fell a silence on the hall,
As the man said:
"I had not seen before
This fair tall man, who in his sword-belt bore
A wondrous weapon, gemmed, and wrought with gold;
Too mean a man I was to be so bold
As in that place to ask about his name.
—Yet certes, mistress, to my mind it came,
That, if tales lied not, this was even he
Men said should wed a bride across the sea
And be a king—e'en Kiartan Olafson."

He looked about him when his speech was done
As one who feareth somewhat, but the word
He last had said, nought new belike had stirred
In those three hearts; Bodli still paced the floor
With downcast eyes, that sometimes to the door
Were lifted; Ospak beat upon the board
A swift tune with his hand; without a word
The gold ring from her finger Gudrun drew
And gave it to the man; and Ospak knew
A gift of Bodli Thorleikson therein,
Given when first her promise he did win.
Yet little wisdom seemed it to those men
About the dais to abide as then,
Though one turned o'er his shoulder as he went,
And saw how Ospak unto Gudrun leant
And nodded head at Bodli, and meanwhile
Thrust his forefinger with a mocking smile
At his own breast; but Gudrun saw him not,
Though their eyes met, nay, rather scarce had got
A thought of Bodli in her heart, for still
'Kiartan come back again,' her soul did fill,
'And I shall see him soon, with what changed eyes!'

And now did night o'er the world's miseries
Draw her dark veil, yet men with stolen light
Must win from restless day a restless night;
Then Gudrun 'gan bestir her, with a smile
Talking of common things a little while,
For Bodli to his seat had come again
And sat him down, though labour spent in vain
It was to speak to him; dull the night went,
And there the most of men were well content
When bed-time came at last. Then one by one
They left the hall till Bodli sat alone
Within the high-seat. No thought then he had

Clear to himself, except that all was bad
That henceforth was to come to him; the night
Went through its changes, light waned after light,
Until but one was left far down the hall
Casting a feeble circle on the wall,
Making the well-known things as strange as death;
Then through the windows came the night's last breath,
And 'gainst the yellow glimmer they showed blue
As the late summer dawn o'er Iceland drew;
And still he sat there, noting nought at all
Till at his back he heard a light footfall,
And fell a-trembling, yet he knew not why;
Nor durst he turn to look, till presently
He knew a figure was beside him, white
In the half dusk of the departing night,
For the last light had died; therewith he strove
To cry aloud, and might not, his tongue clove
Unto his mouth, no power he had to stand
Upon his feet, he might not bring his hand,
How much soe'er he tried, to his sword's hilt;
It seemed to him his sorrow and his guilt
Stood there in bodily form before his eyes,
Yet, when a dreadful voice did now arise
He knew that Gudrun spake:
"I came again
Because I lay awake, and thought how men
Have told of traitors, and I needs must see
How such an one to-night would look to me.
Night hides thee not, O Bodli Thorleikson,
Nor shall death hide from thee what thou hast done.
—What!—thou art grown afraid, thou tremblest then
Because I name death, seed of fearless men?
Fear not, I bear no sword, Kiartan is kind,
He will not slay thee because he was blind
And took thee for a true man time a-gone.
—My curse upon thee! Knowst thou how alone
Thy deed hath made me? Dreamest thou what pain
Burns in me now when he has come again?
Now, when the longed-for sun has risen at last
To light an empty world whence all has passed
Of joy and hope—great is thy gain herein I
A bitter broken thing to seem to win,
A soul the fruit of lies shall yet make vile;
A body for thy base lust to defile,
If thou durst come anigh me any more,
Now I have curst thee, that thy mother bore
So base a wretch among good men to dwell,
That thou mightst build me up this hot-walled hell.
—I curse thee now, while good and evil strive
Within me, but if longer I shall live
What shall my curse be then? myself so curst,

That nought shall then be left me but the worst,
That God shall mock himself for making me."

Breathless she stopped, but Bodli helplessly
Put forth his hands till he gained speech, and said
In a low voice, "Would God that I were dead!
And yet a word from him I hope to have
Kinder than this before I reach the grave!"

"Yea, he is kind, yea, he is kind!" she cried,
"He loveth all, and casts his kindness wide
Even as God; nor loves me more than God
Loves one among us crawlers o'er earth's sod.
And who knows how I love him? how I hate
Each face on which he looks compassionate!
—God help me! I am talking of my love
To thee! and such a traitor I may prove
As thou hast, ere the tale is fully done."

She turned from him therewith to get her gone,
But lingered yet, as waiting till he spake.
Day dawned apace, the sparrows 'gan to wake
Within the eaves; the trumpet of the swan
Sounded from far; the morn's cold wind, that ran
O'er the hall's hangings, reached her unbound hair,
And drave the night-gear round her body fair,
And stirred the rushes by her naked feet:
Most fair she was—their eyes a while did meet,
In a strange look, he rose with haggard face
And trembling lips, that body to embrace,
For which all peace for ever he had lost,
But wildly o'er her head her arms she tossed,
And with one dreadful look she fled away
And left him 'twixt the dark night and the day,
'Twixt good and ill, 'twixt love and struggling hate,
The coming hours of restless pain to wait.

The Yule Feast at Bathstead

Now the days wore, and nowise Kiartan stirred,
Or seemed as he would stir, and no man heard
Speech from him of the twain, for good or ill;
Yet was his father Olaf anxious still,
And doubted that the smouldering fire might blaze,
For drearily did Kiartan pass his days
After a while, and ever silently
Would sit and watch the weary sun go by,
Feeling as though the heart in him were dead.

Kálf Asgeirson came to the Peacock's stead
With Refna, more than once that autumn-tide;
And at the last folk 'gan to whisper wide
That she was meet for him, if anyone
Might now mate Kiartan, since Gudrun was gone.
If Kiartan heard this rumour I know not,
But Refna heard it and her heart waxed hot
With foolish hopes; for one of those she was
Who seem across the weary earth to pass,
That they may show what burden folk may bear
Of unrequited love, nor drawing near
The goal they aim at, die amidst the noise
Of clashing lusts with scarce-complaining voice.
God wot that Kiartan in his bitter need
To her kind eyes could pay but little heed;
Yet did he note that she looked kind on him,
Nor yet had all his kindness grown so dim
That he might pass her by all utterly,
And thereof came full many a biting lie.
Now as the time drew on toward Yule once more,
Did Oswif send, as his wont was of yore,
To bid the men of Herdholt to the feast;
And howso things had changed, both most and least
'Gan make them ready, all but Kiartan, who
That morn went wandering aimless to and fro
Amid the bustling groups, and spake no word.
To whom came Olaf when thereof he heard,
And spake with anxious face: "O noble son,
Wilt thou still harbour wrath for what is done?
Nay, let the past be past; young art thou yet,
And many another honour mayst thou get,
And many another love."
                        Kiartan turned round,
And said, "Yea, good sooth, love doth much abound
In this kind world! Lo! one more loved my love
Than I had deemed of—thus it oft shall prove!"

So spake he sneering and high-voiced, then said,
As he beheld his father's grizzled head
And puckered brow: "What wouldst thou, father? see
Here in thy house do I sit quietly,
And let all folk live even suchlike life
As they love best; and wilt thou wake up strife?"

"Nay, nay, son; but thou knowest that thy mood,
So lonely here, shall bring thee little good;
Thy grief grows greater as thou nursest it,
Nor 'neath thy burden ever shalt thou sit
As it increases on thee; then shall come
A dreadful tale on this once happy home.
Come rather, show all men thou wilt have peace

By meeting them, and it shall bring thee ease,
That sight once over, to think how thou art
A brave man still, not sitting with crushed heart
Amid the stirring world."
Then Kiartan gazed
Long on his father, as a man amazed,
But said at last: "Ah, thou must have thy will!
God wot I looked that the long days would kill
This bitter longing, if unfed it were
By sights and sounds. Now let the long days bear
Their fated burden! I will go with thee."

So like a dreaming man did Kiartan see
That place which once seemed holy in his eyes;
No cry of fury to his lips did rise
When o'er the threshold first he went, and saw
Bodli the son of Thorleik towards him draw,
Blood-red for shame at first, then pale for shame,
As from his lips the old kind speeches came,
And hand met hand. Coldly he spake, and said:

"Be merry, Bodli; thou art nobly wed!
Thou hadst the toil, and now the due reward
Is fallen to thee."
Then, like a cutting sword,
A sharp pain pierced him, as he saw far off
Gudrun's grey eyes turn, with a spoken scoff,
To meet his own; and there the two men stood,
Each knowing somewhat of the other's mood,
Yet scarce the master-key thereto; still stared
Kiartan at Gudrun; and his heart grew hard
With his despair: but toward him Bodli yearned,
As one who well that bitter task had learned;
And now he reached once more to him his hand,
But moveless for a while did Kiartan stand,
And had in heart to get him back again:
Yet with strong will he put aback his pain,
And passed by Bodli, noting him no whit,
And coldly at the feast that day did sit,
In outward seeming; and Gudrun no less
Sat in her place in perfect loveliness,
Untouched by passion: Bodli in meanwhile
From Kiartan's grave brow unto Gudrun's smile
Kept glancing, and in feverish eager wise
Strove to pierce through the mask of bitter lies
That hid the bitter truth; and still must fear,
Lest from the feast's noise he a shriek should hear,
When the thin dream-veil, torn across, should show
That in the very hell he lay alow.

Men say that when the guests must leave the place,

Bodli with good gifts many a man did grace,
And at the last bade bring up to the door
Three goodly horses such as ne'er before
Had Iceland seen, and turned his mournful eyes
To Kiartan's face, stern with the memories
Of many a past departing, bitter-sweet,
And said:
"O cousin, O my friend, unmeet
Is aught that here I have, for thy great fame,
Yet if it please thee still to be the same
As thou hast been to us, take these of me."

But as men crowded round about to see
The goodly steeds, spake Kiartan in low voice:
"Strive not with fate, for thou hast made thy choice;
Thy gifts, thy love, may scarce now heal my heart—
—Look not so kind—God keep us well apart!"

No more they spake as then, but straightway rode
The Herdholt men unto their fair abode;
And so it fell that on the homeward way
'Gan Olaf to his well-loved son to say:

"Kiartan, howe'er the heart in thee did burn,
Unto no evil did this meeting turn;
Yet would that thou hadst taken gifts from him!
Now thou wilt go again?"
"My eyes are dim,
Belike, O father, with my bitter pain;
Yet doubt thou not but I shall go again,
E'en as I doubt not that fresh misery
I there shall gather as the days pass by.
Would I could tell thee all I think, and how
I deem thy wise hand dreadful seed doth sow!"

Kiartan Weds Refna

I think that Gudrun on the morrow morn
Deemed herself yet more wretched and forlorn
Than e'er before; I deem that Kiartan woke
And found it harder yet to bear the yoke
Than in past days—their eyes had met at last,
No look of anger from them had been cast
Sweet words might take away; no look of woe
A touch might turn to pleasure, none can know
But those who know the torturer Love, the bliss
That heals the stripes those bear who still are his.
Who knows what tale had been to tell, if she
Had met his first proud look all tearfully,

With weak imploring looks? Ah, sore she yearned
To cry aloud the things that in her burned,
To cast aside all fear and shame, and kneel
Before his feet, so she his lips might feel
Once more as in the old days; but, alas!
A wall of shame and wrong betwixt them was,
Nor could the past deeds ever be undone.
Sometimes it might be when they were alone
In quiet times—in evening twilight, when
Far off and softened came the voice of men;
Or, better yet, the murmur of the sea
Smote on the hearts of either peacefully,
Each to each kind would seem; until there came
The backward rush of pain and bitter blame
Unanswerable, cold, blighting, as the sea,
Let in o'er flowers—'Why didst thou so to me,
To me of all the world? while others strove
We looked to hold the sweetness of our love.
Yea, if earth failed beneath our feet—and now
How is the sweet turned bitter!—yea, and thou
Art just so nigh to me, that still thou art
A restless anguish to my craving heart.'

Take note too midst all this, that Gudrun heard
Rumoured about this added bitter word,
That Refna, Asgeir's daughter, looked to wear
The coif the Norway queen had meant for her,
When Kiartan left that broken heart behind;
For that tale too her hungry ears must find.
Then would she clean forget all other woe,
In thinking how she dreamed the days would go,
That while she waited doubting nought of him;
Then would the past and future wax all dim
In brooding o'er that unaccomplished bliss,
In moaning to herself, 'twixt kiss and kiss
The things she would have said, in picturing,
As in the hopeful time, how arms would cling
About her, and sweet eyes, unsatisfied
E'en with the fullness of all bliss, would hide
No love from her—and she forgot those eyes
What they were now, all dulled with miseries;
And she forgot the sorrow of the heart
That fate and time from hers had thrust apart.
Still wrong bred wrong within her, day by day
Some little speck of kindness fell away,
Till in her heart naked desire alone
Was left, the one thing not to be undone.
Then would the jealous flame in such wise burn
Within her, that to Bodli would she turn,
And madden him with fond caressing touch
And tender word; and he, worn overmuch

With useless striving, still his heart would blind,
Unto the dread awaking he should find.

Doubt not, that of this too had Kiartan heard,
If nought but idle babbling men had stirred,
But more there was; for the fierce-hearted fools,
The sons of Oswif, made these twain their tools
To satisfy their envious hate; for they
Waxed eviller-hearted as day followed day,
Grudging the Peacock's house its luck and fame;
And when into their household Bodli came,
In such wise as ye know, with hate and scorn,
Which still they had, of his grave face and worn,
A joy began to mingle presently,
A thought that they through him might get to see
Herdholt beneath their feet in grief and shame;
So cunningly they turned them to the game
As such men will, and scattered wide the seeds,
Lies, and words half-true, of the bitterest deeds.
For doubt not, kindly-natured though he were,
That Kiartan too was changing: who would hear
Such things as once he heard, from one who went
'Twixt the two houses, with no ill intent,
But blabbing and a fool, well stuffed with lies,
At Ospak's hands—for in most loving wise
The new-wed folk lived now, he said; soon too
He deemed would Bodli draw to him a crew,
And take ship for the southlands: "Nought at all
Was talked of last night in the Bathstead hall,
But about England and King Ethelred."

"Well, and was Gudrun merry?" Haldor said,
Yet stammered saying it, 'neath Kiartan's frown,
Who cleared his brow though, nor e'en looked adown
As the man answered, smiling, pleased to show
That he somewhat of great folk's minds did know:

"Yea, many, was she merry. Good cause why,
For she will go with Bodli certainly,
And win such fame as women love to do;
Ye well may wot he saith no nay thereto,
If she but ask him; they sat hand in hand
As if no folk were left in all the land
Except themselves."
                        He stayed his talk hereat,
For men looked strangely on him as he sat
Smiling and careless, casting words that bit
Like poisoned darts: no less did Kiartan sit
With unchanged face, nor rose to go away,
Yea, even strove within himself to say:
'Good luck go with them! mine she cannot be,

May she be happy, here, or over sea!
Why should I wish aught ill on them to fall.'

And yet, indeed, a flood of bitterest gall
Swept o'er his heart; despite himself he thought:
'So now, to lonely ways behold me brought,
She will not miss me more—so change the days,
And Bodli's loving looks and Bodli's praise
Shall be enough for her. I am alone,
And ne'er shall be aught else—would I were gone
From where none need me now—belike my fame
Shall be forgotten, wrapped in Bodli's name,
E'en as my kisses on the lips, that once
Trembled with longing through the change of suns—
Those years in Norway shall be blotted out
From song and story—yea, or men shall doubt
If I or Bodli there that praise did win—
What say I, for I deem that men begin
To doubt if e'er I loved my love at all!'

So thought he, mid the clamour of the hall,
Where few men knew his heart, but rather thought
That he began now somewhat to be brought
From out his gloom; withal, time wore away,
And certainly as day comes after day,
So change comes after change in minds of men;
So otherwise he 'gan to be, than when
In early days his pain, nigh cherished, clung
Unto his wounded heart; belike it stung
Bitterer at whiles, now that he knew his life,
And hardened him to meet the lingering strife
'Gainst the cold world that would not think of him
Too much. The kindness of old days waxed dim
Within his heart; he hearkened when men spake
Hard things about his love, for whose dear sake
Had fame once seemed so light a thing to win.
A blacker deed now seemed his fellow's sin
When lesser seemed the prize that it did gain;
Little by little from his bitter pain
Fell off the softening veil of tenderness;
Moody and brooding was he none the less,
And all the world, with all its good and ill,
Seemed nothing meet to move his sluggish will.
And now a whole long year had passed, since he
Stood wildered by the borders of the sea
'Neath his first sorrow. Herdholt late had seen
A noble feast, and thereat had there been
Among the guests Refna, the tender maid;
Gentle of mood, and pale, with head down-weighed
She sat amidst the feast; and Kiartan saw
That much she changed as he anigh did draw,

That her eyes brightened, and a sprightlier grace
Came o'er her lips, and colour lit her face.
And so when all the guests therefrom were gone,
Thurid, his sister, sat with him alone
Close upon sunset; thoughtful now was she,
He gayer than it was his wont to be,
And many things he spake to her; at last
The absent look from off her face she cast,
For she had listened little; and she said;
"Yea, brother, is she not a lovesome maid?"

He started, "Who?" he said, "I noted not."

She smiled, "Nay, then is beauty soon forgot;
Yet if I were a man, not old or wise,
Methinks I should remember wide grey eyes,
Lips like a scarlet thread, skin lily-white,
Round chin, smooth brow 'neath the dark hair's delight,
Fair neck, slim hands, and dainty limbs, well hid,
Since unto most of men doth fate forbid
To hold them as their own."
                            A dark cloud spread
O'er Kiartan's face: "Sister, forbear," he said;
"I am no lover, unto me but nought
Are these things grown."
                        Nigher her face she brought
To his, and said: "And yet were I a man,
And noted how the love of me began
To move within the heart of such a maid
As Refna is, not soon her face would fade
From out my memory."
                     "Nay, nay, thou sayst
Fools' words," he said, "and every word dost waste;
Who shall love broken men like unto me?"

And therewithal he sprang up angrily
And would be gone: she stayed him: "Were it so
That over well she loved; what wouldst thou do?"

"What should I do?" he said; "I have no heart
To give away, let her e'en act my part
And find the days right dreary, yet live on."

"Methinks," she said, "the end will soon be won
For her, poor maid! surely she waneth fast."

And Thurid sighed withal; but Kiartan passed
Swiftly away from her: and yet he went
Unto his bed that night less ill content,
And ere he slept, of Ingibiorg he thought,
And all the pleasure her sweet love had brought

While he was with her; and this maid did seem
Like her come back amidst a happy dream.
The next morn came, and through his dreariness
A sweet thought somewhat did his heart caress;
Howe'er he put it from him, back it came
Until it gathered shape, and took the name
Of pity, and seemed worthy to be nursed.
So wore the days, and life seemed not so cursed
With this to think of—this so set apart
From all the misery that wrung his heart;
Until the sweet ruth grew, until he deemed
That yet perchance her love was only dreamed,
That she was heart-whole, yea, or loved indeed
But for another man was in such need:
And at that thought blank grew the world again,
And his old pain was shot across with pain
As woof hides warp. Ah, well! what will you have?
This was a man some shreds of joy to save
From out the wreck, if so he might, to win
Some garden from the waste, and dwell therein.
And yet he lingered long, or e'er he told
His heart that it another name might hold
With that of the lost Gudrun. Time and sight
Made Refna's love clear as the noonday light;
Yea, nowise hard it was for him to think
That she without this joy would quickly sink
Into death's arms—and she, she to fade thus
God's latest marvel! eyes so piteous
With such sweet longing, midst her beauty rare,
As though they said, 'Nought worthy thee is here,
Yet help me if thou canst: yet, if I die,
Like sweet embalmment round my heart shall lie
This love, this love, this love I have for thee;
Look once again before thou leavest me!'

She died not wholly joyless; they were wed,
When twenty changing moons their light had shed
On the dark waves of Burgfirth, since in trust
Of Gudrun's love, over the bridge new thrust
From out the ship, the much-praised Kiartan ran.
So strangely shift men's lives in little span.

The Sword Comes Back Without the Scabbard

When of this wedding first came tidings true
To Bathstead, then it was that Gudrun knew
How much of hope had been before that day
Within her heart; now, when a cast-away
Upon the lonely rocks of life, she was

With nought to help whate'er might come to pass;
Deaf, dumb, and blind, long hours she went about
Her father's house, till folk began to doubt
If she would ever speak a word again;
Nay, scarce yet could she think about her pain,
Or e'en know what it was, but seemed to face
Some huge blank wall within a lonely place.
And Bodli watched her with a burning heart
Baffled and beaten back, yet for his part
Something like hope 'gan flit before his eyes,
Hope of some change e'en if new miseries
Wrapped it about.

As on a day she went
Slow-footed through the hall without intent,
Taking no heed of aught, of Kiartan's name
She heard one speak, and to her stunned heart came
A flash of hope and pain, against her will
Her foot must stay her, and she stood there still,
And turning round she saw where Ospak stood,
And slowly talking in a sullen mood
Unto his brother Thorolf; but they made
As though they saw her not, and Ospak said:

"Thou art young, Thorolf, and thy words are vain,
So it has been, so it shall be again,
One man shall deem all others made for him,
And 'neath his greatness shall all fame grow dim;
Till on a day men try if he is man
Eh! what then falleth—let him, if he can
Play Thor among the mannikins, and cast
The swords aback when he is caught at last."

"Hist!" Thorolf said; "there sister Gudrun goes!
Kiartan has froze her heart up: stand we close!"

Then Ospak laughed: "She will not hear us yet,
She hath a hope she cannot quite forget,
That he who twice has flung her love aside,
Will come some day to claim her as his bride,
When he has slain our long-faced champion there!
Good sooth, the house of Hauskuld waxeth fair,
We shall have kings in Iceland ere our day
Is quite gone by."
Slowly she gat away
Stung to the heart by those coarse words of hate,
Wondering withal what new thought lay in wait
To change her life; she sat her down alone
And covered up her face, and one by one
Strove to recall the happy days past by,
And wondering why they past so happily

While yet none strove for happiness; at last
She raised her head up and a glance she cast
Unto the open door and down the hall
A streak of sun on Bodli's head did fall
As he turned round and saw her; then she said
Unto herself: 'Nay, then, love is not dead
Since Bodli lives: why should I hate him then
Because he heeded not the shame of men
Amidst his love? but thou, I once called love,
On whom I flung my heart, with whom I strove
For ever, thy weak measured love to make
Equal to mine, what didst thou for my sake?
Thy soul is saved, thy fame is won, and thou
Hast a fair damsel's arms about thee now—
Not mine—and thou art happy. Who can tell,
O Bodli Thorleikson, but down in hell
We twain shall love, and love, and love again,
When the first wave of the eternal pain
Has washed our folly from us, and I know
Why upon earth I loved a weak heart so
That loved me not, while I was ice to thee,
O loving lovesome traitor."
Wearily
She hung her head with parted lips awhile,
Silent she sat, until a bitter smile
Bemocked her face: "Yet if I call thee love,
And kiss thee with sweet kisses, such as move
Great men to great deeds, trust me not too much,
But think of honied words and tremulous touch
As things that slay. If Kiartan lay there dead,
How I should love him!"
Once more sank her head,
And long she sat in silence, till at last
She heard how Bodli toward her bower passed,
And rose and met him coldly, with no sign
That anywise her vexed heart did incline
To ease the bitter burden that he bore.

Unheeding all, the year moved as before,
And autumn came again. What hearts soe'er
The younger folk each unto each might bear
Olaf and Oswif chose to shut their eyes,
And close their ears, as peaceful men and wise,
And make believe that nought amiss there was
'Twixt the two houses; so it came to pass
That Bathstead to the Herdholt feast did go
At autumn-tide once more at least; and though
Kiartan was loth enow those folk to face,
Yet so hard Olaf prayed that he would grace
His father's house with his great fame, and sit,
Yet once again while he might look at it,

A glory to the feast, that he put by
His doubts once more, and there with troubled eye
Noted the twain among the Bathstead crowd,
And Oswif's ill sons, insolent and loud,
And turned pale when the words of greeting came
From out his lips. Meanwhile, with shrinking shame
And anxious heart, did Refna gaze upon
Gudrun's great beauty, deeming she had won
A troublous lot; and Kiartan, noting that,
And how scarce like the mistress there she sat,
Yet to his eyes seemed fairer, because love
Had forged the fear that so her heart did move,
Grew wroth that still so many memories
Must vex his heart, and turn aside his eyes
To Gudrun, the world's wonder there, whose face,
Now coldly watchful, scanned the busy place.

Men say that at this feast three things betid,
Whereby the flame the elders deemed well hid,
Showed through the heap of smouldering love and hate.
First, when the new-come guests did stand and wait
Till they were marshalled to their seats, the maid
Who did this for the women turned and said
To Kiartan, "Who the high-seat fills to-day
Beside the goodwife?"
In most bright array
Stood Gudrun, gazing ever at the bride,
As though she saw not anything beside;
And Kiartan noted her, and therewith deemed
That in her eyes a look of hate there gleamed,
And saw withal Refna's soft eyes fall down
Before hers; then he spake out, with a frown:

"Nay, thou art foolish, damsel: who shall sit
In the best place, if I may deal with it,
Saving my wife?" But as he said the word,
The struggling devil so his vexed heart stirred,
That he must look at Gudrun; their eyes met,
Paler she grew than he had seen her yet,
Then red as blood; but he waxed wroth and said:

"Ah, wert thou e'en so foolish, then, O maid?
For such a guest belike we have got here
As thinketh everything of great or dear,
Honour, and hearts of men, and women's tears
Are but for her." Then tingling took the ears
Of those that stood thereby; as he strode off,
Gudrun's cold smile was bitterer than a scoff
Spoken aloud: but Ospak laughed, and said
In a loud whisper, close to Bodli's head:

"Nay, thou shalt have to fight for Gudrun yet,
Even though Refna did the bride-bed get.
He deems our sister may not quench the thought
Of all the joy she erst to Herdholt brought.
Ah, we shall yet see Refna lie a-cold,
Brother-in-law, unless thou waxest bold."

Such a beginning to the feast there was.

Moreover, the next day it came to pass,
As folk ere supper sported in the hall,
That unto her did goodwife Thorgerd call
The gentle Refna, bidding her as one
Who well might bid, to do the rich coif on,
The wonder of the Greeks, the fair queen's gift:
Then Refna reddened, and her eyes did lift
To Kiartan, e'en as asking him thereof;
But he spake nought, her soft look might not move
His heart from deep thought; so she went her ways,
Scarce happy 'neath his far-off moody gaze,
And came back glittering like a new-born star,
And sat upon the dais seen afar
Down the dusk hall. Then Ospak noted how
Gudrun turned pale, and he his teeth did show
Like a crossed hound, and muttered:
"Past belief,
As men may deem it, sister, yet a thief
Asgeir begat; for longeth not that gold
To Bathstead, if the tale be rightly told?"

Now Kiartan seemed to wake as from a dream,
When in the torches' flare that gold did gleam,
And went across to Refna's side, and said,
Smiling and whispering: "More I love thy head
Uncovered, O my love; yea, and withal,
Sharp swords thy helm from out their sheaths may call:
Look down there, how the sons of Oswif scowl
Around poor Bodli's face; the storm doth growl
Afar already—nay, nay, fear thee nought!—
But good I deemed it thou shouldst know my thought."

Sour and sick-hearted Gudrun turned away,
Noting how Kiartan's hand on Refna's lay,
And how their cheeks were close each unto each.
And Refna's eyes that love did so beseech,
Her soft mouth, tremulous with longing sore
For yet more kisses, long time hung before
Her weary eyes upon that weary night,
Yea, and till mirth of men was slain by light.

Hearken once more: the morn the guests should go,

About the stead Kiartan went to and fro,
Busied in such things, as his father's son,
For honour's very sake, must see well done;
And as he ordered how the folk should ride,
His sword, 'The King's Gift' named, which by his side
Was ever wont to hang, upon his bed
He left awhile, and, when the guests were sped,
Came back to seek the same, and found it gone.
Then questioning there was of everyone,
And mighty trouble; An the Black meanwhile,
A sturdy house-carle, slipped out with a smile,
Just as old Olaf to his son 'gan talk
In such wise:
"Son, hate far abroad will walk
E'en when new-born, although we nurse it not:
Now my heart tells me much must be forgot,
Many words hidden, many sights be seen
By thine eyes only, son, if I, between
Death and the end of life shall see thee last;
And hold thy living hands as life goes past,
Mine eyes a-waxing dim: wait then, and hope:
Thou shalt grow stronger with the world to cope,
If thou sitst down with patience, casting not
Long days and sweet on drawing of a lot."
Such things and more he spake, and Kiartan heard
With kind eyes, if his heart were little stirred.
But, as they sat and talked thereof, came back,
Smiling, but panting sorely, An the Black,
And in his cloak he carried something wrapped.

"Well," Olaf said, "and what new thing hath happed?"

"Soon told," said An; "I followed them afar,
Knowing what thieves those Bathstead skinkers are,
And at the peat moss where the road doth wind
About the dale, young Thorolf lagged behind;
I saw him take a something from his cloak,
And thrust it down just were the stream doth soak
The softest through the peat; then swift again
Ride on: so when they might not see me plain,
O ho, says I, and comes up to the place,
And here and there I peer with careful face
Until at last I draw this fair thing forth;
A pity though, the scabbard is of worth!
Clean gone it is."
Then from his cloak he drew
'The King's Gift' bright and naked. Olaf grew
Joyous thereover, praising An right well.
But Kiartan 'gan to gloom: "Ah, who can tell,"
He muttered, as he took the sword to him,
"But this shall end the troublous tale and dim?—

Well, I at least cast not the sheath away;
Bewail not ye too much, who have to pay
For pleasure gained; his may the worst hap be,
Who best can bear the pain and misery."

The Stealing of the Coif

Now howso Olaf bade An hold his peace,
And Kiartan promised he would nowise cease
To show a good face to the world on all
That 'twixt the houses yet might chance to fall,
Certain it is, that ere long, far and wide
The tale was known, throughout the country-side;
Nay, more than this, to Kiartan's ears it came
That Oswif's sons deemed they had cast a shame
On Herdholt, and must mock him openly
And call him 'Mire-blade,' e'en when those were by
Who held him of the most account; no less
Kiartan was moved not from his quietness,
Nor did aught hap 'twixt autumn and Yule-tide;
Then men at Herdholt busied them to ride
To Bathstead once again, and Olaf said:

"Wilt thou once more be guided by my head,
Son Kiartan, and with brave heart go to face
The troublous things that wait thee in that place?"

"Well," Kiartan said, "if so I deemed, that fate
Might be turned back of men, or foolish hate
Die out for lack of fuel, no more would I
Unto the Bathstead hall-door draw anigh;
But forasmuch as now I know full well,
That the same story there shall be to tell
Whether I go, or whether I refrain,
Let all be as thou wilt; and yet we twain
Not oft again, O father, side by side
Unto this merry-making place shall ride."

Then Olaf sighed, as though indeed he knew
To what an end his latter days now drew.

So now all folk were ready there, but when
The women came their ways to meet the men,
Said Thorgerd unto Refna: "Well, this tide
Thou hast the coif, no doubt, and like a bride
Hast heart to look midst those whose hearts are cold
To thee and thine."
Then Refna did behold
Thorgerd's stern face in trembling wise, and said:

"Nay, goodwife, what fair cloth may coif my head
Shall matter little mid the many things
Men have to talk of: rise and fall of kings
And changes of the world: within my chest
The coif lies."
"There," said Kiartan, "might it rest
For thee and me, sweet; yet I mind indeed
When I, a froward child, deemed I had need
Of some sharp glittering thing, as axe or knife,
But little would my mother raise up strife
With me therefor, and even as I would
I cut myself: so if she think this good
Let fetch the Queen's Gift."
Refna looked adown
Shamefaced and puzzled, Thorgerd with a frown
Turned upon Kiartan, but he smiled in turn,
And said: "Yea, mother, let the red gold burn
Among the lights at Bathstead; great am I
E'en as thou deemst; and men must let pass by
Their hatred to me, whatso say their hearts;
Come, open-handed let us play our parts."

So was the coif brought, and once more they rode
Unto the door of Oswif's fair abode;
And there they feasted merrily enow—
Such of them as were fools, or cared not how
The next week went—and at the highest tide
Of all the feast, sat Refna as a bride
Coifed with the Queen's Gift; Gudrun stern and cold
Scarce would the tender face of her behold,
Or cast a look at Kiartan; rather she
Did press the hand of Bodli lovingly,
Softening her face for him alone of all:
Then would strange tumult on his spirit fall,
Mingled of pain and uttermost delight
To think the whole world had so swerved from right
To give him pleasure for a little while,
Nor durst he look upon his old friend's smile,
Who, glad with his own manhood seemed to be
Once more, once more the brave heart frank and free;
As though at last the trouble and the coil
That wrapped him round, and made him sadly toil
Through weary days, had fallen all clean away,
And smiling he might meet the bitterest day.

So passed the high-tide forth unto its end
But when at last folk from the place would wend,
And Refna fain would have the coif of her
Whose office was to tend the women's gear—
Lo, it was gone—then Refna trembled sore,
And passing through the crowd about the door

Whispered to Kiartan: Ospak stood anigh
And bit his lips, and watched her eagerly,
And Kiartan with a side-long glance could see
His colour come and go, and cried:
"Let be,
Light won, light gone! if still it is 'bove ground,
Doubt thou not, Refna, it shall yet be found."
Folk looked on one another; Thorgerd said,
Turning on Gudrun: "Small account is made
Of great folk's gifts, then; I have seen the day
When Egil's kin a man or two would slay
For things less worth than this."
Her angry frown
Gudrun met calmly: "Was the thing his own?
Then let him do e'en as he will with it;
Small loss it is methinks for her to sit
Without his old love's gift upon her head!"
Ere Thorgerd answered, Kiartan cried, and said:
"Come swift to saddle! Cousin, ride with me,
Until we turn the hill anigh the sea;
I fain would speak with thee a word or twain
That I have striven to think about in vain
These last days that we met."
Bodli flushed red
And looked adown: "So be it then," he said.
Then stammered and turned pale, and said, "Enow
Shall one sword be to-day betwixt us two;
Take thou the rover's weapon, O fair wife."

She looked on him, her lovely face was rife
With many thoughts, but Kiartan's kindly gaze
Seemed to bring back the thoughts of happier days
To both of them, and swift away she passed
Unto her bower; and men were horsed at last,
And sharp the hoofs upon the hard way rung.
So as into the saddle Kiartan swung,
He leant toward Ospak, and said mockingly:
"I love thee—I would not that thou shouldst die;
So see me not too oft, because I have
A plague sometimes, that bringeth to the grave,
Those that come nigh me; live on well and whole!"

Then to his face rushed Ospak's envious soul,
His hand fell on his sword-hilt as le shrank
Back to the doorway, while the fresh air drank
Kiartan's clear laughter, as their company
Rode jingling down unto the hoary sea.

But the last smile from off his face was gone,
When silent, in a while he rode alone
With Bodli silent: then he said to him:

"Thou seest, Bodli, how we twain must swim
Adown a strange stream—thou art weaponless
To-day, and certes bides my sword no less
Within its scabbard—how long shall it last?"

Then Bodli cried, "Until my life is past—
Shall I take life from thee as well as love?"

"Nay," Kiartan said, "be not too sure thereof,
Bethink thee where by thine own deed thou art
Betwixt a passionate woman's hungry heart,
And the vile envy of a dangerous fool;
Doubt not but thou art helpless, and the tool
Of thy mad love, and that ill comes from ill,
And as a thing begins, so ends it still
Nay, not to preach to thee I brought thee here,
Rather to say that the old days are dear,
Despite of all, unto my weary heart.
And now methinks from them and thee I part
This day; not unforgiven, whatsoe'er
Thou at my hands, or I of thine may bear.
For I too—shall I guide myself indeed,
Or rather be so driven by hard need
That still my hand as in a dream shall be,
While clearly sees the heart that is in me
Desires I may not try to bring to pass?
So since no more it may be as it was
In the past days, when fair and orderly
The world before our footsteps seemed to lie,
Now in this welter wherein we are set,
Lonely and bare of all, deem we not yet
That each for each these ill days we have made;
Rather the more let those good words be weighed
We spake, when truth and love within us burned,
Before the lesson of our life was learned.
What say's thou? are the days to come forgiven,
Shall folk remember less that we have striven,
Than that we loved, when all the tale is told?"

Then long did Bodli Kiartan's face behold,
Striving for speech: then said, "Why speak'st thou so?
Twice over now I seem my deed to do,
Twice over strive to wake as from a dream,
That I, once happy, never real may deem,
So vile and bitter is it; may thy sword
If e'er we meet be sharper than thy word,
And make a speedy end of doubt and strife;
Fear not to take much from me, taking life!"

Still seemed the air filled with his words when he
Turned back to Bathstead, and the murmuring sea

Seemed from afar to speak of rest from pain.
Then on a little knoll he shortened rein,
And turned about, and looking toward the hill
Beheld the spear of Kiartan glittering still,
When all the rest of him behind the brow
Was sunken; but the spear sank quickly now,
And slowly home withal did Bodli ride,
E'en as he might the coming end to bide.

Refna Hears Women Talking

So the days wore with nothing new to tell,
Till spring-tide once more on the country fell,
Then on a night as Kiartan to his bed
Would go, still Refna sat with bowed-down head
And stirred not, nor a while would speak, when he
Spake to her in kind words and lovingly;
At last she lifted up a face, wherein
Somewhat did trouble upon sorrow win,
And said:
"Indeed of all thy grief I knew,
But deemed if still thou saw'st me kind and true,
Not asking too much, yet not failing aught
To show that not far off need love be sought,
If thou shouldst need love—if thou sawest all this,
Thou wouldst not grudge to show me what a bliss
Thy whole love was, by giving unto me
As unto one who loved thee silently,
Now and again the broken crumbs thereof:
Alas! I, having then no part in love,
Knew not how nought, nought can allay the soul
Of that sad thirst, but love untouched and whole!
Kinder than e'er I durst have hoped thou art,
Forgive me then, that yet my craving heart
Is so unsatisfied; I know that thou
Art fain to dream that I am happy now,
And for that seeming ever do I strive;
Thy half-love, dearest, keeps me still alive
To love thee; and I bless it—but at whiles—"

So far she spake till her weak quivering smiles
Faded before the bitterness of love.
Her face changed, and her passion 'gan to move
Within her breast until the sobs came fast,
And down upon her hands her face she cast,
And by the pain of tears her heart did gain
A little respite; nor might she refrain
From weeping yet, when Kiartan's arms she felt
About her, and for long her fair lips dwelt

With hungry longing on his lips, and he
Spake to her:
"O poor lover, long may we
Live upon earth, till lover and beloved
Each is to each, by one desire moved;
And whereas thou dost say to me, Forgive,
Forgive me rather! A short while to live
Once seemed the longest life of man to me,
Wherein my love of the old years to see;
But could I die now, and be born again
To give my whole heart up to ease thy pain,
A short while would I choose to live indeed.
But is it not so, sweet, that thou hast need
To tell me of a thing late seen or heard?
Surely by some hap thy dear heart is stirred
From out its wonted quiet; ease thine heart
And 'twixt us twain thy fear and grief depart!"

She looked up: "Yea, kind love, I thought to tell
Of no great thing that yesterday befell.
Why should I vex thee with it? Yet thy fame,
If I must say the word, in question came
Therein. Yet prithee, mark it not too much!"

He smiled and said: "Nay, be the tidings such
As mean my death, speak out and hide not aught!"

She sat a little while, as though she thought
How best to speak, then said: "The day being good,
About noon yesterday in peaceful mood
I wandered by the brook-side, and at last
Behind a great grey stone myself I cast,
And slept, as fate would have it; when I woke
At first I did but note the murmuring brook,
But as my hearing and my sight did clear
The sound of women's voices did I hear,
And in the stream two maidens did I see,
Our housefolk, and belike they saw not me,
Since I lay low adown, and up the stream
Their faces turned; I from a half-sweet dream,
I know not what, awaked, no sooner heard
Their first word, than sick-hearted and afeard
I grew, the cold and evil world to feel
So hard it seemed, love, my life to deal:
Bitterly clear I saw; as if alone
And dead, I saw the world; by a grey stone
Within the shallows, washing linen gear
They stood; their voices sounded sharp and clear;
Half smiles of pleasure and of goodlihead,
Shone on their faces, as their rough work sped;
O God, how bright the world was!"

A flush came
Across her face; as stricken by some shame
She stammered, when she went on: "Thus their speech,
Broken amid their work mine ear did reach
As I woke up to care, for the one said,
'Yea, certes, now has Kiartan good end made
Of all his troubles, things go well enow.'
'Over well,' said the other, 'didst thou know?'
'Know what?' the first one said, 'What knowst thou then?'
'Nay, nought except the certain talk of men.'
'Well, hear I not men too, what wilt thou say?'
She said, 'Men talk that this is latter May,
And Kiartan sitteth still and nought is done
For the two thefts of Bathstead to atone.'
'Fool!' saith the first one, 'shall all fall to strife
For what in no wise maketh worse their life?'
'Well, well, and what will Refna say thereto?
Things had been otherwise a while ago;
Scarce Kiartan's brother had stripped Gudrun's head
Of what she loved, and yet 'scaped lying dead
By this time. Ospak, sure, is safe enow.'
'Ah!' said the other, 'great things sayest thou!'
'True words I speak, when this I say to thee,
That glad would Gudrun and our Kiartan be
If Bodli Thorleikson and Refna lay
Dead on the earth upon the selfsame day;
And this from all men's daily talk I draw;
Old friends are last to sever, saith the saw.'

"This was the last word that I heard, O love,
For from the place softly I 'gan to move
Ere they might see me, and my feet, well taught
To know the homeward way, my body brought
Unto my bower; yet scarce I saw the way,
Rather some place beneath the sod, where lay
A few white bones, unnamed, unheeded, while
Hard by within this bower 'twixt word and smile
Was breast strained unto breast of twain I knew—
—And needs must part awhile, that I might rue
My life, my death, my bitter useless birth.
O Kiartan, over-weary seemed the earth
Yesterday and to-day; too hard to bear
Within thine home to be, and see thee. near,
And think that but for very kindness thou
Must wish me dead—thou didst not note me, how
My face was worn with woe throughout that tide,
Though most men looked on me—for thou must bide
A weary waiting, and thy woe untold
Must make thy face at whiles seem hard and cold.
—Ah me! forgive me that I talk of this!
Think how my heart ached!"

For now kiss on kiss
Did Kiartan shower upon her quivering face,
Yet, even as their arms did interlace,
Despite his love and pity, of past years
He needs must think, of wasted sighs and tears
And hopes all fallen to nought, and vows undone,
And many a pleasure from his life seemed gone;
And sorely his heart smote him for her faith
So pure and changeless; her love strong as death,
As kind as God, that nought should satisfy
Till all the shows of earth had passed her by.

Kiartan Fetches the Price of the Coif from Bathstead

And now a day or two with brooding face
Did Kiartan go about from place to place
And speak few words to any, till one day
He bade his men see to their war-array,
For two hours after midnight all and some
Into the hall to wait his word should come,
And whoso blabbed, he said, the deed should rue.
So thitherward in arms that night they drew;
And Refna trembling lay, while Kiartan clad
His body in the best war-gear he had,
And through the hangings did she watch the spears,
And dreadful seemed the laughter to her ears,
And red the lamps burned, as with twilight grey
They mingled: then he turned to go away,
And kissed her as he spake:
"Refna, this eve,
Most like, a noble gift shalt thou receive;
Do thou thy part to meet it with good grace,
And gather what thou canst into this place
Of fiddlers and of glee-men, and with song
Meet that good gift that comes to heal thy wrong."

Now Refna durst not ask, What wilt thou then,
And whither go to-night these all-armed men?
Because she deemed she knew what word it was
That all this clash of arms had brought to pass,
And sick at heart she grew to think thereof,
And with her fair white arms made strong by love
She clung to Kiartan, but he drew her hold
With gentle hands from off the mail rings cold.
And kissed her sweet mouth opened now to speak,
And gat him gone; and she fell back all weak
Upon her bed, and lying there alone,
Saw how his war-gear in the bright light shone,
And heard his cheery voice as he cried loud,

"To Bathstead, ho!" and then the noisy crowd
Passed clashing from the hall, and nothing there
Within a little while might Refna hear,
But the dawn's noises, and the loitering tread
Of some maid getting slowly back to bed;
So there she lay alone in grief and fear,
But hope's fresh voice shuddering she needs must hear
Whispering wild words, yet sweet, of chance and crime,
Telling the wondrous ways of slowfoot time.

But now at Bathstead ere they rose that morn,
Men deemed they heard the winding of a horn,
And, running straightway to the door, could see
About the stead a goodly company,
And there were Olaf's sons with sixty men
Besetting every gate and door; but when
The men of Bathstead were all armed and went
Unto the door, they saw a gay-striped tent
Just raised upon the slope-side 'gainst the hall
And armed men round about it; one man, tall
Beyond his fellows, stood some yards more near
The hall-door, leaning on a pennoned spear,
Clad in a glittering mail-coat, with a shield
About his neck, where, on a golden field
The holy Rood of God was painted fair;
From 'neath his gilded helm his golden hair
Fell waving down, but hidden were his eyes
By the wide brim: then did great fear arise
Within their hearts, despite their fiery hate,
Because they knew that now at last, if late,
Was Kiartan's might aroused and in the field.
But none the less little would Ospak yield
To any fear; before the rest he strode,
And cried aloud:
"Within this fair abode
Has been thy place, O Kiartan Olafson,
And not without; what ill deed hast thou done
That father Oswif has forbidden thee
Thy honoured seat where it was wont to be?"

The tall man moved not, but a deep voice came
From 'neath his helm: "Thou art right wise to name
A hidden head; grow wiser! sick am I,
And somewhat deadly now to come anigh;
My sword has lost its scabbard 'gainst my will,
Beware then, for its naked edge may kill!"

Then Ospak raised the spear in his right hand
And shook it, but the tall man forth did stand
And pushed his helm aback and showed the face
Of Kiartan, and across the grassy space

Cried mightily: "Be wise, and get ye back!
Of fighting one day shall ye have small lack;
But now beware, because my father's sons
Have sworn to spare no man of you, if once
A drop of blood is spilt! Come ye not forth
Until I bid you, if of any worth
Ye hold your lives; and meantime for the sake
Of what I had and have not, I will take
My due from mead and byre."
And therewithal
He let his helm down o'er his visage fall,
And turned back toward the tent. Back shrank again,
Cowed into sullen rage, the Bathstead men,
And armed but helpless there within the hall
Silent they sat, hearkening the raiders call
The cattle o'er the meads: in high-seat there
Sat Bodli, but his visage worn with care
Of the past days, was sad, but calm and soft,
As if he thought of gentle things, though oft
Fierce eyes would scowl upon his dreamy face
Unnoted of him; in that dreary place
He seemed like some dead king, condemned in hell
For his one sin among such men to dwell
As for their wickedness he hated most
Ere righteous ways and life and all were lost.

And in meantime, 'twixt silent trembling bower
And silent cursing hall, hour after hour
Did Gudrun pace with restless feet, and heart
Betwixt two nameless miseries torn apart,
Whence cold despair was being well fashioned now.
And Oswif sat apart with wrinkled brow,
Unnoted in that house of grief and wrong.
But midst their shame, from outside, laugh and song
Came loud and louder, mingled with the clank
Of mead-horns; the feast's clamour never sank
Till mid-day was well passed; then quieter
It grew without, and yet they still might hear
Lowing of neat and men's shouts. Then a voice
Cried from the slope-side:
"Bathstead men, rejoice
That ye no autumn-feast need hold this year,
For certes else should ye find victuals dear
And hard to come by! Oswif's sons, come out,
Unarmed and peaceable, and have no doubt
Of hurt from us!"
They stirred not for a space;
Then cried the voice: "Lives none within the place?
Are ye all dead of fear? Come out, I say,
Else o'er your roof the red cock crows to-day!"

Then Ospak, cursing, on the pavement cast
His shield and spear, and toward the doorway passed,
And in likewise the others one by one,
Till Bodli and Gudrun were left alone:
And then she said, "And thou—wilt thou not go?
Knowst thou the name of him who shames us so?"

"Yea, yea, I know it!" Bodli cried; "farewell!
Of me, too, shall there be a tale to tell:
I will go forth, but not without my sword."

He drew the thing he named with that last word,
And ran unto the door; against the wall
There stood the sons of Oswif, stout and tall,
Foaming, but helpless: in his saddle now
Sat Kiartan, unhelmed, his bright hair a-glow
With the May sun. His brethren stood around
Beside their horses, and a mighty sound
Came from the herd of neat that thronged the way
Beneath the hill-side; spears with pennons gay
Glittered about them in the sunlight fair,
For Kiartan's company was gathered there
Ready to set forth.

So there Bodli stood
One moment, thinking that the world was good,
Though not for him; then he cried out: "O thou,
Thou son of Olaf, come and meet me now,
For long have I been weary of the earth;
And now to me but one thing seems of worth
That I should win death of such hands as thine."

Then in the sunlight did the bright steel shine,
And Kiartan's brethren soon had ended all,
For Bodli ran forth; yet heard Kiartan call
Across the clash of arms: "Nay, point nor edge
His blood shall redden not; make ye a hedge
Of your strong shields and thrust him back again
Since he knows not that all his might is vain,
E'en to win death; live, foster-brother, yet,
And get despite of all, what thou mayst get
Of joy and honour."
Midway, Bodli stayed,
And in his hand he poised the heavy blade
As he would cast it from him, slowly then
Did he give back face foremost from the men,
Till in the doorway once again he stood.

Then Kiartan said: "Yea, cousin, it is good,
If thou must die by me, that thou shouldst bide
Some noble fight, some glorious reaping-tide,

Where each of each fair fame at least may gain—
God grant a little bliss ere that last pain!—
But hearken, thievish sons of a wise man!
Be taught, ye blustering fools, if yet ye can!
From Yule till now I gave you, a long day,
To pay the debt that needs was ye must pay;
Twice told I take it now, and leave behind
What shall seem shame indeed to most men's mind.
This is my bridal gift, think well of it;
In your own fields it waxed, while ye did sit
Plotting across the meadhorns. Now take heed
That oft henceforth your manhood shall ye need
If ye would live in peace. Blow loud and clear,"
O horns, for Refna waiteth for us there,
And merry shall we be to-night in hall
What things soever afterwards may fall!"

Still Bodli stood with drawn sword in the door
While midst the clang of arms and horn's loud roar,
He saw the herd move up the dusty road;
He saw how Kiartan for a while abode
Behind the rest, and stared at the grey stead
Whose roof so often had been o'er his head;
He saw him turn, and well might deem he sighed,
Then muttered he, "Ah, would God I had died
By thee to-day!" and sheathed his sword, and then
Was hustled by the sullen baffled men
Who shouldered past him back into the hall,
Who heeded him just as they did the wall
Past which they rubbed; but with the last of these
He went in, casting by all hope of peace.

But Refna looking from the Herdholt knoll
That evening, saw a dust-cloud upward roll
And move toward Herdholt, and her heart beat fast
When from the midst thereof bright spear-heads passed,
And then men's helms, and then the guarded herd;
And she bethought her of her mate's last word,
And bade the women in their best array,
And minstrels, stand on either side the way
To greet the new-comers, whose horns blew loud
Close by the garth now, while the beasts 'gan crowd
About the garth-gate; so, the gate past through,
Over the homefield toward the wall they drew,
Tended by gay-clad men-at-arms, who wore
About their helms fair flowers that Bathstead bore,
While of the beasts, sharp horn and curl-browed head,
And dewlapped neck were well begarlanded.
Then from the close loud joyful cries arose,
Tinkle of harps, sharp noise of fiddle-bows,
And all along the line there ran a shout:

Therewith old Olaf to the door came out,
And saw his sons swift from the cattle ride,
Till Kiartan leapt adown by Refna's side
And cast his arms about her, and 'gan cry:

"Now is the Queen's-Gift paid for fittingly;
For these are thine, e'en as my hand and sword,
To put from thee all care, and every word
That grieves thee, sweet. O love, but I am gay!
Sure a fair life beginneth from to-day!"

She gazed at him, and knew not why her heart
Scarce in that joyous scene might play its part—
Why it was not enough—these words of love,
His bright fair face her longing eyes above?
Yet with a loving cry she hid her face
Upon his breast.
Thereat did Olaf gaze
And muttered low: "A goodly price in sooth
For a girl's coif! but yet, for Kiartan's youth,
For his fair hope and glory, and increase
Of good deeds, and mine own old age of peace,
Not too much, not too much! Ah, woe is me
That I should live these latter days to see!"

Thorhalla Tells of Kiartan's Comings and Goings

What should the next move in the strange game be?
Kiartan rode through the country carelessly
With few behind him, but nought hitherto
The sons of Oswif durst against him do,
While he his hand withheld not utterly
From them; so doubtful did the days go by.

And Gudrun? Ah, the black spot in her heart
That rose when first she knew that one had part
In Kiartan's life, and ever greater grew,
When of his love toward this new love she knew,
Now at he last, when over sure she felt
That she no longer in his memory dwelt,
O'erspread her life, till from the foiled desire
Cast back upon her heart, there sprang a fire
Of very hate: true was it, that at first
Bodli, herself, and all around she cursed
Rather than Kiartan—Well, what will you have
That was ere hope had sunk into his grave,
While yet some pleasure clung round Kiartan's name.
Then came the feast at Herdholt; then the shame
About the coif, and fear of shame again,

And many a tale told to make over plain
His love for Refna; then the evil hour,
When she within the darksome hall must cower
Among her trembling brethren: then, when she
Had looked at least a noble death to see,
Of one who loved her, Kiartan sent him back
A baffled man, as who all might did lack,
Yea, even the might to die; still, at each turn
Afresh this weary lesson must she learn;
With the wrong-doers hast thou taken part,
Live then, and die with them, for thy love's heart
Is now no more for thee! still everywhere
Did Kiartan's image meet her; the warm air
Of summer seemed but sent her from his hand,
The sea that beat the borders of the land
Still seemed to bear his fame unto her feet;
All summer sights and sounds, and odours sweet,
Were heavy with his memory: no least way
To 'scape from thought of him from day to day.
Withal, the sight of faces dull with hate
Of that same man, on every step did wait.
Familiar grew the muttering sullen voice
Of those who in no goodhap could rejoice,
Until the very thought and hope of strife,
The use of hate, must grow to be her life.
And shaped therefrom a dreadful longing rose,
That some fell end the weary way would close,
Unto herself she scarce durst whisper what.

Now on a day three of her brothers sat
Within the hall, and talked, and she stood by
Hearkening their eager speech most wearily.
"The gabbling crone Thorhalla has just been,"
Said Ospak, "And whom think you she has seen?"

"Nay, by thy scowl I know well," Thorolf said,
"'Twas Kiartan Olafson, upon my head."

"Well, Thorolf, thou grow'st wise—now, said the crone,
That in her life she ne'er saw such an one
As Kiartan looked, a loving maiden's dream
Of a great king, she said, the man did seem.
'Well,' said I, 'and how long then will it last?'
'Ah,' said the crone, 'till after ye are passed;
Why, the whole country-side is ringing now
With this, that ye had best be wise and bow
Before him humbly, since most kind is he;
Kind,' says the crone, 'certes he was to me.'
'Well, well,' says I, 'but these are fools' words here.'
'Nay, let me speak,' she says, 'for he will fare
Unto the west to Knoll; this know I well,

Because to him therewith I needs must tell
Of one who owed me half a mark thereby.
Well, goody, says he, I shall pass anigh,
And I will fetch it for thee—lo, how kind.'"

"Now may God strike the gabbling idiot blind!"
Said Thorolf. "Nay," said Ospak, "not so wise
Thou growest now; rather, God keep her eyes!
Tidings she told me, saying he would bide
For just three days at Knoll, and thence will ride
Through Swinedale home, close here, nor like that he
Will ride by us with a great company,
Say two at most—good luck go with his pride,
Whereby so fair a chance doth us betide!—
Bodli shall lead or die."

Then Gudrun turned
Sick-hearted from them; how her longing burned
Within her heart! ah, if he died not now,
How might she tell whereto his hate would grow?
Yet a strange hope that longing shot across,
As she got thinking what would be the loss
If Bodli fell 'neath Kiartan's hand. That day,
Like years long told, past Gudrun wore away,
She knew not how; but when the next day came
She cried aloud, "The same, ah, still the same,
Shall every day be, now that he is dead!"
She started as she heard her voice, her head
Seemed filled with flame: she crawled unto her bower
And at her mirrored face hour after hour
She stared, and wondered what she really was,
The once-loved thing o'er which his lips would pass.
Her feet grew heavy at the end of day,
Her heart grew faint, upon her bed she lay
Moveless for many an hour, until the sun
Told her that now the last day was begun;
Then she arose as one might in a dream
To clothe herself, till a great cloud did seem
To draw away from her; as in bright hell,
Sunless but shadowless she saw full well
Her life that was and would be, now she knew
The deed unmasked that summer day should do.
And then she gnashed her teeth and tore her hair,
And beat her breast, nor lightened thus despair,
As over and over the sweet names she told
Whereby he called her in the days of old;
And then she thought of Refna's longing eyes,
And to her face a dreadful smile did rise
That died amidst its birth, as back again
Her thoughts went to the tender longing pain
She once had deemed a sweet fair day would end;

And therewith such an agony did rend
Her body and soul, that all things she forgat
Amidst of it; upon the bed she sat
Rigid and stark, and deemed she shrieked, yet made
No sound indeed; but slowly now did fade
All will away from her, until the sun
Risen higher, on her moveless body shone,
And as a smitten thing beneath its stroke
She shrank and started, and awhile awoke
To hear the tramp of men about the hall.
Then did a hand upon the panel fall;
And in her very soul she heard the ring
Of weapons pulled adown, and every thing,
Yea, even pain, was dead a little space.

At last she woke to see the haggard face
Of Bodli o'er her own: "I go," he said,
"Would God that thou mayst hear of me as dead
Ere the sun sets to-day."
She passed her hand
Across her eyes, as he in arms did stand
Before her there, and stared but answered not,
As though indeed his face were clean forgot;
Yet her face quickened as his eyes she saw
So full of ruth yet nigher to her draw:
She shrank aback, but therewith suddenly
A thought smote through her, with an angry cry
She sprang up from the bed, naked and white
Her gold hair glittering in the sunshine bright
That flooded all the place; his arm she caught
And stared into his eyes:
"What is thy thought?"
She said, "why goest thou with these murderous men?
Ah! dost thou think thou yet mayst save him then?
Ah! dost thou think that thou mayst still be kind
To every one, fool as thou art and blind,
Yet work thy wicked will to pleasure thee?"

Across her passion he began to see
That now she doubted him; he muttered low:
"The work of these my hands what man can know?
And yet at least the end shall be to-day."

She fell aback nor noted more, but lay
All huddled up upon the bed, her hair
O'er her white body scattered here and there,
And as he gazed on her he saw she wept,
And a wild passion o'er his heart there swept,
And twice he stretched his arms out, to embrace
His curse and his delight, twice turned his face
Unto the door that led unto the hall,

Then with a cry upon her did he fall
And, sobbing, strained her to his mail-clad breast,
And to her writhen lips his lips he pressed,
And moaned o'er her wet cheeks, and kissed her eyes
That knew him not; till in his heart 'gan rise,
Now at the last, a glory in his shame,
A pride to take the whole world's bitter blame;
And like a god he felt, though well he deemed
That to an end at last his dream was dreamed.
And she, she knew him not, her arms fell down
Away from him, her drawn mouth and set frown
Were not for him, she did not shrink from him,
She turned not round to curse or bless, when dim
She lay before his burning eyes once more,
Her long hair gilding the white bed-clothes o'er,
As midst low restless moaning there she tossed.
Wildly he cried: "Oh, Gudrun, thou hast lost,
But look on me for I have never won!"
Then from the place he rushed, and with the sun
Burst into the dusk hall, a stream of light,
Neath his dark hair, his face so strange and white
That a dead man dragged up into the day
By wizard's arts he seemed to be, and they
Who waited armed there, and the last cup drank
Looked each at each, and from his presence shrank.

For there were gathered now the murderous band,
Long to be cursed thereafter through the land,
Gudrun's five brethren, and three stout men more.
Then Ospak cried, "Soon shall our shame be o'er,
And thou and we shall be great men and famed,
And Bathstead free; come now, since thou art named
Our leader, husband of Gudrun, lead forth!
For this day shall be called a day of worth,
By those that tell the story of our house."

Flushed were the men, and fierce and boisterous,
And Bodli trembled in his helpless rage
To be among them, but his sin's strong cage
Was strait and strong about him: with no word
He girt to him the rover's deadly sword,
And did his helm on: and so forth they wend
Through the bright morn to bring about the end.

The Slaying of Kiartan Olafson

Now Kiartan rode from Knoll betimes that day,
And goodman Thorkel brought him on the way
With twelve men more, and therewithal they ride

Fast from the west, but where the pass grew wide
And opened into Swinedale, Kiartan stayed
His company, and unto Thorkel said,
"Thanks have thou, goodman, for thy following;
Now get thee back, I fear not anything
'Twixt this and Herdholt."
"Well," the goodman said,
"Time enow is there yet to be waylaid
Ere thou art safe at home; let us ride on."
"Nay," Kiartan said, "the thing shall not be done,
All men of heart will say that heart I lack,
If I must have an army at my back
Where'er I go, for fear of Oswif's sons.
Fare thee well, goodman, get thee back at once!
And therewithal take this to comfort thee,
That Bodli yet is scarce mine enemy,
And holds aback those brethren; wot ye well,
Too strange a story would it be to tell,
If these should overcome my father's son,
Besides, without thee I ride not alone."

So back the goodman turned, misdoubting though,
In spite of all how yet the day would go,
And up the dale rode Kiartan: An the Black,
The man who erst the stolen sword brought back,
Was with him these, and one named Thorarin,
As slowly now the midway dale they win.

Now, as I find it written in my tale,
There went that morn a goodman of the dale,
About those bents his mares and foals to see,
His herdsman with him; these saw presently
Up from the east the men of Bathstead ride,
And take their stand along a streamlet's side
Deep sunken in a hollow, where the mouth
Of the strait pass turns somewhat to the south,
From out the dale; now, since the men they knew,
Much they misdoubted what these came to do;
But when they turned them from the sunken stream,
And saw the sun on other weapons gleam,
And three men armed come riding from the west;
And when they knew the tallest and the best
For Kiartan Olafson, therewith no more
They doubted aught.
Then said the herdsman: "Sore
The troubles are that on the country-side
Shall fall, if this same meeting shall betide;
He is a great chief; let us warn him then!"

"Yea, yea!" his master said, "and all such men
As fate leads unto death, that we may be

'Twixt the two millstones ground right merrily,
And cursed as we cry out! thou art a fool,
Who needs must be the beaker and the stool
For great men's use; emptied of joys of life
For other's joy, then kicked by in the strife
When they are drunken; come, beside the way,
Let us lie close to see the merry play!
For such a swordsman as is Kiartan, we
Shall scarce behold on this side of the sea;
And heavy odds he hath against him too.
These are great men—good, let them hack and hew
Their noble bodies for our poor delight!"

So down the bent they slipped, and as they might
Lurked by the road, and thus they tell their tale:

Ere Kiartan reached the strait place of the dale,
High up upon the brook-bank Bodli lay,
So that his helm was just seen from the way;
Then Ospak went to him, and clear they heard
Across the road his rough and threatening word:
"What dost thou here? thou hast bethought thee then
To warn thy friend that here lurk all-armed men.
Thou knowest Gudrun's mind—or knowst it not,
But knowst that we within a trap have got
Thee and the cursed wretch, the proud Mire-blade,
The Thief, the King's-pimp, the white Herdholt maid.
Come, sister's husband, get thee lower down!"

The foam flew from the lips of the fierce clown
As thus he spake, but Bodli rose and said:
"Thinkst thou I armed because I was afraid
Of thee and thine this morn? If thou knewst well
Of love or honour, somewhat might I tell
Why I am here with thee—If will I have,
Kiartan, who was my friend, this day to save,
Bethink thee I might do it otherwise
Than e'en by showing what in ambush lies!
—How if I stood beside him?".
"Down with thee
And hold thy peace! or he will hear and see."

For so it was that Kiartan drew so near
That now the herd their clinking bits might hear,
Borne down upon the light wind: on he came,
Singing an old song made in Odin's fame,
Merry and careless on that sunny morn;
When suddenly out rang the Bathstead horn,
And sharply he drew rein, and looked around;
Then did the lurkers from the gully bound
And made on toward them, and down leapt all three,

And Kiartan glanced around, and speedily
Led toward a rock that was beside the way,
And there they shifted them to stand at bay.

Most noble then looked Kiartan, said the herd,
Nor ever saw I any less afeard;
Yet, when his watchful eye on Bodli fell,
A change came o'er him, that were hard to tell,
But that he dropped his hands at first, as one
Who thinks that all is over now and done;
Yet, says the neatherd, soon his brows did clear,
And from his strong hand whistled forth his spear,
And down fell Thorolf clattering on the road.
He cried, 'Down goes the thief beneath his load,
One man struck off the tale! I have heard tell
Of such as dealt with more and came off well.'

Silence a space but for the mail rings; then
Over the dusty road on rushed those men;
And, says the herd, there saw I for a space
Confused gleam of swords about that place,
And from their clatter now and then did come
Sharp cry, or groan, or panting shout, as home
Went point or edge: but pale as death one stood,
With sheathed sword, looking on the clashing wood,
And that was Bodli Thorleikson. Then came
A lull a little space in that wild game.
The Bathstead men drew off, and still the three
Stood there scarce hurt as far as I could see;
But of the Bathstead men I deem some bled,
Though all stood firm; then Ospak cried and said;

"O Bodli, what thing wilt thou prophesy
For us, since like a seer thou standest by
And see'st thine house beat back? well then for thee
Will I be wise, foretelling what shall be
A cold bed, and a shamed board, shalt thou have,
Yea, and ere many days a chased dog's grave,
If thou bringst home to-day a bloodless sword!"

But yet for all that answered he no word,
But stood as made of iron, though the breeze
Blew his long black hair round his cheek-pieces
And fanned his scarlet kirtle.
"Time we lose,"
Another cried, "if Bodli so shall choose,
Let him deal with us when this man is slain."
Then stoutly to the game they gat again
And played awhile, and now withal I saw
That rather did the sons of Oswif draw
Toward Thorarin and An, until the first,

From midst the knot of those onsetters burst,
And ran off west, followed by two stout men,
Not Oswif's sons; and An the Black fell then
Wounded to death, I deemed, but over him
Fell Gudlaug, Oswif's nephew, with a limb
Shorn off by Kiartan's sword: then once again
There came a short lull in the iron rain;
And then the four fell on him furiously
Awhile, then gave aback, and I could see
The noble Kiartan, with his mail-coat rent,
His shield hung low adown, his sword-blade bent,
Panting for breath, but still without a wound.

While as a man by some strong spell fast bound,
Without a will for aught, did Bodli stand,
Nor once cast eyes on the waylayers' band,
Nor once glanced round at Kiartan, but stared still
Upon the green side of the grassy hill
Over against him, e'en as he did deem
It yet might yawn as in a dreadful dream,
And from its bowels give some marvel birth,
That in a ghostly wise should change the earth,
And make that day nought. But as there he stood
Ospak raised up his hand, all red with blood,
And smote him on the face, and cried;
"Go home,
Half-hearted traitor, e'en as thou hast come,
And bear my blood to Gudrun!"
Still no word
Came from his pale lips, and the rover's sword
Abode within the scabbard. Ospak said,
"O lover, art thou grown too full of dread
To look him in the face whom thou fearedst not
To cozen of the fair thing he had got?
O faint-heart thief of love, why drawest thou back,
When all the love thou erst so sore didst lack
With one stroke thou mayst win?"
He did not hear,
Or seemed to hear not; but now loud and clear
Kiartan cried out his name from that high place,
And at the first sound Bodli turned his face
This way and that, in puzzled hapless wise,
Till 'twixt the spears his eyes met Kiartan's eyes;
Then his mouth quivered, and he writhed aside,
And with his mail-clad hands his face did hide,
And trembled like one palsy-struck, while high
Over the doubtful field did Kiartan cry:

"Yea, they are right! be not so hardly moved,
O kinsman, foster-brother, friend beloved
Of the old days, friend well forgiven now!

Come nigher, come, that thou my face mayst know,
Then draw thy sword and thrust from off the earth
The fool that so hath spoilt thy days of mirth,
Win long lone days of love by Gudrun's side!
My life is spoilt, why longer do I bide
To vex thee, friend—strike then for happy life!
I said thou mightst not gaze upon the strife
Far off; bethink thee then, who sits at home
And waits thee, Gudrun, my own love, and come,
Come, for the midday sun is over bright,
And I am wearying for the restful night!"

And now had Bodli dropped his hands adown,
And shown his face all drawn into a frown
Of doubt and shame; his hand was on his sword,
Even ere Kiartan spake that latest word;
Still trembling, now he drew it from its sheath,
And the bright sun ran down the fated death,
And e'en the sons of Oswif shuddered now,
As with wild eyes and heavy steps and slow
He turned toward Kiartan; beat the heart in me
Till I might scarce breathe, for I looked to see
A dreadful game; the wind of that midday
Beat 'gainst the hill-sides; a hound far away
Barked by some homestead's door; the grey ewe's bleat
Sounded nearby; but that dull sound of feet,
And the thin tinkling of the mail-coat rings
Drowned in my ears the sound of other things,
As less and less the space betwixt them grew;
I shut my eyes as one the end who knew,
But straight, perforce, I opened them again
Woe worth the while!
As one who looks in vain
For help, looked Kiartan round; then raised his shield,
And poised his sword as though he ne'er would yield
E'en when the earth was sinking; yet a while,
And o'er his face there came a quivering smile,
As into Bodli's dreadful face he gazed;
Then my heart sank within me, as all dazed,
I saw the flash of swords that never met,
And heard how Kiartan cried;
"Ah, better yet
For me to die than live on even so!
Alas! friend, do the deed that thou must do!
Oh, lonely death!—farewell, farewell, farewell!"

And clattering on the road his weapons fell,
And almost ere they touched the bloody dust,
Into his shieldless side the sword was thrust,
And I, who could not turn my eyes away,
Beheld him fall, and shrieked as there I lay,

And yet none noted me; but Bodli flung
Himself upon the earth, and o'er him hung,
Then raised his head, and laid it on his knee,
And cried:
"Alas! what have I done to thee?
Was it for this deed, then, that I was born?
Was this the end I looked for on this morn?
I said, To-day I die, to-day I die,
And folk will say, an ill deed, certainly,
He did, but living had small joy of it,
And quickly from him did his weak life flit—
Where was thy noble sword I looked to take
Here in my breast, and die for Gudrun's sake,
And for thy sake—O friend, am I forgot?
Speak yet a word!"
But Kiartan answered not,
And Bodli said, "Wilt thou not then forgive?
Think of the days I yet may have to live
Of hard life!"
Therewith Kiartan oped his eyes,
And strove to turn about as if to rise,
And could not, but gazed hard on Bodli's face,
And gasped out, as his eyes began to glaze:
"Farewell, thou joyous life beneath the sun,
Thou foolish wasted gift—farewell, Gudrun!"
And then on Bodli's breast back fell his head,
He strove to take his hand, and he was dead.

Then was there silence a long while, well-nigh
We heard each other breathe, till quietly
At last the slayer from the slain arose,
And took his sword, and sheathed it, and to those
Four sons of Oswif, e'en as one he spake
Who had good right the rule o'er them to take:

"Here have we laid to earth a mighty one,
And therein no great deed, forsooth, have done,
Since his great heart o'ercame him, not my sword;
And what hereafter may be our reward
For this, I know not: he that lieth here
By many a man in life was held right dear,
As well as by the man who was his friend,
And brought his life and love to bitter end;
And since I am the leader of this band
Of man-slayers, do after my command.
Go ye to Bathstead, name me everywhere
The slayer of Kiartan Olafson, send here
Folk who shall bear the body to our stead;
And then let each man of you hide his head,
For ye shall find it hard from this ill day
To keep your lives: here, meanwhile will I stay,

Nor think myself yet utterly alone."

Then home turned Oswif's sons, and they being gone,
We slunk away, and looking from the hill
We saw how Bodli Thorleikson stood still
In that same place, nor yet had faced the slain.
And so we gat unto our place again.

So told the herd, time long agone, the tale
Of that sad fight within the grey-sloped vale.

Kiartan Brought Dead to Bathstead

Men say that those who went the corpse to bring
To Bathstead thence, found Bodli muttering
Over the white face turned up to the sky,
Nor did he heed them as they drew anigh,
Therefore they stood by him, and heard him say:

"Perchance it is that thou art far away
From us already; caring nought at all
For what in after days to us may fall—
O piteous, piteous!—yet perchance it is
That thou, though entering on thy life of bliss,
The meed of thy great heart, yet art anear,
And somewhat of my feeble voice can hear;
Then scarce for pardon will I pray thee, friend,
Since thus our love is brought unto no end,
But rather now, indeed, begins anew;
Yet since a long time past nought good or true
My lips might utter, let me speak to thee,
If so it really is that thou art free,
At peace and happy past the golden gate;
That time is dead for thee, and thou mayst wait
A thousand years for her and deem it nought.
O dead friend, in my heart there springs a thought
That, since with thy last breath thou spakst her name,
And since thou knowest now how longing came
Into my soul, thou wilt forgive me yet
That time of times, when in my heart first met
Anger against thee, with the sweet sweet love
Wherewith my old dull life of habit strove
So weakly and so vainly—didst thou quite
Know all the value of that dear delight
As I did? Kiartan, she is changed to thee;
Yea, and since hope is dead changed too to me,
What shall we do, if, each of each forgiven,
We three shall meet at last in that fair heaven
The new faith tells of? Thee and God I pray

Impute it not for sin to me to-day,
If no thought I can shape thereof but this:
O friend, O friend, when thee I meet in bliss,
Wilt thou not give my love Gudrun to me,
Since now indeed thine eyes made clear can see
That I of all the world must love her most?"

Then his voice sank so that his words were lost
A little while; then once again he spake,
As one who from a lovesome dream doth wake:

"Alas! I speak of heaven who am in hell!
I speak of change of days, who know full well
How hopeless now is change from misery:
I speak of time destroyed, when unto me
Shall the world's minutes be as lapse of years;
I speak of love who know how my life bears
The bitter hate which I must face to-day—
I speak of thee, and know thee passed away,
Ne'er to come back to help or pity me."

Therewith he looked up, and those folk did see,
And rose up to his feet, and with strange eyes
That seemed to see nought, slunk in shamefast wise,
Silent, behind them, as the corpse they laid
Upon the bier; then, all things being arrayed,
Back unto Bathstead did they wend once more,
As mournful as though dead with them they bore
The heart of Iceland; and yet folk must gaze
With awe and pity upon Bodli's face,
And deem they never might such eyes forget.
But when they reached the stead, anigh sunset,
There in the porch a tall black figure stood,
Whose stern pale face, 'neath its o'erhanging hood,
In the porch shadow was all cold and grey,
Though on her feet the dying sunlight lay.
They trembled then at what might come to pass,
For that grey face the face of Gudrun was,
And they had heard her raving through the day
As through the hall they passed; then made they stay
A few yards from the threshold, and in dread
Waited what next should follow; but she said,
In a low voice and hoarse:
"Nay, enter here,
Without, this eve is too much change and stir,
And rest is good,—is good, if one might win
A moment's rest; and now none is within
The hall but Oswif: not much will he speak,
And as for me—behold, I am grown weak!
I cannot vex him much."
She stepped aside,

And the dark shade her raiment black did hide
As they passed through into the dusky hall,
Afraid to see her face, and last of all
Went Bodli, clashing through the porch, but he
Stayed in the midst, and turned round silently,
And sought her face and said:
"Thy will is done.
Is it enough? Art thou enough alone
As I am?"
Never any word she spake.
No hate was in her face now: "For thy sake
I did it, Gudrun. Speak one word to me
Before my bitter shame and misery
Crushes my heart to death."
She reached a hand
Out toward the place where trembling he did stand,
But touched him not, and never did he know
If she had mind some pity then to show
Unto him, or if rather more apart
She fain had thrust him from her raging heart,
For now those men came tramping from the hall,
And Bodli shrank aback unto the wall
To let them pass, and when the last was gone,
In the dim twilight there he stood alone,
Nor durst he follow her, but listened there,
Half dead, and but his breathing might he hear,
And the faint noises of the gathering night.
He stood so long that the moon cast her light
In through the porch, and still no sound he heard
But the faint clink of mail-rings as he stirred.
"Ah, she is dead of grief, or else would she
Have come to say some little word to me,
Since I so love her, love her!"

With a wail
He cried these words, and in the moonlight pale,
Clashing he turned: but e'en therewith a shriek
From out the dead hush of the hall did break,
And then came footsteps hurrying to the porch,
And the red flare of a new-litten torch,
And smit by nameless horror and affright
He fled away into the moonlit night.

What Folk Did at Herdholt After the Slaying

Now in the hall next morn did Oswif bide
The while his messengers went far and wide
Asking for help; and all in hiding lay
Whose hapless hands had brought about that day,

Save Bodli; but for him, when back he came
That morn, affrighted, Oswif called his name,
Beholding him so worn and changed, and said:

"Stout art thou, kinsman, not to hide thine head!
Yet think that Olaf is a mighty man,
And though thy coming life look ill and wan—
Good reason why—Yet will I ask of thee
The staff of mine old age at least to be,
And save thy life therefor."
Then Bodli smiled
A ghastly smile: "Nay, I am not beguiled
To hope for speedy death; is it not told
How that Cain lived till he was very old?"

Therewith he sank adown into a seat
And hid his face. But sound of hurrying feet
Was in the porch withal; and presently
Came one who said:
"Oswif, all hail to thee!
From Holyfell I come with tidings true,
That little will the wily Snorri do
To help us herein; for he saith the deed
Is most ill done, and that thy sons shall need
More help than they shall get within the land;
Yet saith withal, he will not hold his hand
From buying peace, if that may serve thy turn."

"Well, well," said Oswif, "scarce now first I learn
That Snorri bides his time, and will not run
His neck into a noose for any one.
Go, get thee food, good fellow. Whence com'st thou
Who followest, thy face is long enow?"

"The bearer of a message back I am
From Whiteriver, where Audun Festargram
Has well-nigh done his lading, and, saith he,
That so it is he feareth the deep sea
But little, and the devil nought at all;
But he is liefer at hell's gate to call
With better men than are thy sons, he saith."

"Good," Oswif said, "that little he fears death!
My sight clears, and I see his black bows strike
The hidden skerry. But thou next; belike
Thou hast ill tidings too: what saith my friend,
The son of Hauskuld? what shall be the end?"

"Oswif," the man said, "be not wroth with me
If unto Herdholt nowise openly
I went last night; I fared with hidden head

E'en as a man who drifts from stead to stead
When things go ill: so shelter there I gat,
And mid the house-caries long enow I sat
To note men's bearing. Olaf—an old man
He looks now truly—sat all worn and wan
Within the high-seat, and I deemed of him
That he had wept, from his red eyes and dim,
That scarce looked dry as yet; but down the board
Sat Thorgerd, and I saw a naked sword
Gleam from her mantle; round her sat her sons,
And unto Haldor did she whisper once
And looked toward Olaf; Haldor from its sheath
Half drew his sword, and then below his breath
Spake somewhat. Now looked Olaf round the hall,
But when his eyes on Kiartan's place did fall
His mouth twitched, though his eyes gazed steadily;
He set his hand unto a beaker nigh
And drank and cried out:
"Drink now all of you
Unto the best man Iceland ever knew!
Son, I am weary that thou hast not come
With gleesome tales this eve unto my home;
Yet well thou farest surely amid those
Who are the noblest there, and not so close
They sit, but there is room for thee beside;
Sure, too, with them this eve is merry tide
That thou art come amongst them—would that I
O son, O son, were of that company!'

"With outstretched hand and fixed eyes did he stare,
As though none other in the hall there were
But him he named; the while mid shout and clank
All folk unto the man departed drank,
And midst the noise, withal, I saw no few,
Who from their sheaths the glittering weapons drew,
And through the talk of Kiartan's deeds I heard,
Not lowly spoken, many a threatening word;
While with the tumult of the clattering place
So gathered white-hot rage in Thorgerd's face,
That long it held her silent: then I saw
A black form from the women's chamber draw
White-faced, white-handed; ever did she gaze
Upon the hall-door with an anxious face,
And once or twice as the stout door-planks shook
Beneath the wind's stroke, a half-hopeful look
Came o'er her face, that faded presently
In anguish, as she looked some face to see
Come from the night, and then remembered all;
And therewith did great ruth upon me fall,
For this was Refna; and most quietly
She passed to Olaf's side, and with a sigh

Sat down beside him there; now and again
An eager look lit up her patient pain
As from the home-men Kiartan's name came loud,
And then once more her heavy head she bowed,
And strove to weep and might not. In a while
She raised her eyes, and met grey Thorgerd's smile
Scornful and fierce, who therewithal rose up
And laid her hand upon a silver cup,
And drew from out her cloak a jewelled sword,
And cast it ringing on the oaken board,
And o'er the hall's noise high her clear voice shrilled;

"If the old gods by Christ and mass are killed,
Or driven away, yet am I left behind,
Daughter of Egil, and with such a mind
As Egil had; wherefore if Asa Thor
Has never lived, and there are men no more
Within the land, yet by this king's gift here,
And by this cup Thor owned once, do I swear
That the false foster-brother shall be slain
Before three summers have come round again,
If but my hand must bring him to his end.'

"Therewith a stern shout did her tall sons send
Across the hall, and mighty din arose
Among the home-men. Refna shrank all close
To Olaf's side; but he at first said nought,
Until the cries and clash of weapons brought
Across his dream some image of past days;
And, turning, upon Refna did he gaze,
And on her soft hair laid his hand, and then
Faced round upon the drink-flushed clamorous men,
And in a mighty voice cried out and said:
'Forbear, ye brawlers! now is Kiartan dead,
Nor shall I live long. Will it bring him back
To let loose on the country war and wrack,
And slay the man I love next after him?
Leave me in peace at least! mine eyes wax dim,
And little pleasure henceforth shall I have,
Until my head hath rest within the grave.'

"Then did he rise and stretch across the board,
And took into his hand the noble sword,
And said, 'In good will wert thou given, O blade,
But not to save my son's heart wert thou made.
Help no man henceforth! harm no man henceforth!
Thou foolish glittering toy of little worth!'

"Therewith he brake the sword across his knee,
And cast it down; and then I minded me
How the dead man there bore not that fair blade

When unto grass of Swinedale he was laid.
But Olaf looked so great a man, that none
Durst say a word against him. Gone is gone,'
He said, 'nor yet on Bodli shall ye fall.
When all is ready Kiartan's voice shall call
For him he loved; but if it must be so,
Then unto Oswif's base sons shall ye show
That him they did to death left friends behind';
For this thing ever shall ye bear in mind,
That through their vile plots did all come to. pass,
And Bodli but the sword they fought with was.'
"And therewithal he sat down wearily,
And once again belike saw nought anigh.

"Well, Oswif, little more there happed that eve,
And I at dawn to-day their stead did leave,
To tell thee how things went."
Now Bodli heard
The man speak, and some heart in him was stirred
When of the woman's oath was told, but when
The tale was ended, his head sank again
With a low moan; but Oswif said:
"Yea, true
Did my heart tell me, when I thought I knew
The nobleness of Olaf Hauskuldson.
What shall be done now?"
As he spake came one
Panting and flushed into the hall, and cried:
Get to your arms in haste; Herdholt doth ride
Unto our stead in goodly company!"
Then was there tumult as was like to be,
And round the silent face of the dead man,
Hither and thither, half-armed tremblers ran
With poor hearts; but old Oswif to the door
Went forth unarmed, and Bodli scarce moved more
Than his dead foster-brother. Soon withal
Did quiet on the troubled homestead fall,
For there was nought come but a peaceful train
To bring back Kiartan to his home again;
And there upon the green slope did they bide,
Whence Kiartan on that other morn had cried
His scorn aloud; wherefrom were six men sent,
Who, entering now the thronged hall, slowly went,
Looking around them, toward the bier; but as
They drew anear it, from the bower did pass
A black-clad figure, and they stood aghast,
For it was Gudrun, and wild eyes she cast
On this and that man, as if questioning
Mutely the meaning of some dreadful thing
She knew was doing there: her black gown's hem
She caught up wildly as she gazed at them,

Then shuddering cast it down, and seemed to seek
The face of Oswif; then as if to shriek
She raised her head, and clenched her hands, but nought
Of sound from out her parched lips was there brought,
Till at her breast she clutched, and rent adown
With trembling hands the bosom of her gown,
And cried out, panting as for lack of air;

"Alas, what do ye? have ye come to bear
My love a second time from me, O men?
Do ye not know he is come back again
After a long time? Ah, but evil heart
Must be in you such love as ours to part!"

Then, crying out, upon the corpse she fell,
And men's hearts failed them for pure ruth, and well
They deemed it, might she never rise again;
But strong are many hearts to bear all pain
And live, and hers was even such an one.
Softly they bore her back amidst her swoon;
And then, while even men must weep, once more
Did Kiartan pass the threshold of the door,
That once had been the gate of Paradise
Unto his longing heart. But in nowise
Did Bodli move amidst all this, until
Slow wound the Herdholt men around the hill;
Then stealthily his white face did he raise,
And turned about unto the empty place
Where erst the bier had stood; then he arose,
And looked into the faces of all those
Who stood around, as asking what betid,
What dreadful thing the quivering silence hid;
And then he staggered back unto the wall,
And such a storm of grief on him did fall,
With sobs, and tears, and inarticulate cries,
That men for shame must turn away their eyes,
Nor seem to see a great man fallen so low.

With such wild songs home to the stead came now
The last load of that bitter harvesting,
That from the seed of lust and lies did spring.

Gudrun's Deeming of the Men Who Loved Her

Thus have I striven to show the troublous life
Of these dead folk, e'en as if mid their strife
I dwelt myself; but now is Kiartan slain;
Bodli's blank yearning, Gudrun's wearying pain,
Shall change but little now unto the end;

And midst a many thoughts home must I wend,
And in the ancient days abide no more.
Yet, when the shipman draweth nigh the shore,
And slacks the sheet and lets adown the sail,
Scarce suddenly therewith all way doth fail
The sea-clasped keel. So with this history
It fareth now; have patience then with me
A moment yet, ere all the tale is told.

While Olaf Peacock lived, his sons did hold
Their hands from Bodli; Oswif's sons must pay
With gold and outlawry for that ill day,
And nothing else there happened to them worse
Than o'er the sea to bear all people's curse,
Nor know men aught more of their history.
Three winters afterward did Olaf die,
Full both of years and honour; then was not
Thorgerd's fierce oath amidst her sons forgot;
The golden ring, whose end old Guest foresaw,
Worn through the weary years with many a flaw,
Now smitten, fell asunder: Bodli died
Manlike amidst his foes, with none beside
To sorrow o'er him, scarcely loth maybe
The end of his warped life at last to see.

Turn back a while; of her I have to tell,
Whose sorrow on my heart the more doth dwell,
That nought she did to earn it, as I deem—
Unto the Ridge, where on the willowy stream
Her father's stead looks down, did Refna go,
That, if it might be, she some rest might know
Within the fair vale where she wandered, when
The bearded faces of the weaponed men
Were wonders to her child's eyes, far away
The wild thoughts of their hearts; her little day
Of hope and joy gone by, there yet awhile
She wandered once again; nor her faint smile
Would she withhold, when pitying eyes did gaze
On the deep sorrow of her lovely face;
For she belike felt strong, and still might deem
That life, all turned into a longing dream,
Would long abide with her—happier she was,
But little time over her head did pass,
Before all smiles from off her face did fade,
And in the grave her yearning heart was laid,
No more now to be rent 'twixt hope and fear,
No more to sicken with the dull despair.

Yet is she left to tell of, some might call,
The very cause the very curse of all;
And yet not I—for after Bodli's death

Too dreadful grew the dale, my story saith,
For Gudrun longer at her house to dwell,
Wherefore with Snorri, lord of Holyfell,
Did she change steads. There dwelt she a long space,
And true it is, that in her noble face
Men deemed but little signs of woe they saw;
And still she lived on long, and in great awe
And honour was she held, nor unfulfilled
Was the last thing that Guest deemed fate had willed
Should fall on her: when Bodli's sons were men
And many things had happed, she wed again,
And though her days of keen joys might be bare
Yet little did they bring of added care
As on and on they wore from that old time
When she was set amidst mad love and crime.

Yet went this husband's end no otherwise
Than Guest foresaw: at last with dreamy eyes
And weary heart from his grave too she turned.
Across the waste of life on one hand burned
The unforgotten sore regretted days
Long left behind; and o'er the stony ways
Her feet must pass yet, the grey cloud of death
Rolled doubtful, drawing nigher. The tale saith
That she lived long years afterwards, and strove,
E'en as she might, to win a little love
From God now, and with bitter yearning prayer
Through these slow-footed lonely days to wear.
And men say, as to all the ways of earth
Her soul grew blind, and other hopes had birth
Within her, that her bodily sight failed too,
And now no more the dark from day she knew.

This one more picture gives the ancient book
On which I pray you for a while to look,
If for your tears ye may. For it doth tell
That on a day she sat at Holyfell
Within the bower, another Bodli there
Beside her, son of him who wrought her care;
A travelled man and mighty, gay of weed,
Doer belike of many a desperate deed
Within the huge wall of the Grecian king.
A summer eve it was, and everything
Was calm and fair, the tinkling bells did sound
From the fair chapel on the higher ground
Of the holy hill, the murmur of the sea
Came on the fitful south-west soothingly;
The house-carles sang as homeward now they went
From out the home-field, and the hay's sweet scent
Floated around: and when the sun had died
An hour agone now, Bodli stirred and sighed;

Perchance too clearly felt he life slip by
Amid those pensive things, and certainly
He too was passed his youth.
"Mother," he said,
"Awhile agone it came into my head
To ask thee somewhat; thou hast loved me well,
And this perchance is no great thing to tell
To one who loves thee."
With her sightless eyes
Turned on him did she smile in loving wise,
But answered nought; then he went on, and said:
"Which of the men thou knewest—who are dead
Long ago, mother,—didst thou love the best?"
Then her thin hands each upon each she pressed,
And her face quivered, as some memory
Were hard upon her:
"Ah, son! years go by.
When we are young this year we call the worst
That we can know; this bitter day is cursed,
And no more such our hearts can bear we say.
But yet as time from us falls fast away
There comes a day, son, when all this is fair
And sweet, to what, still living, we must bear—
Bettered is bale by bale that follows it,
The saw saith."
Silent both awhile did sit
Until she spake again: "Easy to tell
About them, son, my memory serves me well:
A great chief Thorkel was, bounteous and wise, -
And ill hap seemed his death in all men's eyes.
Bodli thy sire was mighty of his hands,
Scarce better dwelt in all the northern lands;
Thou wouldst have loved him well. My husband Thord
Was a great man; wise at the council-board,
Well learned in law—for Thorwald, he indeed,
A rash weak heart, like to a stinging weed
Must be pulled up—ah, that was long ago!"
Then Bodli smiled, "Thou wouldst not have me know
Thy thought, O mother—these things know I well;
Old folk about these men e'en such tales tell."

She said, "Alas, O son, thou askst of love!
Long folly lasteth; still that word doth move
My old worn heart—hearken one little word,
Then ask no more; ill is it to be stirred
To vain repining for the vanished days."

She turned, until her sightless eyes did gaze
As though the wall, the hills, must melt away,
And show her Herdholt in the twilight grey;
She cried, with tremulous voice; and eyes grown wet

For the last time, whate'er should happen yet,
With hands stretched out for all that she had lost:

"I did the worst to him I loved the most."

They too, those old men, well might sit and gaze
Upon the images of bygone days,
And wonder mid their soft self-pity, why
Mid such wild struggles had their lives gone by,
Since neither love nor joy, nor even pain,
Should last for ever; yet their strife so vain
While still they strove, so sore regretted now,
The heavy grief that once their heads did bow,
Had wrought so much for them, that they might sit
Amid some pleasure at the thought of it;
At least not quite consumed by sordid fear,
That now at last the end was come anear;
At least not hardened quite so much, but they
Might hear of love and longing worn away
'Twixt birth and death of others, wondering
Belike, amid their pity what strange thing
Made the mere truth of what poor souls did bear
In vain or not in vain—so sweet to hear,
So healing to the tangled woes of earth,
At least for a short while.

But little mirth
The grey eve and the strong unfailing wind
Might ask of them that tide; and yet behind
That mask of pensive eyes, so unbeguiled
By ancient folly any more, what wild
Strange flickering hopes ineffable might lie,
As swift that latter end of eve slipped by!

William Morris - A Short Biography

British poet, author, thinker and publisher William Morris was born in 1834 in Walthamstow, Essex.
The eldest son of wealthy Londoners Emma Shelton Morris and William Morris, the younger Morris
would become one of the most influential people in the cultural landscape of Victorian England.

Educated at home and at a nearby preparatory school, Morris's childhood was one of privilege, with
books, leisurely excursions and ponies for personal use. The idyll ended (to an extent) with the
sudden death of Morris Senior in 1847 when the younger Morris was just 14 years old. The next
year, Morris began his formal studies at Marlborough College in Wiltshire. After three years of
bullying and homesickness, Morris returned to his family home and was thereafter privately tutored.

In 1852, Morris entered Oxford University to study the Classics. While there he also became
interested in medieval-era history and architecture. Morris would come to identify with medievalist
ideals, as did a growing socio-political movement in England that rejected the values of the

prevailing Victorian capitalist system. Morris would become even more politically active later in life, embracing the socialist values that he had recognized in medievalism as an undergraduate.

Morris made several important and life-long friends while at Exeter College at Oxford, most notably the artist and designer Edward Burne-Jones. Morris and Burne-Jones became part of a group of Oxford thinkers (most of them from the industrial city of Birmingham) who would be known historically as "The Birmingham Set." The group included divinity student William Fulford, poet and theologian Richard Watson Dixon, mathematician Charles Faulkner and scholar Cormell Price – internally they called themselves "The Brotherhood." The members of the group shared literary interests as well as values and were huge fans of Alfred Lord Tennyson, art critic John Ruskin, the Arthurian legends and William Shakespeare.

In 1856, Morris helped fund and start up the *Oxford and Cambridge Magazine*, the first of many cooperative projects in which he took an active role. Twelve issues were published. Also in 1856 – upon completion of his Bachelor of Arts degree - Morris was apprenticed briefly to the Oxford based Gothic revival architect George Edmund Street. Morris would use lessons learned from Street, and supervising architect Philip Webb, during the design process for his own Red House in Kent. Morris lived there with his new family – wife Jane Burdon, who he married in 1859, and daughters Jenny and Mary – until 1865.

In 1858 Morris published *The Defence of Guenvere*, an innovative volume of lyric and dramatic verse, which nonetheless was not well received critically. Morris would not publish again until 1867 when Bell and Dandy published the epic romantic poem *The Life and Death of Jason*. The printing was financed by Morris himself; happily, the book was well received and Morris received a fee for the second edition.

From 1861 Morris commuted from The Red House to London where he had opened a decorative arts firm with Burne-Jones, Webb, Faulkner and other friends: the Pre-Raphaelite painter Dante Gabriel Rossetti, Ford Madox Brown and Peter Paul Marshall. The company – known publicly as Morris, Marshall, Faulkner & Co. and privately as "The Firm" – specialized in locally produced fabrics, furniture, tapestries, wallpaper, architectural carving and stained glass windows. In 1875, Morris assumed total control of the company, now named Morris & Co. Though known in his lifetime chiefly for being a poet, Morris would also achieve posthumous acclaim as a chief architect of the "Arts and Crafts" British design movement.

In 1865, Morris sold The Red House and moved to Bloomsbury in London with his family. By 1870, he was a cultural fixture in that city and a celebrity of some stature.

From 1865 to 1870, Morris worked on another epic poem, *The Earthly Paradise*. Designed as homage to Chaucer, it consists of 24 stories, each with a different narrator from a different cultural background. Set in the late 14th century, it is about a group of Norsemen who flee the Black Death by sailing away from Europe, on the way discovering an island where the inhabitants continue to venerate an ancient Greek god. Published in four parts by F. S. Ellis, the epic gained a cult following and established Morris' reputation as a major poet.

Greatly influenced by his friendship with Icelandic theologian Eiríkr Magnússon and several visits to Iceland, Morris produced a series of English-language translations of the Icelandic Eddas and Sagas (old Norse poems and stories). Morris also taught himself calligraphy and created hand written copies of Nordic tales in translation, including *Frithiof the Bold* and *Halfden the Black*. It was the continuation of a life-long devotion to craft, a feature of many of his subsequent works, including the poetic drama *Love is Enough*, published in 1872 with woodcut illustrations by Burne-Jones.

Though leading a rich life in London, Morris did find the city unhealthy for his young family. He came across and fell in love with a 16th century manor house in Oxfordshire. The Morris family would share Kelmscott Manor with Morris' friend Rossetti (who, it is said, had developed a close relationship with Morris' wife Jane) until their friendship eventually disintegrated. Kelmscott also lent its name to another of Morris' achievements – the Kelmscott Press, which he co-founded, with Emery Walker, in 1891. The bespoke publishing house was dedicated to publishing limited edition, illuminated style fine art books, in keeping with Morris' devotion to the craft of making books as beautiful objects. The Press dovetailed with Morris' continuing design work with Morris & Co. Over the next seven years, it would publish 66 volumes, the first of which was Morris' own novel, *The Story of the Glittering Plain*, in 1891. The Kelmscott Press would go on to publish 23 of Morris' books, but also editions of works by Keats, Shelley, Ruskin, and Swinburne, as well as copies of various Medieval texts. Kelmscott's magnum opus would turn out to be the Kelmscott Chaucer, published in 1896; it took several years to complete and included 87 illustrations and decorative borders from Burne-Jones.

In 1883, Morris joined England's first socialist organization, the Democratic Federation, later renamed the Socialist Democratic Federation (SDF). This was the beginning of years of overt activism on behalf of workers and the poor. In 1884, Morris and a large group of SDF members seceded in order to form the brand new Socialist League (SL). For the rest of the decade, Morris worked tirelessly for the cause; he met several times each week with his comrades from the SL and delivered hundreds of lectures. He was arrested in 1885 for disorderly conduct at the trial of several Socialist protesters, wrote for and edited SL's newspaper, *The Commonweal* and wrote a long series of socialist literary works, including the song collection *Chants for Socialists* (1884); a narrative poem, *The Pilgrims of Hope* (1885); the historical meditation *A Dream of John Ball* (1887); and his most influential work, *News from Nowhere* (1890), a pastoral utopian communist vision of England in the twenty-first century.

Morris also continued as a poet and prose writer. In December 1888, the Chiswick Press published his *The House of the Wolfings*, a fantasy story set in Iron Age Europe, which provides a reconstructed portrait of the lives of Germanic-speaking Gothic tribes. The book contains both prose and poetic verse and was followed by a two-volume sequel, *The Roots of the Mountains*, in 1899.

Morris also embarked on a translation of the quintessential Anglo-Saxon tale, *Beowulf*. Because he could not fully understand Old English, his poetic translation was based largely on that already produced by A.J. Watts. *The Tale of Beowulf* was not well received.

In the last nine years of his life, Morris wrote a series of imaginative fictions usually referred to as the "prose romances." These novels – including *The Wood Beyond the World* and *The Well at the World's End* (1896) – have been credited as important milestones in the history of fantasy fiction, because, while other writers wrote of foreign lands, or of dream worlds, or the future (as Morris had already done in the utopian *News from Nowhere*), Morris's works were the first to be set in an entirely invented neo-medieval fantasy world.

By 1896, Morris was an invalid, not working much but being visited by friends and family at his home. The great man died of tuberculosis on October 4th, 1896. Morris' funeral was held on October 6th, his corpse carried from Kelmscott House, his home in Hammersmith, to Paddington rail station, where it was transported to Oxford, then to Kelmscott, where it was buried in the churchyard of St. George's Church.

Morris lives on with the legacy of the Arts and Crafts movement, in his many fine literary works, essays and translations and through his homes, which have been preserved by the UK's National Trust and the William Morris Society as monuments to the man and the epic period of cultural history in which he flourished.

William Morris - A Concise Bibliography

Collected Poetry, Fiction, and Essays
The Hollow Land (1856)
The Defence of Guenevere, and other Poems (1858)
The Life and Death of Jason (1867)
The Earthly Paradise (1868–1870)
Love is Enough, or The Freeing of Pharamond: A Morality (1872)
The Story of Sigurd the Volsung and the Fall of the Niblungs (1877)
Hopes and Fears For Art (1882)
The Pilgrims of Hope (1885)
A Dream of John Ball (1888)
A Tale of the House of the Wolfings, and All the Kindreds of the Mark. In Prose and in Verse (1889)
The Roots of the Mountains (1890)
Poems By the Way (1891)
News from Nowhere (or, An Epoch of Rest) (1890)
The Story of the Glittering Plain (1891)
The Wood Beyond the World (1894)
Child Christopher and Goldilind the Fair (1895)
The Well at the World's End (1896)
The Water of the Wondrous Isles (1897)
The Sundering Flood (1897)
A King's Lesson (1901)
The World of Romance (1906)
Chants for Socialists (1935)

Translations
Grettis Saga: The Story of Grettir the Strong with Eiríkr Magnússon (1869)
The Saga of Gunnlaug the Worm-tongue and Rafn the Skald with Eiríkr Magnússon (1869)
Völsung Saga: The Story of the Volsungs and Niblungs, with Certain Songs from the Elder Eddawith Eiríkr Magnússon (1870) (from the Volsunga saga)
Three Northern Love Stories & Other Tales with Eiríkr Magnússon (1875)
The Odyssey of Homer Done into English Verse (1887)
The Aeneids of Virgil Done into English (1876)
Of King Florus and the Fair Jehane (1893)
The Tale of Beowulf Done out of the Old English Tongue (1895)
Old French Romances Done into English (1896)

Published Lectures and Papers
Lectures on Art delivered in support of the Society for the Protection of Ancient Buildings (Morris lecture on The Lesser Arts). London, Macmillan, 1882
Architecture and History & Westminster Abbey". Papers read to SPAB in 1884 and 1893. Printed at The Chiswick Press. London, Longmans, 1900
Communism: a lecture London, Fabian Society, 1903

www.ingramcontent.com/pod-product-compliance
Lightning Source LLC
Chambersburg PA
CBHW051943090426
42741CB00008B/1249